# Management Handbook of Computer Usage

R K Sachdeva

British Library Cataloguing in Publication Data

Sachdeva, Rajinder
Management handbook of computer usage.
1. Computer systems. Management
I. Title
004'.068

ISBN 0–85012–769–6

© NCC BLACKWELL LIMITED, 1990

All rights reserved. No part of this publication may be reproduced, stored in a retrieval system, or transmitted, in any form or by any means, without the prior permission of The National Computing Centre.

Published for NCC Publications by NCC Blackwell Limited.

Editorial Office, The National Computing Centre Limited, Oxford Road, Manchester M1 7ED, England.

NCC Blackwell Limited, 108 Cowley Road, Oxford OX4 1JF, England.

Typeset in Times by Bookworm Typesetting, Manchester; and printed by Hobbs the Printers of Southampton.

ISBN 0–85012–769–6

# Contents

# 1 Evolution of Computer Systems

## EARLY COMPUTING DEVICES

The development of computers has followed a long evolutionary path. Man's interest in mechanical computational devices is age old: primitive mechanical computational devices can be traced to Ancient China and Ancient Greece. One of these, the abacus, is still in use in some parts of the world. It consists of a frame with beads sliding on wires to represent and manipulate numeric values.

Logarithm tables were first published by the Scot John Napier in 1614. Every positive number can be associated with a logarithm, with multiplication and division carried out through the simple operations of adding and subtracting logarithms. The slide-rule, based on the concept of the logarithm, was developed by William Oughtred in 1622. This mechanical device allows multiplication and division to be performed by sliding a moving rule against fixed calibrations. The slide-rule is an early example of an *analogue* device which employs continuous physical quantities, like length or voltage, rather than discrete numbers as in *digital* calculators and computers.

The arithmetic engine (the 'Pascaline'), produced by Blaise Pascal in 1642, was the first real calculating machine. Digits from 0 to 9 were arranged on wheels. Turning one wheel a full revolution caused its neighbour to be advanced one notch. The arithmetic engine worked on a similar principle to mechanical milometers or the taxi meter. Later, in 1694, a more sophisticated mechanical calculator was invented by Wilhelm Gottfried von Leibniz. But it was not until the nineteenth century that mechanical computation took a major step forward. The Difference Engine, built by Charles Babbage, was unveiled to the Royal Astronomical Society in 1821. It calculated the differences between numbers to compute and check mathematical tables.

Babbage then began development of a new device, the Analytical Engine, that was intended to function as a program-controlled machine. This design provided 'architectural' concepts that were to prove important for modern electronic digital computers. The design for the Analytical Engine contained five elements: input, store, arithmetic unit, control unit and output. These, in one form or another, are intrinsic to all computer systems. Input was accomplished by means of punched cards, a facility originally developed by Joseph Maria Jacquard in France to control looms automatically.

The Unit Record System, also using punched cards, was developed by Hermann Hollerith in the 1880s. He won a competition to find an efficient way of analysing the 1890 American census. The 80-column card designed by Hollerith was still the main input medium in most electronic computers until the 1970s. The presence or absence of a hole in particular positions on a card would be used to indicate the presence or absence of particular characteristics of the individuals in the census. In order to read the cards, rods were passed through them. The rods then made contact with a bowl of mercury to form an electrical contact, causing a counter to advance by one. The Unit Record System consisted of a 'sorter' for arranging the punched cards in a desired sequence, a 'collator' to selectively merge the cards and a 'tabulator' to tabulate the contents of the cards.

This device was the first electromechanical computing system. Use was made of hard-wired programs to control the operations of the individual machines, and control panels could be wired with different programs to achieve different results from the same machines. Dr Hollerith's work eventually gave birth to International Business Machines (IBM) in the US and to International Computers Limited (ICL) in the UK.

## DEVELOPMENTS IN COMPUTER HARDWARE

The concept of *stored program control* was further developed by John von Neumann in 1945 and this helped to lay the foundation for modern electronic computers. He built a machine – EDVAC, the Electronic Discrete Variable Automatic Computer – based on this principle, in 1951. An earlier device – ENIAC, the Electronic Numerical Integrator and Calculator – developed in 1946, is now seen as one of the first general-purpose computers. It was a gigantic machine with eighteen thousand valves. It consumed many kilowatts of power, had to be water cooled and had a very high failure rate compared to modern computers.

The earliest computers, built from electronic valves, are now depicted as *first-generation*. The introduction of transistors, in the late-1950s, resulted in *second-generation* computers. These were typified by the ICT (a forerunner of ICL) 1301 and the IBM 1401. *Third-generation* computers are based on integrated circuits where large numbers of transistors and other electronic components are carried on semiconductor *chips*. The ICL 1900 series, System 4 and the IBM 360, introduced in 1964, are examples. The development of large scale integration (LSI) and very large scale integration (VLSI) led to *fourth-generation* computers. (It was semiconductor technology which facilitated the emergence of microcomputers in the early-1970s). *Fifth-generation* computers, currently being developed, are intended to embody artificial intelligence (AI) and other features. They will, for example, be able to imitate common human functions like vision, natural language comprehension and the use of specialised knowledge.

The internal computer storage ('memory') was, in the 1940s, built from vacuum tubes. These were relatively large (a few inches in length), and each was able to hold only one binary digit, called a *bit* (a 0 or 1). The storage capacity of such first-generation systems was tiny by present standards. The most popular computer in the mid-1950s (the IBM 650) used a rotating drum coated with a magnetisable material as the primary storage medium. Between 1960 and 1975, however, the dominant computer storage design used tiny rings or 'cores' of magnetisable material in the primary storage section. Current flowing in one direction represented a 0 while flow in the opposite direction represented a 1. Since the core permanently retained its magnetic state in the absence of the current, it was a non-volatile storage medium. Core storage was popular for 15 years because it was safe, durable and reasonably fast. However, the new storage devices that appeared in the 1970s offered even faster performance at a lower cost and so the popularity of cores quickly faded.

Virtually all today's computers use semiconductor elements in their primary storage sections. Semiconductor storage elements are tiny integrated circuits (ICs). Both the storage cell circuits and the support circuitry needed for data writing and reading are packaged on chips of silicon. The chips used for the primary storage section usually employ metal-oxide semiconductor (MOS) technology. In third-generation computers, the level of integration was of the order of 200 transistor components on one IC. The LS chips had a level of integration of 10,000 components. Present-day VLSI chips integrate one million or more components and can store that many bits of data. These chips are available for a few dollars each. This represents a reduction, from second-generation times, in the cost-to-performance factor of more than one thousand.

In the earliest electronic computers the feeding of input data to, and output from, the computer was via the medium of punched paper cards or punched paper tape. Such facilities were very slow compared to present standards. Second-generation computers used magnetic tapes which could store 800 characters of data per inch of tape length. Hard magnetic disks could store up to two million characters of data.

Miniaturisation of the central processing unit of the computer was also reflected in the input and output devices. Magnetic tape gave way to the cassette tape and the hard magnetic disk to the floppy in the smaller mini and microcomputers. Today 3½ inch-diameter floppy disks can store more than a million characters of data, and magnetic tapes with the capacity to store more than 6000 characters per inch are quite common. Hard disks used on larger computers can store more than 500 million characters. Similarly, rates of data transfer between the input/output devices and the central processing unit have increased from a few thousand characters per second in the second generation to more than a million characters per second in today's systems.

Another popular modern input/output device is a visual display unit (VDU) or visual display terminal (VDT). The terminal has given rise to interactive computing – with on-line access to computer data and to the computing power needed to manipulate the data. Specialised input devices – such as optical readers in the point-of-sale terminal – have made it possible to directly feed data from the point of activity, instead of transcribing it onto paper cards or magnetic tape.

## DEVELOPMENTS IN COMPUTER SOFTWARE

Earlier computers were sold as bare machines consisting of hardware alone. While the computer devices, such as the central processing unit and the input/output devices, form the hardware of the computer, processing procedures are necessary to solve user problems on the computer. These procedures (*programs*) are specified in special computer languages, and constitute the computer software. Modern computers are sold along with a wide variety of software designed to aid the computer user. Over the years, computers have become increasingly 'user-friendly'.

Communication with earlier computers was by means of highly complicated machine languages. Each instruction in a machine language consisted of a long string of binary digits (0 and 1). Each machine instruction performed a very elementary operation – such as moving one digit of data from one place in the memory to another or adding or subtracting two digits. The user operations had to be broken down to series of such elementary operations which could be directly executed by the machine. So programs for simple jobs consisted of a large number of instructions, each instruction in turn consisting of a long string of 0s and 1s. Each computer model had its unique machine language, and programming a different model of computer meant learning a different machine language. The machine languages are referred to as first-generation languages.

Second-generation languages replaced the binary codes with 'mnemonic codes' and 'symbolic addresses' consisting of alphabets and numerals. However, there was still a one-to-one correspondence between the program instructions and the corresponding machine-language instructions. So the program still consisted of a large number of instructions performing elementary steps. Such languages are referred to as *low-level languages* and are also unique for each computer model. The program in such a language has to be first translated into the machine language before it can be executed; the translation is carried out by the computer itself using the software supplied. Examples of second-generation languages are AUTOCODER used on IBM 1401 computers and PLAN used on ICL 1900 series of computers. Third-generation languages are procedure oriented and machine independent, ie a program written in such a language can be executed on any computer, provided the software is available to translate the program into the machine language of the respective computer.

Using *high-level languages* the programmer concentrates on the problem to be solved rather than on the design features of the machine to be used. He describes the procedure for solving the problem in terms of the natural steps used by humans. Each step in a high-level language may be translated into a series of steps in the machine language before execution by the computer. Examples of high-level languages are BASIC, FORTRAN, COBOL and Pascal. These languages have been standardised by the International Standards Organization and are widely used.

Third-generation languages still needed vast numbers of lines of codes for typical commercial programs. They were designed for data processing professionals rather than for end-users. It was very time-consuming to test the accuracy of programs (to 'debug' them). Modification of complex programs was very difficult and huge investments went into maintaining them. A variety of software development tools have now been developed to solve this problem. These tools range from simple query languages to application program generators (APLs). Such tools are referred to as fourth-generation languages or 4GLs. In addition to employing sequential statements, as do third-generation languages, they employ a diversity of other mechanisms such as form filling, screen painting, questionnaire with menus, commands, etc. The focus in these languages is to specify what is required to be done rather than how it is to be achieved. If the problem can be specified in computable specifications, machine code can be generated from it mechanically. A large number of such tools are currently available; for example, ORACLE, PROGRESS, SEA-CHANGE, etc.

## EVOLUTION OF OPERATING SYSTEMS

Early computers could handle only one program at a time. The operator had to perform a number of tasks manually between every two jobs. The job program and input data would be loaded on input devices, the storage areas in the processor would be cleared of any data remaining from the previous job, appropriate switches would be set, and the job would run alone in the processor until it was completed. After completion, the job program, input data, and output results would be unloaded by the operator and the entire ritual would begin again for the next job. Because the computer sat idle while the operator loaded and unloaded jobs, a great deal of processing time was lost. The situation was further degraded when a fault occurred during the running of a program. The operator had to collect diagnostic information in an attempt to pinpoint the fault. This was very time consuming.

The operating system (OS) software was designed to perform routine housekeeping operations and to manage the computer resources for their optimal utilisation. The early mainframe operating systems reduced the idle time by allowing jobs to be stacked up in a waiting line. When one job was finished, system control would branch back to OS software which would automatically perform the housekeeping duties needed to load and run the next job. This automatic job-to-job transition is still one of the major functions performed by a modern mainframe OS.

The operating system has also made it possible to process more than one program concurrently on the same computer. This feature is called 'multiprogramming'. The input and output operations in any computer are generally many times slower than the processing speed in the central processor. Thus when the computer is busy executing only one program, the processor has to wait for long intervals when the data is being read into the memory or the results are being transferred to an output device. This considerably reduces the processor utilisation. The operating system software can switch control between programs so that each program is processed for short periods in an appropriate sequence. The program that has to wait for an input/output operation relinquishes control in favour of other programs until it has completed data transfer.

## APPLICATION PACKAGES AND DEVELOPMENT AIDS

While system programs such as compilers (language translators) and operating systems are designed to operate, control and extend the processing capabilities of the computer itself, an application program is needed to solve a specific data processing task for a user. Conventionally, application programs are custom-made according to the specific processing requirements of the user. This requirement has often involved heavy investment and long development periods. Internal expertise was required in the organisation to develop such programs or at least to maintain them. With the proliferation of computers, multiple users trying to solve similar problems on computers became common. To meet this situation, independent software suppliers started developing application packages to supply them as prewritten programs to prospective users.

Application packages are designed for use in more than one environment or organisation to perform specific functions which are common to these organisations and are performed similarly, eg accounting, payroll, sales order processing, etc. The functions performed by the package may be generalised to meet the requirements of a large number of organisations but parameterised to cater for the individual needs of each organisation. The cost of developing the package gets distributed over the user organisations. The application packages involve low capital cost, are available for immediate implementation, and eliminate the need for internal expertise of developing and maintaining software.

A large variety of application packages are currently marketed. These include: basic accounting functions (general ledger, accounts receivable, accounts payable, payroll, fixed assets, etc); manufacturing operations (bill of materials, inventory control, materials requirement planning, production scheduling, cost accounting, etc); distribution operations (order entry, sales analysis, route scheduling, etc); finance functions (budgeting, projections, economic analysis, etc); and a host of other functions. In addition, general-purpose application packages like spreadsheet, word processing, data management, office systems. etc can be used for a wide range of tasks.

A number of software tools have been developed to support and/or automate the process of software development. Significant among these are the 'code generators' and 'application generators'. Code generators produce applications in the form of a high-level language program (or possibly a low-level language program), usually for subsequent translation and/or execution independent of the parent tool. Therefore the application is a separate piece of stand-alone software which could have been produced by hand-coding techniques. Application generators, on the other hand, incorporate a translator and also control execution of the generated application. Hence the generator and the application are both required to be present at run time. The code generator produces commonly used high-level languages such as COBOL or BASIC. The application generator either has an internal translation facility which generates the machine code or, more usually, interprets parameter tables at run time. The user feeds the requirements through an interactive terminal under the control of the tool, by the methods of form filling, screen painting, questionnaire or a set of commands.

*Screen painting* uses a video display screen to simulate a screen or a page which is to be developed for an application. The generator allows the developer to configure the layout of the applications display or page (for a report) by presenting a blank screen initially on which the developer 'paints' or places, using cursor commands or keys, the required information in the appropriate positions.

*Form-filling* (or fill-in-the-blanks) is another widely used technique for accomplishing a software component definition. This method also assumes that the generator utilises a visual display unit, and in this case the screen presented to the developer is not blank, as for screen painting, but is pre-formatted with available options.

The *questionnaire* approach again presumes that the developer is working at a visual display terminal. The particular aspects of the application under development are presented in the form of a series of questions requiring usually an affirmative or a negative response from the developer. Otherwise, it may present a set of options in the form of a 'menu' to the developer who may select the option(s) from the menu by depressing selected keys.

The *command language* approach is the same as that used in conventional high-level language programming except that the commands used are likely to be less procedural. This method can be used for any of the components of an application software package and can also be used off-line (non-interactively) as well as on-line (interactively); so in that sense it is a very flexible method.

## DEVELOPMENTS IN TELECOMMUNICATIONS

Telecommunication systems such as telephone, telegraph or radio transmission systems have existed for many decades. The early communication systems used *analogue* signals to carry information. An analogue signal is continuously variable: the waveform is analogous to the information being transmitted. For example, the loudness and the pitch of the speech are reflected in the variation of the amplitude and frequency of the corresponding speech signal. An analogue signal is generated by an analogue device such as the microphone in a telephone handset.

Analogue transmission is not very suitable for transmitting data over long distances. Firstly, the transmission environment is sensitive to outside interference which affects the signal waveform and distorts the message being transmitted. Secondly, analogue signals need to undergo staged amplification to restore signal strength when transmitted over long distances and this creates a cumulative build-up of errors due to noise interference.

The need for utmost accuracy in data communication led to the concept of digital transmission. Digital transmission is far more tolerant of the effects of outside interference because the receiver simply needs to distinguish between discrete signal levels. Digital transmission also makes more efficient use of the transmission medium so that many times more information can be sent on the same line. Analogue messages, such as voice and picture, can also be converted to a *digital* form and then transmitted as digital information.

The initial transmission medium was a pair of twisted insulated wires. Such lines are quite inexpensive and easy to install. They are still in use for local short-distance communication. However, they are sensitive to environmental interference and their information-carrying capacity is limited. Co-axial cables provide much higher capacity and suffer relatively little outside interference. But these cables are bulky, difficult to install and more expensive. They are in use for trunk transmission lines. Wired lines have their own problems of installation and maintenance particularly when they have to pass through cities and cope with natural obstacles. Microwave lines are wireless and can communicate via line-of-sight – up to about 50 km on the earth's surface. They have very high capacity but are sensitive to environmental interference.

The 1960s and 1970s saw the emergence of the satellite as a major communication medium linking distant countries and continents. Satellites revolving at a height of 36,000 km from the earth's surface have the same orbit time as the earth's revolution and hence appear from the earth's surface to be stationary. Such satellites are known as geostationary and are extremely useful as a communication medium. A satellite relays microwave signals from one earth station to another. They have very high capacity and can broadcast messages to a large number of receivers.

The information-carrying capacity of a signal depends on the frequency of the signal – which is why microwave signals have a high capacity. Light is of even higher frequency, and the 1980s have seen the development of a new communication medium, the 'fibre optic cable'. Its central core is made of very transparent glass surrounded by a glass cladding of lower refractive index which causes total internal reflection of the light rays as they pass through the core. Very fine cables of optic fibre provide an immensely high carrying capacity which is quite free from environmental interference. Optic fibre lines are still expensive but are useful in high-traffic areas.

The early computers were stand-alone machines where the

entire computer system, consisting of the processing device and the input/output devices, was housed in a single room or in at most a single building. Long-distance data communication lines and their interface with the computer systems have now made it possible to connect remote input/output terminals to the computer located thousands of miles away. From remote distances, a user may use the full processing capacity of the computer. Also, computers can be connected together to pool their hardware and software resources. One may like to utilise, at a local computer, some special facilities available on a distant computer, or large complicated problems may be solved co-operatively by a number of computers interconnected in a computer network.

## OBJECTIVES OF COMPUTERISATION

Computer systems have been used by different organisations for a wide variety of applications. The objectives of using the computerised systems have, however, varied for different organisations and for different applications. Most applications would aim to achieve some or all of the objectives of accuracy, precision, completeness, conciseness, throughput, turnaround time and response time.

*Accuracy* is the ratio of correct information produced over a period. If 1000 items of information are produced and 950 of these give a correct report of the actual situation, then the accuracy level is 0.95. Whether this level is high enough depends on the information being produced. Fifty incorrect bank balances in a mailing of 1000 bank statements are intolerable. But, if physical inventory records kept on large quantities of inexpensive parts achieve an accuracy level of 0.95, this might be acceptable. Greater accuracy *could* be achieved, but the additional value to managers of having a more accurate inventory might be less than the additional costs required to gather it.

*Precision* refers to the amount of error which can be tolerated in a certain value or action. An accounting statement may be required to be precise to the last penny. But in an expenditure report for the purposes of budgetary control, values less than a hundred pounds may be considered meaningless; precision to the nearest hundred pounds may be considered good enough.

Nobody may be interested in the population of a country to the last individual; the value to the nearest million may be good enough. On the other hand, if the computer system is controlling the movement of a satellite, very precise information is necessary.

Information available in bits and pieces is generally not useful unless it can be integrated into a *complete whole*. Conclusions about integrated systems can be drawn only when information is available on all the different aspects. Incomplete information may lead to wrong conclusions.

There is a limit to the amount of information one can easily comprehend. Over-ambitious systems have concentrated on generating piles of reports. Important information, along with relatively useless data, is often buried in stacks of paper. People are then faced with the problem of extracting those items of information that they need. *Concise* information that summarises the relevant data and points out areas of exception to normal or planned activities is what is often needed.

*Throughput* refers to the number of jobs processed per hour. It is related to the efficient utilisation of the computing resources. It is necessary to achieve a reasonable level of throughput to recover the investment in computing resources. A casual job with occasional use of the computer system may not be able to justify the establishment of the facility.

*Turnaround time* is the amount of time the user must wait for the results of processing to be delivered to him. Depending on the nature of the job, the user may have a certain expectation of a reasonable turnaround time. Usually, the results obtained from the computer system are used to control some process or activity in the organisation. In that case, the expected turnaround time is related to the response time required for the control of the activity. Jobs may be processed in the order they arrive at the computer centre or in some order of priority according to their needs. Generally it is desirable to process the shorter jobs first in order to achieve better overall turnaround.

*Response time* is understood as the gap between the time a condition needing control action is created and the time when the corresponding control action is initiated. In a chemical plant, response time may be the interval between reading instruments and making appropriate adjustments to valves, temperature controls, etc. In the context of an interactive computer system, the response time is understood as the time between feeding a query to the system and obtaining the reply from it or between feeding a command and the execution of the command by the system. Such response times must be optimised to meet the users' demands, according to each type of application. In some applications the value of having a fast or real-time response is only marginally better than that of a slow response. In other applications a fast response is vital, ie a computerised system without fast response time would not be viable. This is particularly true when the public is directly involved; for example, at a railway reservation counter or a bank counter. By contrast, the demands on a monthly production planning system may not be that pressing.

The response time required in a specific application may be 'immediate', 'conversational', 'as convenient', 'deferred', 'daily' or 'non-urgent'. Systems controlling a technical process may need to give a very fast response to certain events. A switch closing, or a temperature being exceeded, may cause an immediate interruption of the process being run. A program to deal with such a condition is expected to give the fastest response possible. Conditions requiring conversational response include answering user enquiries, making an airline booking, debugging a program, or processing a bank transaction. In these cases, the response time must be geared to human reaction time. Less than one second is unnecessarily fast and may even be intimidating. More than 10 seconds is too long, and the human terminal operator will become impatient. If the operator is carrying on a complex conversation with a computer, the response needs to be within two or three seconds. Users of a terminal judge the performance of the entire system from the response which they themselves obtain, even though the computer may well be concurrently processing many tasks.

Some terminal-based transactions may need to be processed quickly but are not subject to the constraints of conversational-mode working. Management reports, for instance, might fall into this category where the response may be provided 'as convenient'. Some computers receive jobs from the computer room and/or from distant terminals which can wait in a queue to be processed. These jobs are processed on a basis of priority. Nevertheless the system will be designed so that the job queues do not become too large and the items will normally not have to wait longer than an hour or so.

With many types of transactions, it is desirable to complete the processing on a daily basis. Cost figures may be produced daily. Tomorrow's delivery schedule may be determined by today's events. The collection and distribution of the necessary data will often involve data transmission, particularly if long distances are involved. Some other functions are not urgent and can be dealt with in batches of weekly (or longer) cycles. Output can be distributed by post.

## BATCH PROCESSING SYSTEMS

Batch processing was the original method of data processing. Batch techniques were used almost exclusively until the 1960s to process computer applications. The procedures involved in data entry, batching, controls, processing, dissemination and distribution of results were dictated by the limitations of hardware (and associated software) available at the time.

Whilst major advances have been made, it is worth noting that batch processing may in some circumstances still be the best solution. However, the methods of data capture and subsequent transmission of output are more sophisticated than those employed originally. Furthermore, the batch processing is likely to be carried out in a mixed environment where on-line systems take priority and batch processing is performed in the background. The characteristics of a batch processing system are:

- large volumes of data;
- turnaround times which are not critical;
- a series (suite) of programs which processes one set of data;
- the passing of the complete set of data through each program in turn;

- processing efficiency considered to be more important than rapid turnaround of results;
- data processed at a rate determined by the computer, not by the operator.

An obvious feature is delay due to periodicity of processing. For example, a sales engineer might know that inventory was available at the end of the last processing period (say, the first of the month) to fill an order, but he could not assume on the fifth that his order could still be filled.

Batch processing is basically a periodic processing system with the cycle of processing repeated at the end of each period. Data is captured on paper documents as in a manual processing system. Use is often made of preprinted forms which may be modified versions of those used in the earlier manual system to facilitate orderly punching in the codified form. Users are often expected to fill in data in code numbers to avoid unnecessary punching effort and the ambiguities that descriptions can create. The alternative code numbers are either preprinted on the form or supplied in the form of code directories to respective users. The transaction documents are collected into convenient batches for despatch to the data processing centre at the end of a prescribed period or as and when convenient.

Batch processing systems generate periodic reports, at the end of each period, to indicate the status of the application system at the cut-off date of the period. The reports generated may be either 'detailed', 'summary', or 'exception'. *Detailed reports* may indicate the status of each item in the system in a desired sequence. *Summary reports* may sum up the details for a group of items on the basis of some common parameter, like department-wise summary, territory-wise summary, etc. The *exception reports* highlight only those items where the status is widely different from the expected. Exception reports are very useful to management for exercising control in the functioning of the organisation.

Batch processing does not make too much demand on the hardware and software resources. Conventional centralised computer systems, without a communication interface and on-line terminals, are quite suitable for batch processing. However, a multiprogramming facility is quite useful for the efficient utilisation of the computer. Batch processing programs are comparatively simple in nature as they do not involve dialogue between the user and the computer but only reading of records from input devices, processing them, and writing results on output devices. In any application where minute-to-minute information is not necessary, and periodic information on a daily, weekly or monthly basis is good enough, batch processing is always recommended. Many real-life applications fall into this category. Payroll and accounting systems are common examples.

Another important area is that of management reports for planning and control. Planning in organisations is generally a periodic exercise. This includes financial plans, marketing plans, etc. While it may be a weekly, monthly or annual exercise in the functional areas, annual and five-year plans are prepared at corporate and national levels. Information systems to support such planning and control procedures need also to be able to serve such periodic requirements.

## ON-LINE AND REAL-TIME PROCESSING SYSTEMS

*On-line* refers to the direct contact of the computer system with its users, a feature that offers many tangible benefits. The lengthy data preparation, submission, error detection, correction and resubmission cycles are cut out by enabling the originator of data to record it directly into the computer system. This approach saves elapsed time and avoids many system complexities needed to minimise the incidence of error. If the originators of data also enter it, they will understand its meaning better than will data preparation staff and computer operators. Consequently they will make fewer mistakes in entering data. Also, the system can refer to them for adjudication on feasibility violations. There is, moreover, an opportunity for programs to suspend processing until doubtful data is checked, rather than unfounded assumptions being made, simply to avoid a programmed halt.

Error detection and subsequent processing becomes conversational, with computer contributions made in time to assist in the execution of a live task. For example, the computer may check the customer's credit status before accepting an order. The operator may then be given the option to accept an order, despite an unsatisfactory credit position, or to have that order put on a rejected list to be reported later.

On the other hand, the loss of data preparation stages removes a number of opportunities for exercising control over the use of the system. An on-line system must therefore include security features within the computer programs. There are three aspects to be incorporated: security of access to facilities, security of data files, and the audit trail. The first involves the employment of techniques to ensure that unauthorised persons are not able to use the system, in total or in part. The second implies the protection of data which is personally or commercially private (this level of protection is particularly important in the age of hackers and computer viruses). The third is concerned with maintaining a record of what actions have been carried out. Provision of an audit trail is particularly important if the terminals used make no automatic record of activity in a permanent form.

The term '*real-time*' covers a wide range of computer (and other) systems, but all share the common feature that results of some kind are demanded by deadlines imposed by the 'real' world outside the system. Real-time systems are basically on-line systems with tight constraints on response time and availability. In these systems the data is processed to make results available within a timescale that can influence external events. The range of timescales may vary from microseconds, as in a digital signal processor, to a couple of seconds in an airline reservation system.

'Real-time' is used to describe two very different kinds of systems. The older usage applied to such things as airline reservation systems and message-switching systems. These systems were regarded as real-time because an operator sat at a terminal waiting for a response. Such systems are also commonly called 'interactive'. The other kind of real-time system was once less common; for example, the 'process-control' system, in which the computer is directing or monitoring some ongoing physical process.

## DISTRIBUTED PROCESSING SYSTEMS

Distributed processing systems represent an evolutionary path from early centralised systems. Developments in technology, and the consequential rapid fall in prices, have demolished the economies of scale that existed in centralised systems. Earlier distribution was in the form of resource sharing networks. In the late-1960s, it became possible to link autonomous computers into 'networks' through which information could be exchanged and resources shared; for example, ARPANET was developed to link universities and research centres both within America and throughout the rest of the world.

The main use of resource-sharing networks is to allow users to transfer data files from one site to another, or to log onto one site from another because a needed hardware or software resource is available at the other site. However, many a job can be processed locally using local data at the user location. Such jobs have to be transmitted to the central computer and results retransmitted to the user in a centralised on-line system. Some of this communication can be avoided, using distributed processing, without disturbing the logical integration of the system.

A distributed processing system is one in which there are several autonomous but interacting processors and/or data stores at different geographical locations. A distinction should be drawn between distributed and networking systems. In networking systems the objective is to transport tasks efficiently to an optimum processing resource which is not usually sited at the point of user activity. By contrast, the objective of distributed systems is to process as many tasks as economically possible or administratively desirable, at the point of user activity. A network provides only for transporting tasks to desired locations for processing, whereas in a distributed system a task may be processed co-operatively by two or more locations sharing processing capacity, stored data and software.

# 2 Information Technology Today

Developments in computer technology and communications technology and their merger have given rise to information systems that are geographically spread but functionally integrated. The underlying technology has come to be known as Information Technology. In this chapter we shall have a closer look at this technology and its current state.

## ORGANISATION OF COMPUTER SYSTEM COMPONENTS

A computer system, like any other system, receives input, processes input and delivers the processed input as output. The computer receives data as input, processes it into useful information and delivers information as output. Some input devices allow direct human/machine communication, while others require data to be recorded on an input medium such as a magnetisable material. Punched paper cards and paper tape have been widely used in the past as input media. The magnetic media commonly used now are the specially coated plastic flexible or 'floppy' disks and magnetic tapes. The keyboard of a workstation connected directly to a computer is an example of a direct input device. The other input devices are the mouse, light pen, touch screen, microphone, etc.

The heart of any computer system is the central processing unit commonly known as the CPU. The CPU contains the primary or main storage, arithmetic-logic, and control sections. The main storage, also know as 'memory', is used for storing data fed as input, the program to be used for processing, data being processed and results of processing before they are transferred to an output device. All calculations are performed and all comparisons (decisions) are made in the arithmetic-logic section of the CPU. By selecting, interpreting, and seeing to the execution of program instructions, the control section of the CPU maintains order and directs the operation of the entire system. Although the control section does not process data, it acts as a central nervous system for the other data-manipulating components of the computer.

Output devices, like input devices, are instruments of interpretation and communication between humans and computers. In personal computer systems, display screens and desktop printers are popular output devices. Larger and faster printers, many on-line workstations, and magnetic tape and rigid disk units often accept the output of larger systems.

Secondary (or auxiliary) storage devices are used in most computer systems to supplement the limited storage capacity of the primary storage section. Secondary storage devices, like input and output devices, are connected or are on-line to the CPU. Rigid magnetic disks, floppy disks and magnetic tapes are commonly used for secondary storage. Input/output and secondary storage units are sometimes called peripheral devices or just peripherals, because they are often located around the processing unit.

Once the program is fed into the computer memory, the computer works under the control of the program and the data is processed as specified in the program instructions. A computer program consists of a series of steps called instructions, each instruction involving a basic arithmetic or logic operation. The speed at which a computer performs processing is based on its 'cycle time'. For a typical small computer the cycle time would be in the order of 500-600 nanoseconds (ns), and much less for larger computers going to less than 10 ns for a supercomputer, a nanosecond being one billionth or thousand-millionth of a second.

## MAIN STORAGE OR MEMORY

The main or primary storage section of a computer has many small storage areas called locations or words. A word can store a specific number of binary digits (0 or 1), called bits, depending on the architecture of the computer. The word length may generally vary from 8 bits for a very small computer to 64 bits for a very large computer. A group of 8 bits is also called a byte. Each word is assigned an address – a built-in and unique number that identifies the word location. A word or storage location can hold either a data item or an instruction, and its identifying number remains the same regardless of its contents. A group of binary digits is used to represent alphabetic and numeric characters using a data representation coding scheme. The user does not have to bother about data representation coding schemes as coding and decoding from alphanumeric to binary and vice versa is automatically handled by the computer itself. Retrieving data from a storage location is non-destructive, but entering data into a location is destructive, ie the previous contents of the location are automatically erased and replaced.

The first general-purpose electronic computer (ENIAC), built in 1946 and already mentioned, used vacuum tubes to build memory. These tubes were relatively large, and each was able to hold only a single bit. Storage capacity was thus tiny by present standards. The most popular computer in the mid-1950s (the IBM 650) used a rotating drum coated with a magnetisable material as the primary storage device.

Between 1960 and 1975, however, the dominant computer storage design used tiny rings or cores of magnetisable material in the primary storage section. These tiny rings could be magnetised in the clockwise or anti-clockwise direction by passing current through a wire passing through the ring in either direction to represent a 0 or a 1. Today virtually all computers use semiconductor elements in their primary storage sections. Semiconductor storage elements are tiny integrated circuits. Both the storage cell circuits and the support circuitry needed for data writing and reading are packaged on chips of silicon. The chips usually used for the primary storage section employ metal-oxide semiconductor (MOS) technology. These primary storage components are often referred to as random access memory (RAM) chips because any of the locations on a chip can be randomly selected and used to directly store and retrieve data and instructions. RAM chips provide volatile storage, ie the data stored are lost in the event of a power failure.

Other types of memory include read-only memory (ROM) chips which are used by manufacturers to permanently store some programs. Such chips have found wide application as a program storage medium in video games and personal computers. Users can 'burn-in' their own frequently-used programs on a programmable read-only memory (PROM) chip. Once operations have been written into a PROM chip, they are permanent and cannot be altered.

With developments in technology over the last fifteen years, the number of bits that can be stored on a chip has quadrupled every three years. During the same period, the cost per bit of storage has been cut in half every three years. Today, many chips are available that store one million bits and cost only a few dollars each. The speed of processing can be considerably enhanced with the use of high-speed buffer called 'cache' memory. Cache memory is both faster and more expensive per character stored than primary storage. This high-speed circuitry is used as a 'scratch pad' to temporarily store data and instructions that are likely to be retrieved many times during processing. Once found only in larger systems, cache memory is now available in some of the tiny microprocessor chips used in personal computers.

For many years, the size of a program was effectively limited by the size of the computer's primary storage section because the complete program was held in primary storage during its entire execution. If the program size did not exceed the limited primary storage capacity, then there was no problem. But if, on the other hand, the task required thousands of instructions, then the programmer might be forced to find ways to trim the program or to divide it into separate jobs. This can be a tedious and time-consuming chore. To avoid this situation, operating systems with virtual storage capability have been developed. The basic approach is to divide the total program into small sequences of instructions called either 'pages' or 'segments'. Then, only those program pages or segments that are actually required at a particular time need be in the primary (or real) storage. The remaining pages or segments may be kept temporarily in on-line (or virtual) storage, from where they can be rapidly retrieved as needed following a program interruption. The operating system handles the swapping of program pages or segments between primary and on-line secondary storage units. Thus, from the application programmer's point of view, the effective (or virtual) size of the available primary storage may appear to be unlimited.

## DIRECT ACCESS DEVICES

Magnetic disks are by far the most popular direct-access storage medium. They are typically made of thin metal plates coated on both sides with a magnetisable recording material. These disks may remain permanently in their cabinets or they may be packaged in portable or replaceable assemblies called 'disk packs'. Regardless of whether disks are permanently mounted or portable, they are placed on a vertical shaft which rotates at a high constant speed. A space is left between the spinning disks to allow access arms with small read-write heads to move to any storage location. Data are organised into a number of concentric circles on the disk surface called 'tracks'. Each track has a designated location number. There are typically 200 to 800 tracks on the disk surface. The track is divided into 'sectors' (or 'blocks') that are fixed in size. The unit of transfer of data may be one or more of these fixed-size sectors.

The disks, once in the drive, spin continuously, often at thousands of revolutions per minute. The read-write heads are capable of crossing the disk surface from track to track very quickly, so a data file, or even a page in the file containing a given record, may be reached in milliseconds. Thus the disk and its drive give the computer user 'direct access' not only to files on the disk but to particular items of data within those files. On command from the CPU to read data from a specified sector, the read-write head moves axially to the position of the respective track. This involves axial delay or seek time. Then it waits for the specified sector to spin under the head. This involves the rotational delay or latency. The actual reading may take place at the rate of 256 kilobytes per second or more. But the total time to read an isolated sector consisting of seek, latency and actual read may be of the order of 50 to 100 milliseconds. While a floppy disk may store about one million bytes or one megabyte of data and costs only five dollars, a rigid disk may store up to 500 megabytes or more and costs a few hundred dollars.

The drives that allow a disk or disk pack or a cartridge to be removed are called exchangeable disk drives whereas those that do not are called fixed disk drives. Disks may either be rigid or flexible; the latter are also known as floppy disks and sometimes diskettes. Rigid disks come in four main standard diameters for large computer systems and are often used in packs of up to twelve. Large computers normally use rigid disks of 14 inches in diameter. The smaller computers may use disks that are only 8 inches, 5 ¼ inches, or 3 ½ inches in diameter. These smaller disk units are also known as Winchester drives. Flexible disks also come in four diameters: 8 inches, 5 ¼ inches, 3 ½ inches and 3 inches, although there is as yet no standard for the format of the smaller ones.

Optical disks use storage techniques based on light instead of magnetism as with other disks. Optical disks are being widely used in consumer electronics today. The 12-inch disk is used for audio-visual recording while the smaller compact disk (CD) of 4.7-inch diameter records high-quality music. In both cases, tiny pits visible only under the microscope are burned or pressed into a thin coating of metal or other material deposited on a disk. The pit patterns represent the streams of digital data that are used to encode images and sounds. A beam of laser light is used to read the pit patterns and convert these patterns into audiovisual signals. The bits burned or pressed into optical disks cannot be erased, and the disks cannot be reused to record new signals.

The same optical disk technology used in consumer products is also used to store and retrieve data. CD-ROM (compact disk, read-only memory) optical storage disks and drives based on the same technology are used with personal computers. The storage density of optical disks is enormous, the storage cost is very low, and the access time is relatively fast. Just one CD-ROM disk stores about 550 megabytes which is equivalent to the capacity of more than 500 floppy disks or 15 magnetic tapes.

In addition to the CD-ROM, there are also laser-based writable optical storage devices. With write-once read-many, or WORM, systems users record their own data on blank optical disks.

## MAGNETIC TAPE DEVICES

Magnetic tape has been used as a backing storage medium since the very early computers were produced. Because of its relatively fast transfer rate, magnetic tape is still a very popular input medium for high-speed, large-volume applications. In addition to providing rapid input and output, it is the most widely used secondary off-line computer storage medium. Today there are two basic types of magnetic tape devices in general use. The first is the standard computer tape which consists of ½-inch wide plastic tape with a magnetic surface. Data characters are coded in the form of magnetised bits across the width of the tape. A standard tape today may store as much as 800 to 6250 characters per inch of tape length. A full length tape running into 2400 feet may store a few million characters. The rate of transfer of characters from the magnetic tape into the CPU storage and vice versa during the read and write operations may typically be in the range of 20,000 to 200,000 characters per second.

The other type of tape is the cartridge or cassette tape which is similar to the ordinary cassette tape used in modern audio or video tape recorders. Data is stored on this in a serial fashion, ie one bit following another. Accordingly, the recording density and the rate of transfer of characters for the cartridge is much less than on the standard tape.

Tapes are ideally suited to serial processing of large volumes of data. They are also inherently more secure than fixed disks as the only time they can be accessed is when they are loaded onto the computer. This is normally done by an operator who can check that the program requesting the file is authorised to do so. Tape formats are more standard than disk formats. This makes them a good medium for the transfer of information between machines. Being smaller in size and physically less susceptible to damage than rigid disks, they can be easily transported between sites. Backing-up data on tape is also a cheap and effective way of providing security copies of files which can be stored off site.

## VISUAL DISPLAY UNITS

The Visual Display Unit (VDU) is an interactive device linking the user directly with the computer. It consists of a keyboard for manual input of characters and a screen or cathode ray tube (CRT) which displays the characters held in the VDU's character store for output. The input and output features of the VDU allow a response to be sent by the computer to the point at which the data originated. This is a 'conversational' facility, giving immediate acknowledgement to the user, together with prompts and comments on any errors. VDUs are often called 'terminals' since in medium- and large-scale computer systems they may be situated at locations remote from the CPU, although the operators may also interact with the system via local connections. In small computer systems such as minis and micros, the VDU is often local to (and sometimes integral with) the processor. A terminal is described as local when it is connected, often by a cable, to a computer in the same building. It is a remote terminal when it is connected to the computer via an external circuit supplied by the telephone authority.

The VDU is very useful for increased speed, silence and convenience when one does not necessarily need hard-copy records of messages received and sent. A small matrix printer may, however, be used with a VDU to provide a hard-copy facility.

The input to the VDU is supplied by manually typing in on the keyboard of the VDU. The keyboard is basically the same as the mechanical typewriter keyboard in that it has keys for printing upper- and lower-case letters, numbers and a variety of symbols. However, since it is not used to just print out letters and numbers, it needs to have extra keys to perform these additional tasks. These are generally the Function keys, Control/Alt keys, Cursor keys, Return key, ESC key and Numeric keypad keys.

The output from the VDU is displayed on the television-like screen (the CRT, cathode ray tube). Screen size varies considerably, but may be typically 8 inches high by 10 inches wide providing 40 or 80 characters per line and 20 to 25 lines for a 2000-character display. There is also considerable variety in format and size of displayed characters. Brightness and contrast controls are usually provided to enable the operator to adjust the image intensity. A blinking (flashing) field facility is available on some terminals which can be used to draw the user's attention to a field. Other terminals offer a different image intensity, a reverse negative effect, or a different character font to identify selected fields. The colours offered vary according to supplier – common ones are green/black, orange/brown and white/black.

Graphics terminals may be low-resolution or high-resolution. Graphs, charts, maps, and other visual aids prepared from pages of statistical data are better able to capture and hold the interest of viewers. Data showing the relationships, changes, and trends that are often buried in piles of alphanumeric reports can be highlighted with a few graphic representations using package software. The screen of an engineering workstation is often used by designers, engineers, and architects to display preliminary sketches. Workstation programs analyse the sketches and report on certain characteristics. Designers and engineers then interact with their workstations to produce finished drawings. This is commonly referred to as Computer-aided Design (CAD). Another allied application on the shop floor is Computer-aided Manufacture (CAM).

Office personnel use graphics software packages to convert alphanumeric input data into colourful and informative pictures on their VDU screens. A growing office market for PCs capable of producing high-resolution images in multiple colours has also developed. After engineering drawings or office graphics aids have been displayed on a screen to a user's satisfaction, permanent copies can be prepared using dot-matrix printers, plotters or film recorders. Graphical information can also be fed as input through the VDU. This can be done using a 'light pen', a 'joy-stick', a 'mouse' or a 'tablet' which may be available with the VDU.

## WORD PROCESSING AND DESKTOP PUBLISHING

Word processing systems use hardware and software to create, view, edit, manipulate, transmit, store, retrieve and print text material through the VDU. Desktop publishing systems combine computers and suitable peripherals with software that can produce attractive page layouts complete with pictures and text printed in a variety of typefaces or fonts.

There are two categories of desktop publishing systems. The more capable and more expensive (over $20,000) units are the dedicated publishing systems built around powerful engineering workstations. These stations have a large storage capacity, and are equipped with high-resolution screens that can be divided (or 'mapped') into thousands of dots or picture elements. Each picture element, or pixel, may be turned on or off by software to create pictures and text in different fonts and formats. 'Digitisers' or scanners are commonly used to convert art, photo, and text images into a digitised map of 'on' and 'off' pixels that can be fed into the station's processor. Bundled into each dedicated system is the sophisticated software that allows all the hardware components to work in a unified way with text processing, page layout and other program elements.

In the second desktop publishing category are those that use general-purpose PCs to run off-the-shelf desktop publishing packages. These packages combine text and graphics manipulating capabilities to allow users to combine charts and pictures with text and headlines. Desktop publishing packages give PCs many of the general capabilities found in dedicated publishing systems. Both types of system accept digitised text and picture input; both accept data imported from WP (word processing), page format, and graphics files; both allow users to create, edit, format and enter text and graphics into documents; and both then send these documents to laser or other graphics printers, or to phototypesetting or other output machines.

## PRINTERS AND PLOTTERS

Printers are the primary output devices used to prepare permanent documents for human use. There are four types of printers in use: character printers, line printers, page printers and graphics printers and plotters. Character printers are one-character-at-a-time devices used with personal computers and other workstations for low-volume printing jobs. They are usually of the impact type where the print is created by pressing a typeface against paper and inked ribbon like in a common typewriter. The impact character printers often use a 'daisy-wheel' or a 'dot-matrix' printing mechanism. The daisy-wheel printer uses a print wheel with a character embossed on each 'petal' of the wheel. In the dot-matrix printer, letters are formed by a combination of dots produced by the striking of tiny hammers.

Dot-matrix printers are usually faster than daisy-wheel devices and are often less expensive, but their print quality is not as good. They print from 30 to 600 characters/second and are available for less than $300. Daisy-wheel printers are available in the 10 to 90 characters/second range and cost from $500 upwards. Non-impact printers are also available that use thermal, electrostatic, chemical, or ink-jet technologies.

Line printers use impact methods to produce line-at-a-time printed output, some are dot-matrix devices, but others typically use rapidly moving chains or bands of print characters or some form of print drum to print lines of information on paper. From 300 to over 3000 lines can be printed each minute depending on the printer used. Line printers cost upwards of $2000.

Non-impact desktop printers that use laser light to produce the dots needed to form pages of characters have become popular PC output devices. Blending printer and office-copier technologies, these 'laser printers' write the desired output image on a copier drum with a light beam that operates under computer control. High-speed page printers can produce documents at speeds of over 20,000 lines per minute. Each page is an original, since there can be no carbon copies.

Although they come with a five- or six-figure price tag and thus cost more than many entire computer systems, high-speed printers can be economical when hundreds of thousands of pages are printed each month. A dot-matrix printer can produce effective pictures through its ability to generate hundreds of lines of tiny dots on an inch of paper. Even many of the inexpensive dot-matrix printers used with PCs have a graphics capability. Some ink-jet and thermal-transfer printers also have impressive multicolour graphics capabilities. The dot density of laser printers, about 300 dots per inch, exceeds that of dot matrix devices, so laser systems can produce excellent graphics images. Graphics plotters are also available that use pen or ink-jet approaches. These plotters are able to produce large drawings, mounted on a flat-bed table or a drum, containing many colours. Plotters can produce complete drawings at a rate of several inches per second at a resolution of a few thousandths of an inch.

## POINT-OF-SALE TERMINALS

Point-of-sale (POS) terminals are used in retail or wholesale organisations such as supermarkets as the customer transaction occurs. They are replacing cash registers as they can do everything a cash register does plus many other things. Manufacturers print a Universal Product Code (UPC), consisting of light and dark bars, on most items sold in grocery stores. When bar-coded items are received at a supermarket's automated checkout stand, they are pulled across a fixed scanning window. As items are scanned, the bars are decoded by an Optical Character Reader (OCR). The data are transmitted to a computer that looks up the price, possibly updates inventory and sales records, forwards price and description information back to the checkout stand, and prints a sales receipt.

Other POS terminals in department stores can be used to (a) make a direct enquiry about the credit status of the customer, (b) improve inventory control, and (c) produce faster and more accurate sales information. Such a POS terminal may be equipped with a handheld 'wand reader' that can be used to speed up the sales transaction. A special tag called the 'kimball tag' is in effect a miniature punched card containing details of the goods to which it is attached. The kimball tag and the customer credit card can be read by the point-of-sale terminal.

## MAGNETIC-INK CHARACTER READERS

Magnetic-ink character recognition (MICR) is widely used by banks to process the tremendous volume of cheques being read each day. The cheques are precoded along the bottom with the bank's identification number and with the depositer's account number. These numbers and other special symbols are printed with a special ink that contains magnetisable particles. The reading station is used to sense and identify the magnetic characters as they pass through. The data being read can be entered directly into a computer, or they can be transferred to magnetic tape for later processing. As up to 2600 cheques pass through the machine each minute, they are also sorted into pockets according to their identification code numbers. People can easily read the magnetic ink characters. But the amount of information that can be contained on each document is limited and it can only be located in special predetermined positions. MICR uses only ten digits and four special characters needed for bank processing. No alphabetic characters are available.

## OPTICAL CHARACTER READERS

Unlike MICR, optical character recognition (OCR) techniques permit the direct reading of *any* printed character. No special ink is required. This OCR flexibility makes it possible for organisations to eliminate or reduce the input keying bottleneck. In addition to reading bar codes and merchandise tags, which has already been discussed, readers designed to interpret handmade marks and machine printed characters are commonly used in off-line operations to prepare data for processing. Most of these will recognise machine printed characters in a single selected typeface or 'font', although some are switchable between fonts. This method of input is ideally suited to documents which can be used as 'turnaround' documents. Gas and electricity bills are good examples. The bills are printed with all the information necessary for re-input to the system in an OCR font. If the customer pays the amount stated on the bill (which happens in well over 90 per cent of cases) then the portion of the bill with the OCR data on it can be returned for direct input to the system.

## OPTICAL MARK READERS AND SCANNERS

Optical mark readers are often used to read documents with objective multiple choice information like examination papers, survey questionnaires, etc. The marks can be made mechanically so that the document can be part of a turnaround system. Where marks are made clerically, the intermediate stage of keypunching is eliminated. Optical scanners can also read certain handmade letters and numbers, but these characters must usually be precisely written. The automatic reading of handwritten script is still some years away in the future.

## SENSORS AND FACTORY TERMINALS

For industrial computer applications, such as process control, the computer is required to interact directly with the plant. Sensors are designed to detect such physical (analogue) variables as temperature, pressure, flow rate, light intensity, electric voltages, electric currents, angular velocity, switch positions, etc and feed their values into the computer. The computer performs an output function by having its electrical signals converted to the required physical values, eg to operate an electric motor (which in turn could operate a wide variety of equipment), or to switch equipment 'on' or 'off'.

## CASH DISPENSERS AND SMART CARDS

Cash dispensers have become a familiar sight in our high streets. A plastic embossed card with information such as the customer's account code and credit limit encoded on a magnetic strip is inserted into a slot and a security number input on a small numeric keyboard together with the amount required to be withdrawn. The whole transaction is prompted by instructions shown on a small display screen. Details of the transaction are recorded and used either immediately or later for updating the customer's account. Smart cards are an alternative to magnetic-strip cards. Smart-card technology substitutes a built-in micro-computer chip for the magnetic strip. The chip stores information to reduce the chances of fraud and abuse. Data representing a specific amount of cash can be stored in the chip before the card is issued to a customer. As the card is used to make purchases, the purchase amount is deducted from the stored balance by special electronic registers used by merchants. These electronic registers periodically communicate with the card-issuing company's computer. In effect, customers gradually 'cash in their chips' and use up their electronic money. The card holder may then be able to replenish the stored balance at an automatic banking machine. Smart cards can also store a record of more than 100 purchases.

## VOICE AND SPEECH

Computers can be programmed to recognise sounds. A microphone or telephone is used to convert human speech into electric signals. The signal patterns are recognised by comparing a 'dictionary' of patterns that have been previously stored in the computer. The voice pattern must resemble the one the computer has been trained to recognise. Existing systems cannot recognise an unlimited number of words spoken in a continuous stream. Audio-response systems are also available to respond to human enquiries that are transmitted over telephone lines to a central computer. Such a response may be generated by assembling the pre-recorded sounds in the proper sequence and transmitting them back to the station requesting the information.

Machine vision systems have been developed which can recognise a limited set of objects. Such a system uses a TV camera to 'see' images and details, and a computer to then compare the scanned patterns with the stored images that it has been programmed to recognise. Most machine vision systems in use today are found in factories. Some robots with machine vision are programmed to recognise and separate the various components in a bin of parts. Other machine vision systems check the quality of assembled items as they pass an inspection point; or are able to recognise the various components needed in the assembly of some products. It is expected that the rapid development of robots with machine vision will permit the widespread automation of future quality control and assembly processes.

## RANGE OF COMPUTER SYSTEMS

In the 1970s the application of microelectronics led to decreases in the size and price of computers whilst increasing their capabilities. A wide range of 'microcomputers' was developed and marketed to the small user in industry and commerce. At one end of the scale, the microcomputer is small and cheap but has limited power; at the other end, it cannot be distinguished from a mini, either in cost or facilities. The range of computers marketed today can be loosely classified into home computer, personal computer, microcomputer, minicomputer, mainframe and supercomputer.

The real breakthrough for the 'home computer' was the Sinclair ZX80, designed by the British electronics entrepreneur Sir Clive Sinclair. It was launched in 1980 and cost about £150. Its successors, the ZX81 and Spectrum also proved immensely popular. Home computers are designed for personal domestic applications and are also widely used by students. 'Personal computers' for business applications are now very popular. Some of the widely used models are the IBM PCs and their compatibles and the Macintosh II. Personal computers may be used by individual professionals: a doctor may maintain computer-based records on patients; a small retail store may use PCs to maintain financial and stock accounts; and individual managers in large corporations may use PCs as part of a network linked to other computers.

Before the advent of the micros, small computers were called minis. Today a 'minicomputer' would be a multiterminal, multiuser system. A minicomputer may be used for a dedicated real-time application such as a reservation or banking system or for a mix of real-time and batch processing applications. It may be used in a medium-size organisation for a range of applications such as payroll, financial accounts, costing, sales administration, production planning, etc.

Because of the large size of the early computers they were called 'mainframes'. The term still applies to the large computers used by corporations as the main computers to which the minis and micros, in different departments and sections, may be connected.

Some of the complex scientific applications such as weather forecasting and nuclear research require a large volume of data to be manipulated within a short time. This is accomplished by 'supercomputers' able to perform hundreds of millions of calculations every second.

## COMPUTER NETWORKS

Computer systems at two or more locations (nodes) which are connected together using communication links form a computer network. Depending on the topology of the interconnecting communication network, they may form a star, bus, loop or mesh network. In a *star* network, a number of small terminal computers are individually connected to a large central computer. In a *bus* network, the computers are all individually connected to a communication link or bus. Computers may be connected to one another in the form of a *loop* or, using an irregular interconnection of computers, to form a *mesh* network. The network topology is selected according to the required nature of use and the required sharing of information and other resources.

Networks can also be categorised according to the geographical area they cover: Local Area Network (LAN) and Wide Area Network (WAN). A LAN is a shared local data communications facility contained within a small geographical radius of up to a few kilometres. Typically a LAN serves a single department or links several departments throughout an office building. LANs, usually owned and managed by a single private organisation independent of the telecommunications authorities (PTTs), are characterised by ease of interfacing through standard interfaces, modern transmission methods, high-speed data transfer and low error rates.

A LAN may interconnect a variety of devices such as microcomputers, personal computers, office workstations, mini-computers, mainframes, terminals, printers, plotters, etc; and may provide shared hardware resources.

Printers and disk storage devices may be shared among all the network users, such that each device can communicate with every other device on the network. LANs may also provide shared software resources. Single networked versions of popular software may be held centrally and loaded into each user's microcomputer when the application needs to be run. General application packages such as word processing, spreadsheets and database management are typical examples of applications accessed in this way. Shared data resources may also be provided so that users have access to multiuser databases.

Local area networks are used for a wide variety of applications in different organisations. They include office automation (electronic mail, electronic messaging, database access, etc). In industry they may be used for manufacturing and factory floor communications, CAD/CAM, and process control. They are used for electronic publishing in newspapers, TV news, document publishing and document imaging. In retail stores they may provide a network of point-of-sale terminals. They are also used in banking, insurance, stock exchanges, educational institutions and libraries.

## TRANSMISSION FACILITIES

### Electronic Data Interchange

Wide area networks are used by large corporations having operations at many distant locations; different business organisations forming trading partners; and universities or government institutions – to exchange data, share hardware, software and data resources.

Electronic Data Interchange (EDI) is the name given to the exchange of structured data between the computer systems of trading partners. It is predicted that this method of 'paperless' trading will revolutionise the way companies do business. EDI covers trade data interchange (invoices, purchase orders, acknowledgements, delivery instructions, etc), product data interchange (CAD/CAM, engineering design, etc), interactive enquiry/confirmation messages, and electronic funds transfer. EDI is now being implemented, nationally and internationally, for organisations of every size in many different business sectors, including retail, manufacturing, commerce, transport and shipping.

EDI speeds up the trading cycle, enabling a faster response to customer orders and requests. In addition, by using agreed message (or data exchange) standards, EDI simplifies the customer's data processing task by accurately supplying only that minimum amount of data that is required by the customer. In addition to document printing and mailing cost savings, the effort required for verifying and keying outgoing and particularly incoming documentation, such as invoices, is unnecessary. Shorter order, delivery and payment cycles imply lower stock levels, the release of valuable capital and improved cashflow. 'Just-in-time' manufacturing relies on a close link between the manufacturer, the supplier and the customer. EDI forges this link by providing the timely and accurate information required on a daily basis, whilst promoting the trust and commitment required on a long-term basis. EDI software packages are now available for handling incoming and outgoing data and for linking to internal company applications.

## Teletex

Teletex is a recent text transmission facility which offers transmission speeds up to thirty times faster than Telex. Users operate Teletex over public communication networks. Teletex offers point-to-point communication between terminals such as electronic typewriters, word processors and suitably equipped PCs. It offers document transfer with a high degree of accuracy and speed (one A4 page can be sent in about 20 seconds), and 24-hour service with unattended receipt of messages (as with Telex).

## Facsimile

Facsimile is concerned with the transmission of text and graphics in image form. This facility is becoming very popular commercially with more than two million machines sold worldwide. In certain business sectors the facsimile machine is as indispensable as the photocopier.

## Viewdata

Viewdata has become a familiar public information service as well as finding use in the travel, motor, insurance and banking trades. The attraction of Viewdata is its ease of use, particularly where users have minimal computer or technical literacy. Use is made of colour displays and graphics. A domestic colour television set fitted with a suitable adaptor can be used to provide a low-cost terminal into the service. Alternatively the facility can be used as a dedicated Videotex terminal or as a PC with Viewdata software. In a Viewdata system the vast amounts of data are stored on the host computer as pages. Users follow a routeing from one index page (menu) to another until the required page of information is reached. On the Viewdata terminal, information is presented in character frames divided into a number of rows and columns; eg Prestel, developed by British Telecom, uses 24 rows and 40 columns. Each character position can be occupied by either an alphabetic or numeric character or by a graphic mosaic cell used to construct chunky graphics.

## Electronic Mail

Electronic mail services (E-mail) can be set up over wide area networks for use in providing a private (within one organisation) or public messaging service. Electronic messaging has become very popular with an estimated 80,000 users in the UK at the end of 1986. The user of this service is able to prepare messages locally and send the resultant messages via a network of other users. Equally the user is able to receive messages. Messages are stored in a user's mailbox which is simply an allocated area of storage on the host computer where the mail software resides. Each user has password control over access to his mailbox. Messages can be read or updated by the mailbox holder and transmitted to other users if required.

In the UK, public electronic mail services operate under the Value Added and Data Services licence. The leading provider of this in the UK is Telecom Gold operated by BT. Other licensed service providers in the UK are Comet (Istel), Mercury Link 7500 (Cable and Wireless), One To One (Comtext International), and Quik-Comm (Geisco). Most of the services have the ability to access the Telex network. The basic ingredients typically required to access an electronic mail service comprise a terminal, modem, telephone line and relevant access authority. Terminals such as word processors, PCs, Viewdata sets and VDUs are suitable providing they are capable of asynchronous communication.

### CCITT X.400 Message Handling Service

One of the drawbacks of current electronic mail services is that mailboxes can only be reached by users of the same service (although links can be made to Telex). The X.400 provision, which is currently being introduced by the majority of PTTs in Western Europe and the United States, will provide a link between public and private electronic mail services. It will provide worldwide, vendor-independent, open systems interconnection for millions of users of messaging services, stand-alone terminals and personal computers.

# 3 Impact on Organisation Management

## PROCESS OF MANAGEMENT

The process of management has been described as Planning, Organising, Staffing, Leading and Controlling.

*Planning* is deciding in advance what to do, how to do it, when to do it, and who is to do it. Planning bridges the gap from where we are to where we want to be in a desired future. It strongly implies not only the introduction of new things, but also sensible and workable innovation. It makes it possible for things to occur that would not otherwise happen. Although the future situation can seldom be predicted with accuracy and unforeseen events may interfere with the best-laid plans, unless there is planning, actions of people tend to be aimless and left to chance.

*Organising* is that point of management that involves establishing an intentional structure of roles for people in an enterprise to fill. It is intentional in the sense of making sure that all the tasks necessary to accomplish goals are assigned and, it is hoped, assigned to people who can do them best.

*Staffing* involves filling, and keeping filled, the positions provided for by the organisation structure. It thus necessitates defining manpower requirements for the job to be done, and it includes making an inventory of, appraising and selecting candidates for positions; compensating and training or otherwise developing both candidates and current job holders to accomplish their jobs effectively.

*Leading* has to do with the predominantly interpersonal aspect of management. It involves motivation, leadership styles, approaches and communications.

*Controlling* is the measuring and correcting of activities of subordinates to ensure that events conform to plans. It measures performance against goals and plans, shows where negative deviations exist and by putting in motion actions to correct deviations, helps assure accomplishment of plans.

## Planning

Planning is the most basic of all managerial functions since it involves selecting from among alternative future courses of action. Also, planning is essential to the other four functions of organising, staffing, leading and controlling.

A manager organises, staffs, leads and controls in order to assure the attainment of goals and the plans designed to achieve them. Planning is an intellectually demanding process; it requires the conscious determination of courses of action, often in a highly complex environment. An important aspect of the managerial revolution of the past few decades has been a tremendous interest in planning.

Production managers discovered early that, without planning, their mistakes showed up within days – as production lines came to a halt because of a misfit point or absence of a needed component. Also, well-managed companies have long planned to meet cash needs before their cheques bounce. But, generally speaking, planning as a widely recognised and actively pursued managerial function is a fairly recent development.

Planning is carried out at various levels in the organisation. Plans can be classified as, or closely associated with, purposes, missions, objectives, strategies, policies, rules, procedures, programmes and budgets. Every organisation has, or at least *should* have, a *purpose* or *mission*, a basic function or task assigned to it by society. The general purpose of an organisation is the production and distribution of economic goods and services. The purpose of a state highway department is the design, building and operation of a system of state highways. The purpose of the courts is the interpretation of laws and their application. The purpose of a university is teaching and research. And so on.

*Objectives*, or *goals*, are the ends toward which organisational activities are aimed. Objectives constitute the basic plan of the enterprise. *Strategies* often denote a general programme of action implying commitment of emphasis and resources to attain broad objectives. Policies – general statements or understandings which guide or channel thinking and action in decision making – limit the area within which a decision is to be made and assure that the decision will be consistent with, and contribute to, the objectives.

*Policies* tend to predecide issues, avoid the necessity of repeated analysis and give a unified structure to other types of plans, thus permitting managers to delegate authority while maintaining control. *Procedures* are plans in that they establish a required method of handling future activities. They are truly guides to action, rather than to thinking, and they detail the exact manner in which a certain activity must be accomplished. Their essence is a chronological sequence of required actions. *Rules*, also, are predecided courses of action. A rule reflects a managerial decision that some action must be taken – or not be taken.

*Programmes* may be regarded as a complex of goals, policies, procedures, rules, task assignments, steps to be taken, resources to be employed and other elements necessary to carry out a given course of action. They are ordinarily supported by necessary capital and operating budgets.

A *budget* is a statement of expected results expressed in numerical terms. It may be referred to as a 'numberised' programme. It may be expressed either in financial terms or in terms of labour-hours, units of product, machine-hours or any other numerically measurable item. It may deal with operations, as the expense budget does; it may reflect capital outlays, as the capital expenditures budget does; or it may show flow of cash as the cash budget does.

## LEVELS OF MANAGEMENT

Management activity can be described in terms of the kinds and levels of decisions involved. Anthony (1965) views managerial activities as falling into three categories and argues that each is sufficiently of a kind to require distinctive planning and control systems. The first of these categories is 'Strategic Planning'. It is the process of deciding on the objectives of the organisation, on changes to these objectives, on the resources used to attain the objectives, and on the policies that are to govern acquisition, use and disposition of resources. Defining objectives implies an emphasis on scanning the organisation's environment.

The strategic planning process typically involves senior managers and analysts and often requires innovation and creativity. The complexity of the problems that arise and the non-routine manner in which they are handled make it difficult to appraise the quality of the planning process and to define rules for it.

The second category is 'Management Control'. This is the process by which managers ensure that resources are obtained and used effectively and efficiently in the accomplishment of the organisation's objectives. Anthony stresses three key issues in management control:

(1) the activity involves considerable interpersonal interaction;

(2) it takes place within the context of the policies and objectives developed in the strategic planning process;

(3) its paramount aim is to ensure effective and efficient performance.

The third category is 'Operational Control'. This is the process of ensuring that specific tasks are effectively and efficiently carried out. Operational control is concerned with performing predefined activities (such as manufacturing a specific unit) whereas management control more often relates to the organisation's policies. There is much less judgement required in the operational control area because the tasks, goals and resources have already been carefully defined.

The three levels of management described above can be considered only as a general framework. The actual levels of management in a specific organisation may be three, four or more, with suitable division of responsibilities. The combined levels of management can be depicted as the management system of the organisation (in which each level is concerned with planning and decision making). However, the function of management involves the fulfilment of the organisation's goals through the effort of other people. Management is concerned with the planning, leading, directing and controlling of the activities of its staff. The direct physical activities leading to the production of goods and services in the organisation are performed by the staff. This can be termed the operational activity system of the organisation. It is here that the direct resources of the organisation – manpower, materials, machinery, etc – exist and are utilised for the production of goods and services.

## PROCESS OF DECISION MAKING

A decision is a conscious choice from a set of possible alternative courses of action to achieve a desired goal. In a decision situation, the manager is confronted with the need to reach some goal that cannot be attained without positive action. He must have a clear understanding of alternative courses by which the goal could be reached under existing circumstances and limitations. He must have the information and the ability to analyse and evaluate alternatives in the light of the goal. And he must have a desire to achieve the best solution by selecting the alternative that is most likely to reach the goal.

Herbert Simon describes the process of decision making as comprising four steps: Intelligence, Design, Choice and Review. *Intelligence* is used to mean gathering information. The manager must have a continuous system of gathering and scanning information to be aware of the developments taking place within the organisation and its environment. This is necessary for him to identify situations calling for decision. For example, if the expenses are significantly in deviation from the budget, this calls for investigation. Similarly, if an export organisation finds that government has changed the rates of export duty, there is a need for re-evaluation of the company's policies.

*Design* refers to the design of alternative courses of action. It is rare for alternatives to be lacking for any course of action; indeed, a sound adage for any manager is that if there seems to be only one way of doing a thing, that way is probably wrong. In such a case, the manager probably has not considered other ways – which is necessary if the decision is to be the best possible. The ability to develop alternatives can be as important as selecting correctly from among them. On the other hand, ingenuity, research and common sense will often yield so many choices that not all of them can be adequately evaluated. Once appropriate alternatives have been found, the next step is to evaluate them and select the one that will best contribute to the goal. This is referred to as *choice*. The evaluation of alternatives has to be based on the prediction of outcome from each of the alternatives and their value in terms of the goals to be achieved.

This requires a clear understanding of the objectives or goals and a search for relationships among the more critical variables, constraints and premises in order to make predictions. In the past, experience was the only basis for evaluation. But today a number of operations research models, methods of cost-benefit analysis and system simulation are available to the manager to facilitate the making of predictions from possible alternatives and evaluating these predictions. Past choices can be subject to *reviews* to enable the manager to learn from mistakes.

## BUSINESS ORGANISATION AS A SYSTEM

It is useful to understand the function of a business organisation as a system. Like any other system, the business organisation operates through the medium of information. A simple model of the organisation as a system is shown in Figure 3.1.

Because the outputs of the system identify the purpose for which the system exists, we first examine the outputs of the business organisation. These objectives are multiple, but for a manufacturing organisation they must necessarily include the manufacture and sale of a product at a profit. Other organisations may produce services instead of products. If no objective is established, the organisation has no stated reason for existing, and therefore no system can be described or designed. Inputs to the organisation include the four classic items: men, money, materials and machinery – plus the vital fifth input of information.

What controls operate on the output of the organisation? There are considerations outside the firm, such as custom,

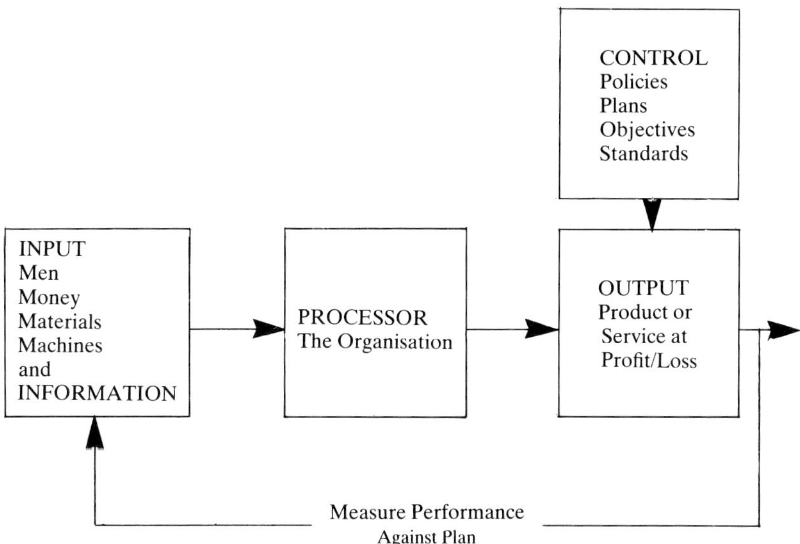


**Figure 3.1 Organisation as a System**

competitive environment, and government regulation that imply external control. These must be considered limitations on the operation of the system and information measures must be designed to measure output against them. However, for most design purposes, the internal controls are more important. Each subsystem has one or more measures of control and, as in the control process, these consist of standards of performance or some other measure of whether the output is within the limits previously established in the control measures (standards of performance) that operate on them. These elements are shown in Table 3.1.

| Subsystem | Output | Control |
|---|---|---|
| Sales | Sales orders | Quota |
| Industrial relations | Employee morale | Turnover |
| Quality control | Quality product | Rejections |
| Accounts receivable | Collections | Bad debts |

**Table 3.1**

The final element of feedback is essential for system operation and for self-regulation or correction of deviations. If sales quotas are not met, if labour turnover is high, if bad debts exceed expectations, this information must be fed back into the system as input so that corrections can be made. The feedback provides information for system self-correction.

## INFORMATION, DATA AND PROCESSING

In a business organisation, many events take place in the course of a single working day. When the facts about such events are recorded, they become *data*. Data comprises the raw facts concerning occurrences or happenings in a business. The problem with raw data, however, is that it is too voluminous to be of use for planning any action. A particular item of data relevant to a decision may be hidden in masses of data. In order to overcome this problem, a system is needed which will transform raw data into meaningful *information* which is relevant and concise. Such a system is a Data Processing system. Thus data processing generates meaningful information from raw data.

An important distinction between information and data is that information affects the behaviour of men or machines. Data consists of recorded observations that are not currently affecting behaviour. However, data may become information if behaviour becomes affected. The database for computer systems consists of masses of data items that are not affecting behaviour. Until the data are actually viewed, and properly organised for a user so that he reacts to them, they are not information. For example, items of data may consist of the number of hours worked by any employee on a particular machine; his rate of pay, the amount and type of materials consumed in a particular process; the number of tons of finished product produced in a day or week. But, when they are transformed into an efficiency report to plan the future course of action, it becomes information.

## INFORMATION FLOW IN ORGANISATIONS

Every organisation consists of a number of business functions: sales, production, accounting, etc. In order to co-ordinate these functions effectively, information must be passed between them.

Information is needed to enable a business to produce and sell its products, to assist decision-making and to enable controls to be effected, both at the functional level and overall. Since the advent of computers, the data processing (DP) function has become a major provider of information to the other functions in the organisation, and to corporate management. Consider credit control as an example.

Basically the credit controller needs to have customer information. In the first instance, perhaps, this will be bank references and other background data relating to a customer so that credit worthiness can be assessed. Then, as a continuing process, data relating to customer orders and payments are checked, so that credit worthiness can be continuously checked, and if necessary, readjusted in the light of new information. The credit controller may decide how he wants the information presented. He may want a full payment history for everyone, or only details of when someone reaches his credit limit, or when debts exceed a certain age.

In the total business context, what is information at one level is data at another level. To pursue the credit control example, the credit controller will be interested in individual debts. At a higher level, however, the financial director will probably want to know how the total debt problem is going to affect the company's cash flow position, and therefore a summary of all outstanding debts will be more relevant to him. Normally, items of data have to be related to one another to provide information for the next level up in the organisation structure. Thus the major information flows in the organisation follow the line structure; instructions pass down from management and information flows up to management.

The other information flows in the organisation are horizontal and external. Horizontal information flows between people at similar levels in the hierarchy. For example, the sales order office will check credit levels with the sales ledger department and stock levels with the stock records office. Often horizontal information flows are informal and include interaction such as rumour and gossip.

Some information reaches the organisation from outside. It can consist of customers' orders, suppliers' invoices and information about environmental activity (for example, government legislation or new products introduced by competitors). Again, external information flows can also be informal. Figure 3.2 provides a summary of information sources and flows.

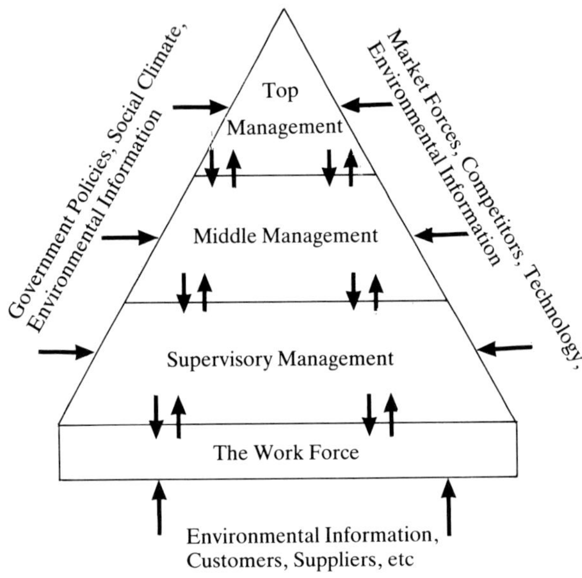


**Figure 3.2 Information Flow in Organisation**

## TYPES OF INFORMATION

At the lowest level of the organisation, staff handle operational transactions such as orders, time-sheets, delivery notes, sickness notes, production work-sheets, inspection advices, stock records, etc. These documents are the working papers of the operational systems. For example, to obtain payment from customers for their purchases an invoice is needed; to pay an employee for hours worked a time-sheet is needed; or to reorder goods for the warehouse a requisition is used. These operational documents are used to provide summaries of operational activity to the next level in the hierarchy. The summary information is compared and analysed to provide management reports at the next level and so on.

Thus, the payroll clerks handle time-sheets to produce the payroll, the time-sheets are summarised to provide details of time spent on different activities in different departments, and the time analyses are related to costs and production achieved. Therefore, the information flowing up the organisation is based on the events at the lowest levels. At the higher levels in the hierarchy, increasing importance is placed on horizontal and external types of information until, at the top management level, these are at least as important as internal management reports.

## TYPES OF INFORMATION SYSTEMS

Information systems in organisations are primarily of two types. The ones that support the operational activities in the organisation can be called Operational Information Systems (OIS). Many real-time systems fall into this category. Airline reservation systems, teller systems in banks and process control systems in industrial plant are all examples of operational information systems.

The other types of information systems that support managerial functions in the organisation are Management Information Systems (MIS). These are designed to generate information that helps management decision making. The information generated may be 'suggestive', 'predictive', 'decisive' or 'systemic'. Here we are primarily concerned with this second kind of information system, MIS.

Mason and Swanson (1981) describe four basic types of management information system. The classification is based on the level of support the information system provides in the process of decision making or the point of articulation between the information system and the decision maker, ie where the information system leaves off and the decision maker begins. A description is given of the sequence of activities that begin with the state of the business itself and end with the actual taking of a decision. This sequence of activities can be summarised as follows:

1 A 'source' consisting of the physical activities and objects which are relevant to the business.

2 The observation, measurement and recording of 'data' from the source.

3 The drawing of 'inferences and predictions' from the data.

4 The evaluation of inferences with regard to the 'values' (objectives or goals) of the organisation and the 'choosing' of a course of action.

5 The taking of a course of 'action'.

Based on this description of activities leading to a management decision and action, and on how many of these activities are performed by the information system, the four types of systems may be called Databank Information Systems, Predictive Information Systems, Decision-making Information Systems, and Decision-taking Information Systems.

A Databank Information System (Figure 3.3) performs only the first two activities described above, ie it observes the objects and activities in the organisation, measures and records them and maintains a pool of data for use by the decision maker.

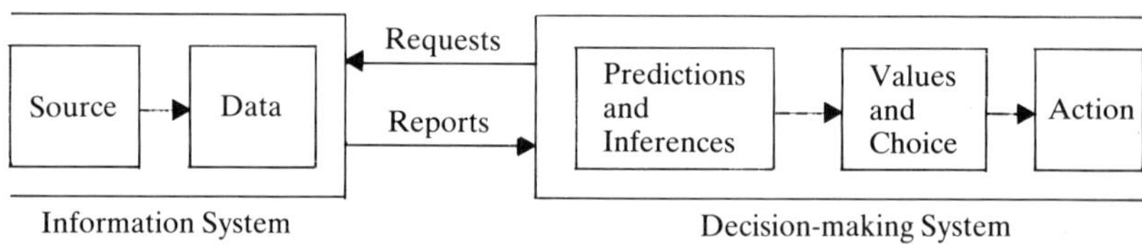


**Figure 3.3 Databank Information System**

The responsibility of the information system is to observe, classify and store any item of data which might be potentially useful to the decision maker. It is incumbent on the user to request the data items he needs and to determine what their implication is for the decision problem he faces. The information system's designer must specify the data inputs required for a variety of subsequent uses.

The decision maker utilises the data by accessing those data items that are relevant to the problem at hand. He may obtain these items of data in the form of prestructured periodic reports (eg a weekly sales or production report) or by making ad-hoc retrieval requests such as the cost of repairing a machine that has suffered a major breakdown. How the decision maker interprets this information or makes use of it for his decision making is left to him. This type of approach is useful where the decision is not of a repetitive nature, and hence its information needs cannot be precisely predetermined; or the structure of the decision problem is not clearly understood and no reasonable methodology for making interpretations from the data can be prescribed. Many strategic planning decisions fall in this category. The databank information system has also been dubbed a 'suggestive information system' since the data provided only 'suggests' a decision to the manager and does not reflect the cause and effect relationships between the possible courses of action and their expected outcomes, or judge between the value of possible outcomes. One danger in a databank information system is that too much data may be stored because its utility is not clearly known in advance.

A Predictive Information System (Figure 3.4) extends the system from the activities of pure data collection and filing to include the drawing of inferences and predictions that are relevant to decision making. The predictions are made on the basis of cause and effect relationships that are assumed to exist and have been programmed into a descriptive or simulation model of the system. The decision-making system inquires as to 'what-if?' certain actions are taken and certain assumptions are true. The information system responds in the vein of 'if' he does that 'then' this is what he can expect to occur. No attempt is made to evaluate the outcome. Much of the recent development has been in this type of information system. Interactive systems of this type are called 'Decision Support Systems'.

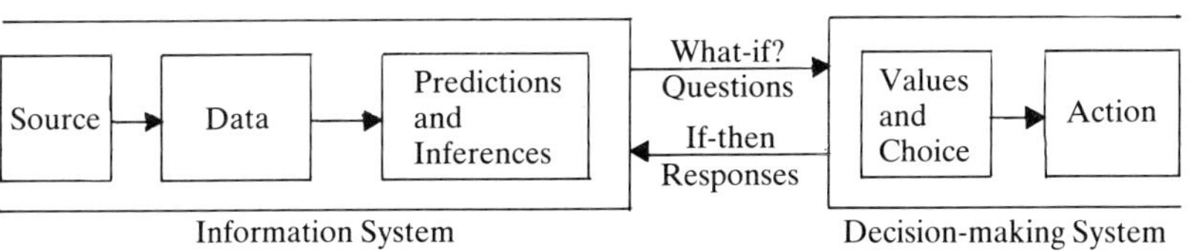


**Figure 3.4 Predictive Information System**

A manager sitting at a remote terminal of the computer can interact with such a system. He may like to study the financial planning choices available to him before arriving at his decisions. Through the remote terminal he can call for the current financial status of his organisation (depicted by such databank type items as financial statements and charts of accounts). He then assumes forecasted levels for certain important economic indicators which affect his business (such as population and GNP) and feeds them into the computer system if they are not already stored.

He also assumes structural relationships between such items as sales and expenses, accounts receivable and collections, etc – which are stored in the computer system in the form of a simulation model. He then feeds in the alternative choices he wants to simulate or study. For example, one choice may be to finance through equity and another to finance through borrowing. He may also like to study alternatives on which division of the company will manufacture what products; by what methods they will distribute them; or alternative manufacturing techniques and their attendant costs.

Given various assumptions, the simulation model then predicts the levels of sales, cost of materials and other variables by means of the cause and effect relationships programmed into the model. The program may then predict future financial statements and produce pro formas for them. Similar simulation models may predict the implications of alternative project schedules, production plans or alternative inventory policies. These simulations inform the decision maker as to what is expected to happen under a given set of circumstances. The decision maker may, of course, pose as many different conditions to the model as he thinks will be useful and obtain their separate implications.

However, an evaluation of the outcomes – by applying a criterion or objective function to rank one potential outcome above another – remains with the decision maker. The capacity to make this evaluation is not built into the model, not least because it could not be defined in precise quantitative terms. The decision maker makes the ultimate choice based on predictions he receives about the alternatives tested and his subjective understanding of the objectives or goals.

The predictive information system is particularly advantageous in those situations where the number of data items to be considered is large and their interrelationships are complicated. The resulting predictive model relieves the decision maker of the burden of having to make these calculations and thereby frees him to consider other more important matters. A well-designed predictive system should be able to take into account more data items, make more accurate calculations and produce predictions faster than can the unaided manager. Moreover, it allows him to test many more alternatives quickly and economically than would be possible at the databank level. The danger lies in the possibility that the inferences are based on assumptions that are not in accord with the best judgement of the decision maker and that these assumptions are 'hidden' from him by the information system design.

The Decision-making Information System (Figure 3.5) goes one step further in the process of decision making and incorporates the value system of the organisation or choice criteria from amongst the alternatives. This is possible only if the objectives or goals of the organisation are clearly defined and fed to the system in precise terms. A linear program for, say, production scheduling is one example of a decision-making information system. In developing this model the designer begins by specifying a group of functional relationships (eg 'constraints') about machine output rates, cost coefficients, market demands, etc. This is the predictive or implicative aspect of the information system. But now the objective function (in this case to maximise profits) is added to the problem specification and it is built into the information system. In effect (although this is not precisely

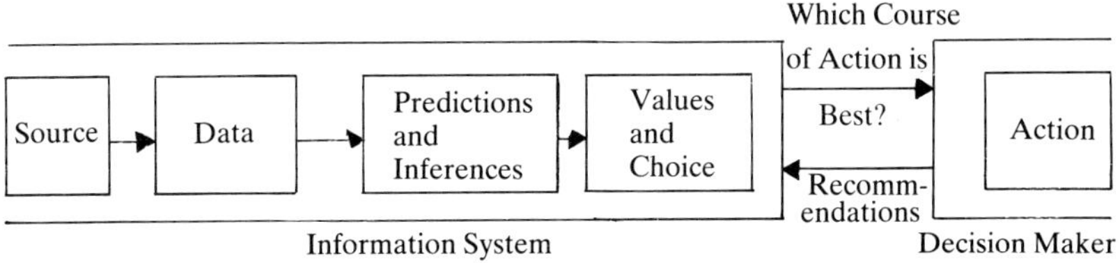


**Figure 3.5 Decision-making Information System**

how the algorithms work) the objective function serves to 'rank' the predicted outcome from each alternative and to select the best or 'optimal' policy. In this example, the objective function determines the most profitable product mix for the company to produce.

Cost-benefit models and economic order quantity models are other examples of such an optimisation approach. Here the information system presents the best choice to the manager instead of a set of alternatives and their expected outcomes. This could be represented as the 'expert advice' offered by the information system to the decision maker. But the decision maker still has the option to modify or reject the expert advice. The manager may be aware of the assumptions made in the model and the special circumstances of the situation which invalidate the assumptions. In most cases, however, he may accept the advice.

The Decision-taking Information System (Figure 3.6) is one in which the information system and the decision maker are one. Management is so confident in the assumptions incorporated in the system that it sees fit to relegate even its veto power to the information system. Process-control computer applications represent good examples of decision-taking information systems. The computer is programmed to know the preferred state of, say, a petroleum cracking process. For many situations that can occur in the process, the computer can 'decide' which course of action to take and initiate action. It can, for example, change the temperature or regulate the flow of input materials. There is relatively little human intervention because the managing body for the organisation has confidence in the premises upon which the computer acts.

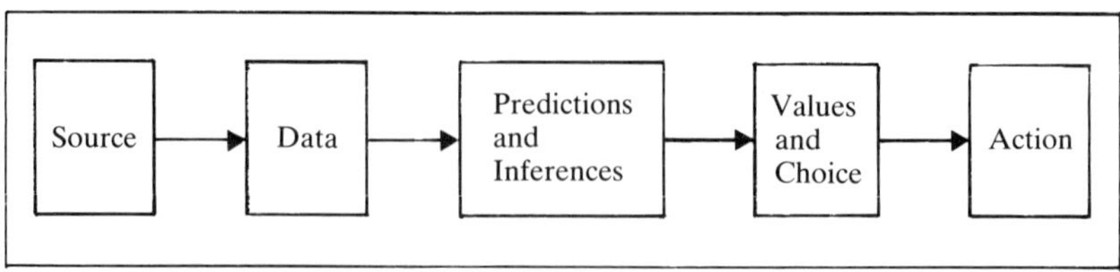


**Figure 3.6 Information (and Decision-making) System; Decision-taking Information System**

There are similar examples of decision-taking information systems in the office. Some systems automatically initiate a purchase order when inventory has dropped below the reorder print; or send a letter to a customer when he has been overdue for some prespecified period of time; or automatically create loans for bank customers who are overdrawn. These are relatively trivial decisions within the overall context of management decision making.

The complete elimination of human discretion in the decision-taking information system limits the system to an operational status. This may not have been possible without the ability of the computer to execute complex programs quickly and precisely. So the use of computers helps to relegate decisions to lower and lower levels, and frees senior management to concentrate on strategic issues.

Mason and Swanson (1981) describe also two other types of information system: the Feedback (Cybernetic) Information System, and the Systemic Information System. Feedback or cybernetic systems can be formed through combinations of databank, predictive, decision-making and decision-taking information systems.

The basic cybernetic model includes some norm or target set by a decision-making information system. Then action is taken pursuant to this goal. Subsequently, observations are made to measure the effect that the action has upon the source, and the resulting 'feedback' is recorded in a databank. These databank items are then compared with the target to generate a variance, error or mismatch signal which shows the degree of deviation. The mismatch signal is, in turn, processed through the predictive-inferential and decision-making stages. Finally, action is taken with the intent of reducing the deviation to zero.

This cycle is repeated to maintain the system 'on course', ie to keep the deviation from the goal near zero. For example, most inventory control systems determine a 'recommended' reorder quantity but the decision maker has final veto power and the responsibility to take action. Thus, they are decision-making information systems.

Some managerial techniques provide what is in reality a kind of sophisticated databank information system by relating current data to some previous goal. For example, budgetary planning systems produce data which describe the variance between budgeted and actual quantities. But it is up to the decision maker to make the appropriate predictions and inferences from this data and to reconsider the organisational values that apply before taking corrective action. Quality control methods are similar in this respect.

The control chart reports the occurrence of an out-of-control state. The decision maker must determine the cause of this deviation and then weigh the cost and benefits of several alternatives before taking action.

Systemic Information Systems are those which apprise the manager or the information systems designer about the assumptions or view-of-the-world which underlie decisions. Consideration of the other classes of information systems suggests the need to examine assumptions carefully. One point of emphasis in each of the preceding classes of information systems centres on the extent and kind of assumptions which are intrinsic to the information system. The key differentiating distinction between a databank information system and a predictive one is that additional managerial assumptions are built in to the predictive system. The same principle holds as one moves along continuously until, in the decision-taking information system, essentially all assumptions concerning the domain of choice are contained within the information system itself. The purpose of a systemic information system is to expose these assumptions so that they may be examined and reconsidered.

## ORGANISATION OF DATABANK

Information systems in organisations largely depend on organised databanks. Most of the data processing applications make use of some kind of databank. A databank represents the physical reality as it exists in the organisation and in its environment. Data is captured as the physical reality is measured. The resources (ie employees, materials and machinery) and the activities in the organisation constitute the entities in the organisation system.

The entities are measured by their various characteristics or attributes. For example, an employee has a name, a date of birth, designation, scale of pay, qualifications, etc. A machine has speed, power consumption, production capacity, etc. The value of each attribute of an entity constitutes a data item. The databank for an organisation (or for a part of an organisation) consists of a large collection of data items of various entities.

The status of physical reality can be measured at a given time and stored in a databank. This constitutes status data. But the status of physical reality continuously changes as the transactions take place. Transactions may take place between the organisation and its environment (as with receiving goods from the supplier, receiving payment from the customer, making payment to the supplier or paying taxes to the government, etc). Transactions may also take place between departments or sections within an organisation (as with the issue of material from store to shop floor, the payment of salaries to employees, or the transfer of an employee from one department to another). Measures of transactions are captured in the form of transaction documents or direct keying in from the computer terminals. Transactions form the basis of changes to, or updating of, the databank.

Data is generally organised into records and files for the purpose of organised storage and retrieval. A record is a group of related data items, generally the different attributes of the same entity, a resource object, an activity or a transaction. The data items in a record are also often referred to as the 'fields' of the record. One of the data items in the record may constitute the key attribute of the entity used to identify the entity or the record.

The collection of records of the same entity type constitutes a file. For example, the collection of employee records for all the employees in the organisation may be called an employee file. Here we should distinguish between a logical record and a physical record unit and between a logical file and a physical file unit. While a logical record is a collection of all the data items within the record, depending upon the length of the record, it may actually be stored on one or more than one disk sector or punched card. On the other hand, in the case of very small records, more than one record may be stored on a sector or a card. Similarly, very long files may be stored on more than one tape reel or floppy disk while a number of short files may be stored on the same floppy disk or hard disk.

**Types of Files**

The five broad categories of data files used in any information system are Master File, Transaction File, Work File, Security (or back-up) File, and Audit (or history) File. A master file is a permanent file in the sense that it is never, apart from at the time of its creation, empty. A master file contains the status of a set of entities at a given point of time. Since the status keeps on changing from time to time, the master files need to be updated from time to time. The transactions form the basis of such updates. Master files can be static or dynamic. Dynamic master files are more volatile than the static ones. Volatility is a measure of the extent to which the file contents change with time. Dynamic files describe entities that are of transitory importance to the business, customer orders, work orders, job tickets, projects, etc. Static master files describe business entities that are of a permanent or semi-permanent nature, eg products, suppliers, customers, employees, etc.

Transaction files are those in which the data relating to transactions (or business events) are recorded. Transaction data may be used to update master files, or the archiving of the transactions for audit purposes. After the transaction file is processed, it is usually reinitialised and further transactions are then recorded in it. Examples of transaction files are: customer's orders for products (to update an order file); details of price changes for products (to update a product file); and details of cash postings to customer accounts (to be held for audit purposes).

Work files are generated between the stages of processing created in the previous stage to be used in the next stage. Any other file created for temporary use may also be called a work file.

Security files are generated in order to provide back-up for the important data in case it gets destroyed due to some accident or mistreatment. It should be possible to re-create, with minimum effort, the destroyed data. In case of periodical updating of files, a new version of the file is created by processing the previous version along with the transaction file for the last period. In such a system, the new version created is called the child of the previous version and the files used to create the child are called the parent files. The parent files, if preserved, provide a good back-up for the current version. At the end of the current period, when the current file is updated, it gives birth to a new version which then becomes the child file and the current version becomes the parent file. The parent files become grandparent files. For very important files, three generations of data, ie grandparent files, parent files and current files may be stored at any point of time. In case of on-line updating, the master file may be copied periodically and the copy stored. In addition, a log of transactions may be maintained for the back-up purposes.

Audit files are a particular type of transaction file. They play the same role in computerised information systems as the postings in a traditional manual ledger. They enable the auditor to check the correct functioning of the computer procedures, by storing copies of all the transactions which cause the permanent system files to be altered. For example, in a sales ledger system, the transactions to be recorded might be: invoice number, date, cash amount for each invoice raised; date and amount of cash received; credit note number, date, amount of money credited; account adjustment, amount of money, cross-reference to authorisation, adjustment code, etc. These files will normally be serial, the records being created at the time of the master file update and accumulated, in the sequence of the update, on the audit file.

**Retrieval from Databank**

The retrieval from a databank may be in the form of a 'direct' or 'inverted' query. A direct query is one where the user can identify the entity in which he is interested. He may like to know some of the particulars or attributes of that entity. An example of a direct query would be where a salesman wants to know the amount and location of stock of a particular product in the organisation. He is able to identify the product by product name or product number and this identification is used as the key for making the query which is also the primary record key. So, the basic purpose of the direct query is to know the attribute values of already identified entities.

An inverted query is one where the user does not know the identification of the entities in which he is interested. He wants to identify the entities by some criteria or attribute values. An example of an inverted query would be the purchase department trying to find the list of items for which the stock level is below the desired level. In this case, the user does not know the identities of the items already, but wants to find them. He is only specifying a criterion as the basis of the query. Here, obviously, the primary record key cannot be used for retrieval as it is not available. Some other attribute like stock level has to be used for the retrieval of records.

**Models of File Organisation**

The databank files should be organised in a way to ensure efficient maintenance and fast retrieval. These two requirements can be mutually exclusive. In any particular case, a trade-off must be made between one and the other. It is also generally necessary to achieve a practical balance between storage and processing costs of data. Processing costs can be reduced if the data organisation suits the characteristics and applications of the logical data. Storage costs can sometimes be reduced only at the expense of the processing costs. The model of file organisation adopted in a particular case would depend on the nature and frequency of data usage, the types of queries made and the type of file media used for storage, whether sequential or direct access. Various models of file organisation on direct access file media include Pile File, Sequential File, Indexed Sequential File, Direct File, Inverted File and Multi-ring File. Sequential access media support only the first two categories.

Pile file organisation is one where the records are not stored in any particular order. They are just stored in the order they are received. New records are added at the end of the file. This method of organisation is used when the usage of the records is not clearly known, or as a prelude to organising the file in another order. For example, transactions may be punched and stored on a pile file. The file may be subsequently sorted into a desired sequence.

Sequential file organisation is one where the records are stored in the sequence of the values of one of the fields or attributes in the record. For example, the parts records on the parts file may be stored in the sequence of parts number. The key used for sequencing the records may be the identification field of the record like parts number or may be any other field. For example, the parts records may also be stored in the sequence of their location in the organisation. The rearrangement of records from one key sequence to another key sequence is called 'sorting'. The sequence key may also consist of a concatenation of two or more fields. It is important that the sequence key completely identifies the record; otherwise the sequence of records would remain uncertain. For example, if the parts records are arranged in the location sequence, the order of different parts stored at the same location will remain uncertain in the file.

However, if the location is used as the major key and the parts number as the minor key within the location, then every record has a definite location in the file. The sequence key, in that case, becomes location/parts number. Addition and deletion of records in a sequential file is handled in such a way that the logical sequence of the file is not disturbed. Search and retrieval of a desired record from a sequential file is handled by using various search techniques; for example, sequential search, binary search, skip search. The binary search method is known to be the most efficient.

In the indexed sequential file organisation, records are stored in the sequential order as in the sequential organisation. But, in addition to the data, an index containing pointers to the records in the data file, is also stored. The index helps in locating a record in the data file. The index basically consists of two columns. The first column contains the value of the record key and the second a pointer to the physical location of the record in the data file. Since the data records are stored in a sequential order of the record key in the data file, it is not necessary to have an index entry for every record in the file. The data can be divided into pages so that each page contains records with a range of keys. The highest key in each page is then indexed.

If the records on the file are going to be accessed by more than one key, multiple indexes may be maintained. The index on the attribute or field in which the file is sequenced would then be called the 'primary index' and those on other attributes 'secondary indexes'. For example, if the purchase order records are stored in the sequence of part number, the primary index may be maintained on the part number and an additional secondary index may be maintained on the order number. This will facilitate the retrieval of records either by parts number or by order number. Since the records are not stored in the order of the secondary key (in this case, the order number), the records cannot be grouped into pages, and there would essentially have to be an index entry for every record in the file.

In the direct file organisation, also sometimes known as random or relative file organisation, the records are not stored in any particular sequence. Instead a mathematical relation is established between the record key value and the address of its physical location. For the storage of records in the direct file organisation, the record key is transformed or 'hashed' using some hashing algorithm. Various hashing methods or algorithms are in use. The location and retrieval of a desired record can be made using the same hashing algorithm on the record key value. This method of organisation is most efficient for handling direct queries. However, indirect queries cannot be handled with this organisation. This method is also very useful for on-line transaction processing using only one record key.

Inverted file organisation is a special case of indexed sequential organisation where an index is maintained for every attribute in the record. The main file itself may not be stored if direct queries are not to be handled. The entire file data is in any case stored in the indexes. Inverted file organisation is very useful for handling inverted queries.

Multi-ring file organisation is also very useful for handling inverted queries when sets of records have the same attribute value. In this method of organisation, each set of records with the same attribute value is linked into a ring. One record in each ring has an index entry in the index file so that it provides an entry point to the ring. If it is desired to retrieve the records with a particular attribute value, the index of that attribute is read first. The reference to the index provides the entry to the ring and all the records with that attribute value can be easily located.

## DATABASE SYSTEMS

A database on a given subject is a collection of data on that subject that observes three criteria: exhaustivity (completeness), non-redundancy, and appropriate structure. Exhaustivity means that all the data about the subject are actually present in the database. Non-redundancy means that each individual piece of data exists only once in the database. Appropriate structure means that the data are stored in such a way as to minimise the cost of the expected processing and/or storage.

Technology of database organisation is of more recent origin than the file systems and was evolved to overcome some of the shortcomings of the latter. The computer file system was a natural outcome of the mechanisation of manual data processing systems. File systems tended to organise the data on magnetic media hitherto organised on paper media in a similar manner. Computer files were necessary as new applications in the business organisation were computerised. Each file was designed to meet the specific data requirements of a particular application program. As more and more applications were computerised, new files were designed to meet their needs without relating them to the existing files in the organisation. This led to a number of problems.

## OBJECTIVES OF DATABASE SYSTEMS

The objectives of the database systems – in overcoming the problems in conventional file systems – include non-redundancy, integrated view, data independence and security protection.

Take the example of two separate files, ie PAYROLL and PERSONNEL, designed for two different applications and maintained separately by different application programmers. The PAYROLL record may contain data items NUMBER, NAME, DEPARTMENT and SALARY. On the other hand, the

PERSONNEL record may contain NUMBER, NAME, ADDRESS, AGE, SKILL and DEPARTMENT. Note that the data items NAME and DEPARTMENT appear in both the files. Now, if an employee is transferred from one department to another, the change must be brought about in both the files. Since the files are being maintained separately, it is quite possible that the PAYROLL file is updated on the 25th day of the month while the PERSONNEL file is updated on the 10th day. So, between the 10th and 25th of the month, the two files show different status. So, redundancy leads to the problems of inconsistency or lack of integrity of data. Entering and storing multiple copies of data and multiple updates for a single physical transaction leads to waste of time and resources. Database systems aim to eliminate this redundancy by storing each data item only once and making it available to all the users.

In the above example of PAYROLL and PERSONNEL files, suppose the management wants to know the total pay bill of each category (skill) of employee; it cannot be obtained from either of the files because SALARY is stored on one file while the SKILL is stored on the other. Such requests for information cutting across various files may not be readily met in the file system. A database system may store all the relevant information about employees in an EMPLOYEE database and provide a different 'view' to each user. A view is a part of a database as seen by an application programmer. In addition to storing the values of data items, the database system also stores the relationship between data items. Such relationships are unknown in the file system.

One study showed that a typical organisation was spending as much as 60% of its programming effort in maintaining existing programs and only 40% on the development of new programs. This was considered a major problem with the file systems. For example, if an additional field has to be added or the size of a field has to be increased in the existing record, all the application programs referring to the file have to be modified and recompiled. Database systems achieve data independence by having separate software, a Database Management System (DBMS), to manage the database. The storage structure of data and/or access mechanism may be changed without changing application programs because data is made available to the application programs through the DBMS.

Data security refers to the protection of data against accidental or intentional disclosure to unauthorised persons or unauthorised modifications or destruction. Security is closely related to the issue of privacy of data. Privacy refers to the rights of individuals and organisations to determine for themselves when, how and to what extent information about them is to be transmitted to others.

Database systems bring all data under the central control of a 'database administrator'. The database administrator controls the overall structure of the data. He encourages standardisation of data items and determines what data structures and layouts will be best for the data users as a whole. He provides controlled access of data to various users according to their needs and authorisation. Centralisation of data makes it easier to implement various protection measures against the unauthorised use or destruction of data.

## DATA MODELS

One of the important features of a database system is that it stores relationships between data items in addition to data values. Data values stored in various files, by themselves, are not meaningful. A given set of values of house addresses and another of colours does not really communicate anything, except perhaps that the addresses and colours exist somewhere. However, if one is informed that the house at 125 Lincoln Avenue is painted red, the house at 4 Bridgetown Drive is painted blue, etc, the two sets of values immediately convey some information. The information is available because a relationship has been established between the values of addresses and colours. The relationship structure amongst data items is represented by a data model. A data model is a pattern according to which data are logically organised. It consists of named logical units of data and expresses the relationships amongst the data as determined by the interpretation of a model of the world. One of the several data models can be used to represent the interpretation of a model of the world. The main difference between them is the manner in which they represent certain relationships among the data.

A relationship is a correspondence, or mapping, between the members of two sets. There are many relationships that can be identified in our perception of the real world. For instance, each of 'father of', 'age of', and 'residence of' defines relationships between a person and a person, age and address respectively. A relationship may be one-to-one, one-to-many or many-to-many. A one-to-one relationship, for example, is the relationship between a department and its manager if each department is managed by one and only one manager and each manager is in charge of one and only one department. A one-to-many relationship exists between the manager and his staff if the manager has several staff members working with him and each staff member reports to one and only one manager. Similarly a one-to-one relationship exists between husband and wife, and a one-to-many relationship between a mother and her children. A many-to-many relationship exists between teachers and students in a college where each teacher teaches many students and each student attends the classes of many teachers. The data models used by DBMSs can be distinguished mainly according to how they represent relationships among data. There are three main approaches: hierarchical, network and relational.

The relational model is by far the most popular. It has an immediate appeal to traditional computer practitioners in that it is based on the use of the tabular form of data collection similar to files. The tables in the relational model are known as 'relations' and rows of tables or records as 'tuples'. The three basic operations performed by a relational DBMS to respond to users' needs are called SELECT, PROJECT and JOIN. SELECT is straightforward. It means having the ability to select any record from a table, given some predefined criterion. It is a fairly basic requirement in any databank. PROJECT is the function whereby simplified data may be extracted from a table and output in summarised form. So by using PROJECT it is possible to extract the data on a national sales file to give the totals by area. The result is a table (or relation) in its own right, consisting of the summarised entries on the searched table. The JOIN function is, as its name implies, a means of joining two tables and producing a third. For example, two tables giving respectively the salary of each employee and the skill of each employee may be joined together to produce the category-wise pay bill of the organisation or the average salary of employees in each category.

## USER INTERFACE WITH DATABASE

The Conference on Data Systems Languages (CODASYL) has made recommendations as to the facilities that an ideal DBMS should have. Chief among these are the concepts of the schema and sub-schema. The schema is the overall model of the data, and it usually exists in some form of network diagram. This is the 'conceptual schema' which reflects the real-world disposition and use of data. Because it is only concerned with data and its use, the conceptual schema should not change if the computer hardware changes or even if the company reverts to manual systems. The conceptual schema should change only if the concepts change. Below this level the computer must deal with practicalities of physical data storage or the physical schema that are not visible to the users.

Since the conceptual schema reflects all the company's data, it is bound to show more confidential data. Obviously it is not desirable that this should be visible to all, and it is even less desirable that everyone should be able to update it. For this reason, sub-sets of the schema are all that are made available to the programmers or users. These sub-sets, which are called sub-schemas, are also stored centrally within the computer. Each program or user, depending on his purpose, will access one of these, and this will give only a limited view of the data. For example, the invoicing department will have no knowledge of the salary information; the payroll department will be able to see the salary information and update it when required, whereas the personnel department will be able to view it but not update it.

So the sub-schema concept allows a greater measure of control, and it is of great benefit to data security.

# 4 Computers at the Competitive Edge

## GENERAL

Organisations have to remain competitive in order to stay in business. There is ever-increasing pressure on organisations to provide more value for money to their customers. Governments often legislate and formulate policies to encourage competition in industry in order to maximise consumer welfare.

An organisation can be competitive in marketing its products only if it is also competitive in acquiring and exploiting its factors of production, in addition to supporting a vigilant marketing strategy. This represents a great challenge to the organisational management. In this chapter attention is given to some of the computer applications in various functional areas of management which have contributed to the competitiveness of the organisations, which have provided them with the competitive edge.

## SALES ADMINISTRATION

The main function of sales administration is the processing of orders. In addition it may perform the functions of sales analysis, inventory management and route scheduling for distribution. Sales Order Processing (SOP) is the activity which accepts customers' orders, allocates and obtains the items or services ordered, initiates their despatch, records the supply and informs the accounting functions. Invoicing may be regarded as part of SOP, or may be separate from it. The characteristics of sales order processing are high-volume, high-speed, many outputs, and access to many records. Sales order processing systems may use on-line or batch processing or have elements of both on-line and batch processing within it, for different aspects of the work to be done.

In an on-line SOP system, each order is input to the computer usually through a keyboard. The computer system identifies the customer and ensures that he has credit available. Unless it is a new customer, the computer may already have his invoice as well as delivery address. The items ordered are identified by the system and the quantities are input. Other instructions such as delivery mode to be used, insurance, etc are recorded. Once the order is entered, the computer checks the availability of stock from its inventory records. It would then either allocate the stock or back order for a later date when the supply becomes available or advise if the order cannot be met. The system then prints out documents like confirmation of order, 'picking list' and 'despatch/advice note'. If invoicing is part of SOP, it will be triggered by the return of the picking list/customer receipt.

The usual '*price times quantity less item discount*' calculations are performed and the invoice total/order discount plus carriage or similar charges, is made up. VAT is added, and the grand total completed. If there is an early payment discount offered, and customers normally take it, this may be shown on the invoices, and the appropriate VAT calculations after discount may be printed on the invoices as well. If invoicing is treated as part of a different system (say the accounting system), then the details of the items supplied and that of the customer are sent to the accounting system. Analyses such as sales representatives' commission and target reports usually follow invoicing because they may contain money information as well as quantities.

The purpose of the sales analysis system is to provide timely summaries of historical data, to facilitate market analysis and forecasting and to produce commission statements. It would be able to generate:

- product category sales analysis and forecast;
- salesman sales analysis (by salesman, customer and territory);
- customer sales analysis (by customer type, territory, salesman, alphabetical);

- product analysis by salesman;
- salesman commission statements;
- market analysis by industry type, geographic territory, product line, type of customer and sales listing totals.

Some companies use common carriers for deliveries while others maintain a fleet of company operated trucks. The primary objective of the route scheduling system is to enable the fleet to be used in the most effective manner. It would generate:

- truck loading statements;
- route scheduling statements indicating vehicle assignments, territory, distance, customers, driver, load, inventory, etc;
- truck breakage report;
- route reconciliation report (to help eliminate shrinkage).

## MARKETING FUNCTIONS

Marketing is a crucial function of organisations in the competitive world: it helps to determine the revenue of the organisation. Marketing management is required to plan, implement and monitor the marketing activities. Marketing planning involves the steps of Diagnosis, Prognosis, Objectives, Strategy and Tactics. Analysis of sales and financial statements help to diagnose the present market position. These statements are analysed to make projections or prognoses. The objective of selecting the market areas for action and setting revenue targets is done on the basis of diagnosis and prognosis. Strategy requires careful assessment of numerous alternatives relating to quality, price, advertising, customer services, etc. Tactics or specific procedures can then be evolved for the implementation of the policy. Monitoring reports generated compare the actual performance to prior period and plan. Marketing may relate to advertising programmes, sales contact effort, market share, new business or customer awareness.

Marketing databases can support management by assisting in marketing efforts (mailings, seminars, invitations, contracts, etc) and reporting information regarding potential clients. A marketing database may draw information from trade association membership listings, chamber of commerce membership listings, research organisations, annual reports of public companies, telephone directories, newspaper reports, acquaintances and other referred sources like attorneys, bankers, etc.

## MANUFACTURING OPERATIONS

Applications in manufacturing operations include Resource Scheduling, Bill of Materials Explosion, Production Scheduling, Materials Requirement Planning, Inventory Control, Cost Accounting, Warranty, Factory Automation, Computer-aided Design (CAD), Computer-aided Manufacturing (CAM), and Computer-integrated Manufacturing (CIM).

The resources of a manufacturing organisation are the people concerned, the machines and equipment used and, most important of all, the time for which those resources are available. People are never a totally predictable resource. At different times some people will work more or less quickly, more or less accurately, more or less willingly. Moreover, people need, and are entitled to, holidays. Sometimes overtime working is an option.

If a computer is used to keep records of personnel availability, and these are accessed during the scheduling process, the system can at least cope automatically with planned holidays or such other planned absences as hospital visits, dentist appointments, and so on. Machines and equipment are more predictable than people, although they can still break down, requiring what is sometimes called breakdown maintenance. They also require regular preventive maintenance and overhauling. Schedules for routine maintenance, planned overhauls and machine replacements can be held on a computer file, and the scheduling system will not then attempt to load work onto a machine which is known to be unavailable.

The materials required to meet the production schedules can be estimated to the minute. So, it is possible for the system to predict the precise moment at which a resupply will be required. One name for this approach is 'Just in Time' stock control. The advantage of buying in this way is that not only is the minimum amount of capital tied up in stock, but also the minimum amount of space is required to hold it.

Most manufacture takes one or more materials and bought-in parts, and, through a series of operations, transforms them into a finished saleable product – or several products. If this information is put into the computer for every product, then whenever a product (or batch of products) is added to the production plan, the total effect can be calculated by the computer very quickly and accurately. For any product, lists can be produced showing the operating sequence as well as material sequence.

First, a list can show every operation needed from the beginning to the end of the production process. The plant required (machines and equipment) and the personnel required at each stage can be specified. The details can also include the components of batch set-up time and the component operation time. Secondly, every part or material can be listed, together with the operation at which it will be required. Usually some wastage will be automatically allowed for. The computer can do these calculations and pass the information on predicted demand to the stock control system. This is usually referred to as the 'Bill of Materials Processing'.

Now the first stage of scheduling can be carried out. It is decided that in the weeks or months ahead, a certain quantity of each product must be made; and the time or times when each is to be available can be stated. This may be done on the basis of known orders, with promised delivery dates, or may be a forecast based on market research, recent demand, the launch of a new product or whatever. Using a computer in this stage of setting up the manufacturing plan can give considerable benefits. A 'spreadsheet' type of approach is often taken, in which the known capacity of the factory can be held, and by entering desired finished products and dates, the computer can do an instant recalculation of the effect of that entry, and compare the result with the capacity available. This is a form of 'What-if?' planning, allowing considerable flexibility in the planning process. If a particular product order and due date give an overload situation, different due dates and quantities can be tried out, to see the effect.

Where factories are completely automated, the result of the

scheduling process will be the on-line instructions to the various machines to handle whatever work is presented to them. Manufacturing robots are machines which are programmed – or directly controlled – to do specific tasks. Numerically Controlled (NC) machines are similar in concept, and are basically machine tools, such as a lathe, a drill, a milling machine or a grinding machine, which do not need hand operating, but can be instructed via a tape and/or a keyboard to perform a specific task. Many have automatic feeding systems attached, allowing the machine to do the same operation(s) as many times as there are parts to be machined.

Computer-aided Design (CAD) is based on the technique of computer graphics. A picture on a display device can be created, manipulated, modified and stored. The stored image can be used to produce final drawings for manufacture. All the details of the picture – which may simulate a three-dimensional image – are held digitally (ie as numbers), and the compiler can perform all kinds of manipulations on the display, including apparent rotation so that the image can be viewed from all angles. Components of items can be stored as elements, and recalled with a few key depressions. This means that complex objects can be constructed very quickly and accurately by assembling the components. A design can be created, stored and then modified, so that two or more forms of a design can be considered and accessed very quickly. The computers which support this kind of activity range from a fairly standard micro – with limited but real CAD facilities provided by off-the-shelf software packages to large powerful machines with almost unlimited capabilities, and impressive speed.

Computer-aided Manufacture (CAM) started with the numerically controlled machines. The numerical control was often provided, in the early days, by a punched tape, which could be hand punched, or output from a computer, and which simply fed to the machine the co-ordinates and actions required. These developed into CNC (Computer Numerically Controlled) machines, when a computer (a PLC, Programmable Logic Controller) was added to the machine. The computer could be reprogrammed as often as needed and had many functions. Such manufacturing systems have come to be known as Flexible Manufacturing Systems (FMS). As the number, type and facilities of CNC machines increased, so CAM became a reality, with some systems operating under direct numerical control from the control computer. When systems (such as planning facilities) are linked through CAD and CAM systems to the production of finished products, with the main human involvement being brain work rather than pen-pushing and physical labour, Computer-integrated Manufacturing (CIM) is a realistic option.

The purpose of inventory control is to minimise inventory investment while maintaining sufficient levels to support manufacturing and marketing goals, and to reduce elapsed time from customer order placement to shipment. The inventory control system is able to answer stock status enquiries for selected items, including value of inventory. It would perform A-B-C analysis that documents inventory by usage to determine order policies, demand control codes and frequency of reorders. Shortage reports and purchase requisition reports are generated for making purchase orders.

The purpose of the cost accounting system is to integrate the results of manufacturing and other activities into the general ledger reporting system. While the manufacturing systems facilitate establishing and monitoring quantities, the cost accounting system attaches money to these quantities. It would generate detailed cost information for all open work orders and perform budgeting and variance analysis. It implodes cost up through the product structure to arrive at a cumulative cost for each sub-assembly and end product and calculates variances on work orders partially completed.

Many manufacturing companies incur significant costs to repair defects for products under warranty. The objectives of an adequate warranty system are to identify (and quantify in money terms) unfavourable trends that may be developing, summarise the nature of repairs, determine whether the warranty period has expired, monitor repair department performance and calculate warranty reserves.

## BASIC ACCOUNTING SYSTEMS

Basic accounting systems represent the building blocks of any organisation's accounting and information systems. The introduction of computers in most organisations starts with the basic accounting system. The general ledger system involves the preparation of chart of accounts, preliminary trial balance, general ledger reports, balance sheets, income statements, changes in financial position (cash or working capital), and cost-centre reports. The accounts receivable system helps to monitor the collection of debts and maintain cash flow of the company. Ageing analysis of debts due and overdue by different periods helps to concentrate efforts in appropriate directions. The payroll system involves the preparation of payroll cheques, cheques register, reports for taxation and other activities, deduction summary reports by deduction type, overtime and similar exception reports. Fixed assets need to be depreciated to know their current value. Fixed assets cost records are also required for insurance and property tax purposes. A fixed assets system would maintain the master file of assets and update it from time to time. It would generate depreciation reports indicating by category, by asset and in total the original cost, current period depreciation, accumulated depreciation, net value, etc.

## FINANCE FUNCTIONS

The finance function in an organisation involves budgeting for the next year, continuous monitoring of current results and analysis of expenses including alternatives for reducing costs. Preparation of budget involves the preparation of estimates of revenue, cost of revenue, personnel costs, selling expenses, cash flow and consumption (fuel, supplies, etc). Decisions on these issues are made by generating alternative scenarios using decision support models. Budgetary control is exercised by comparing budget to actual, analysing variances, revising the assumptions for the remaining months of the year and rerunning the budget preparation model.

Projections are forecasts based on historical data. Analysis of the past financial statements helps to make projections. In addition to financial statements, projections may be applied to market share, profit contribution, inflationary effects, manpower requirements, capacity planning, new locations for offices or territories, maintenance programmes, productivity and training. Economic analysis involves making cost-effective choices from possible economic alternatives. Alternatives may relate to debt/

equity, short-term/long-term finance, lease/purchase, make/buy, payback period, portfolio investment analysis, and rate of return analysis.

## PERSONNEL FUNCTIONS

People are the most important asset of any organisation. Management of personnel is as important, if not more so, as the management of cash, receivables and inventory. Computers are used to maintain the history of remuneration to employees and details of remuneration planning. The trends of remuneration amounts and percentage increases can be analysed to study their effect on future profitability. Computers can be used to monitor compliance with statutory training requirements, to maintain an information base of courses attended, including course evaluation and to assist managers to plan training in areas in which additional skills are needed. Performance evaluation data can be stored on computer files. It can then be used to identify poor performers who need counselling regarding improvement and to assist in determining remuneration adjustments.

In a growing organisation, a key consideration is the number of personnel required to accomplish that growth. Requirement planning models make assumptions regarding employee turnover, total man-hours to be worked (regular, overtime, etc), and work to be performed. The program can then calculate the number of personnel required for each set of assumptions. The results could then be used to determine short- and long-term policies (overtime, new hires, etc), to accomplish overall goals. Applications in the recruiting process include interview scheduling, interview results, form letters and campus statistics.

Scheduling models deal with the assignment of people to tasks in the organisation according to their abilities in order to optimise the overall production in the organisation. The skills inventory maintained for the purpose can also be used to identify areas where additional skills are required.

## OFFICE SYSTEMS

Office systems are a recent addition to the range of business computer applications. Personal computers and local area networks have helped to improve office efficiency considerably. A computer workstation in the manager's office can provide a means of real-time information exchange with other offices inside and outside the organisation. He may like to exchange information with his co-workers, his home, the office database, public databases and business associates. In this context, viewdata services and electronic mail are just two examples of information flow.

The various documents prepared in the office often contain duplicated information. Identical letters may be sent to different recipients; and similar or dissimilar letters may be repeatedly sent to different recipients. Duplication of keying operations is avoided if the repeating information is stored in the word-processing system and extracted at the time of preparing individual documents. Common examples of recurring documents are engagement letters, mailing lists, mailing labels, etc.

## GENERAL-PURPOSE APPLICATION PACKAGES

Electronic spreadsheet packages are very useful for analysing different scenarios. They help the user to (1) perform repeated calculations automatically (foot, crossfoot, extend figures, dependent variables, etc), and (2) perform 'what-if?' calculations by changing assumptions. The spreadsheet can be pictured as a columnar work-sheet with many rows and columns. Each intersection of a row and column is referred to as a cell. Each cell is capable of storing numeric constants, formulae or words/characters. The formulae are the means by which mathematical and 'what-if?' calculations are performed. Any change by the user in the value of a cell automatically recalculates the values of all other cells which are functionally dependent on the first cell. An electronic spreadsheet is a very useful tool for the analysis of financial and costing options.

Word processing packages for desktop micros permit the (1) editing of draft documents easily and quickly (move, add, or delete paragraphs, sentences and words), and (2) retrieval of standard and recurring text and quick modification of it as necessary. Graphics packages facilitate the display of numeric data (perhaps the results of spreadsheet calculations) in the form of bar charts, pie charts and so on.

A graphics capability provides a unique tool to illustrate rates of growth, trends, proportions, etc. It is also very useful in performing graph-related functions such as curve fitting, frequency distribution, trend generation, etc.

Data management packages (often referred to as 'database management systems') enable users to manipulate and/or retrieve large volumes of related data. Data can be organised in large collections for various purposes; examples include contact/target lists, customer/client lists, mailing lists, membership lists, personnel records, subscriber lists, telephone directories, vendor lists, etc. In all such cases there is a requirement for effective data management.

## INFORMATION TECHNOLOGY FOR COMPETITIVE ADVANTAGE

In one interpretation, the state of competition in an industry depends on five basic forces: (1) bargaining power of suppliers, (2) bargaining power of buyers, (3) threat of new entrants into the industry segment, (4) threat of substitute products or services, and (5) positioning of traditional intra-industry rivals. In a specific industry, not all forces are of equal importance. Some industries are dominated by suppliers (for example, the impact of OPEC on the petroleum industry), while other industries are preoccupied with the threat of new entrants and/or substitute products (such as the banking and insurance industries).

Each competitive force has its own implications. For example, when new entrants move into an established industry segment, they generally introduce significant additional capacity. They frequently have allocated substantial resources to establish a beachhead in the new industry. Typically, the result of new entrants is reduced product prices or increased costs for incumbents. The bargaining power of buyers leads to prices being forced down, demand for higher quality and more services; competition is encouraged. The effect of the suppliers' bargaining power results in prices being raised, reduced quality and services (see Figure 4.1).

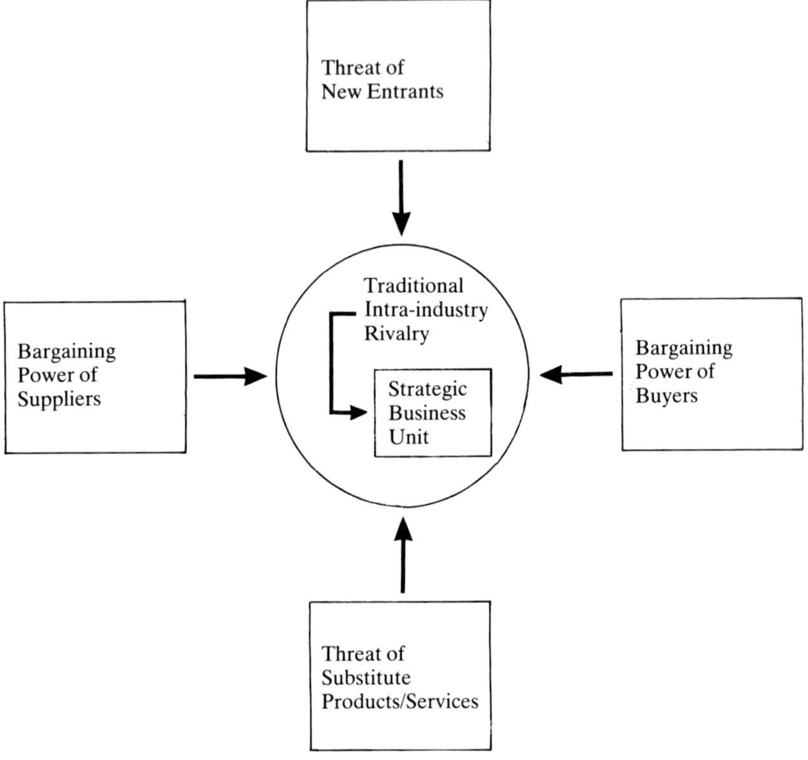


**Figure 4.1**

James Cash (1988) has described a three-era model of the use of information technology as a strategic competitive force. The model creates an image of overlapping categories, or types, of corporate computing. These types of computing applications are distinct, have appeared sequentially, and have therefore, been designated as 'eras'. The primary characteristics of each era include its administrative framework, primary clients, and sources for justifying systems development.

Era I, beginning in the early-1960s, focused on the dominant, transaction-oriented, backbone corporate information systems like those for order entry, personnel records, payroll, and sales data. They were generally written in-house by emerging data processing departments in COBOL or some other third-generation language and had long development cycles. The monolithic data processing departments, in concert with other organisational units, determined priorities for which systems were developed, modified, or placed in ever-lengthening queues. The primary clients for Era I systems are either the corporate organisation as a whole, or large administrative units. Justification for prioritising Era I systems development has been based on the productivity efficiency, cost-benefit models.

Era II corporate computing was introduced around 1980 with the advent of the stand-alone personal computer. Whereas Era I computing focused on the processing of the organisation's records, Era II has, as its clients, individual managers and their needs for decision support. These information management and decision support systems are developed either by, or under the close supervision of, the end user. In many cases, such end-user systems have been comparable, or superior, in function to systems for which corporate MIS/DP departments had projected multiyear development cycles.

One result of Era II computing has been the development of small-scale Era-I-type systems that have been waiting with a low priority in the MIS queue. More importantly, however, entirely new forms of computing, designed specifically for managerial decision support, have emerged. These include the variety of spreadsheets and other modelling tools that had no real counterpart in the mainframe MIS environment. Era II applications have had a powerful impact on managerial views of computing applications have largely been defined as managerial effectiveness competitive applications of computing in general, and for new computing technologies in particular. Era II applications, for the most part, have not been under the control of a central information system organisation. The means of justifying Era II applications have largely been defined as managerial effectiveness as opposed to the administrative efficiency arguments used to justify Era I systems.

Era III computing is closely tied to the concept of strategic competitive analysis. In its simplest form, this application of computing is concerned not with the general objective of making the internal, organisational operations of a business unit more efficient, nor with making the individual managers and/or management teams more effective. Rather, the focus is on using information technology to gain a competitive advantage. The competitive forces model, described earlier, is a popular and appropriate conceptual framework for classifying the unique characteristics of Era III computing.

Two basic types of competitive advantage, cost leadership or market differentiation, combined with the scope of activities for a firm seeking to achieve them, lead to three 'generic strategies' for achieving performance in an industry: cost leadership, differentiation, and focus. The focus strategy has two variants: cost advantage, and differentiation. Each generic strategy involves a fundamentally different route to competitive advantage, combining a choice about the type of competitive advantage sought with the scope of the strategic target in which competitive advantage is to be achieved. The cost leadership and differentiation strategies seek competitive advantage in a broad range of industry segments, while focus strategies aim at cost advantage (cost focus) or differentiation (differentiation focus) in a narrow segment.

In assessing the ultimate impact of IT, companies can begin by addressing the following four questions:

- *Can IT build barriers to competitors?* A successful system of this type not only offers a new service to appeal to customers but also offers features that keep the customers 'hooked'. The harder the service is to emulate, the higher the barrier for competition. Electronic tools that increase the scope and speed of price quotes for salespeople is an example of such a service.

- *Can IT build-in switching costs?* Are there ways to encourage customer reliance on the supplier's electronic support, to build it into their operations so that increased operational dependence and normal business inertia make switching to a competitor unattractive? Electronic home banking is a good example of this. When customers have learned to use such a system and have coded all monthly creditors for the system, they will be much more reluctant than before to change banks.

- *Can IT change the balance of power in supplier relationships?* The development of inter-organisational systems can be a powerful asset. For example, just-in-time delivery systems can drastically reduce inventory levels in the automotive and other industries, thus permitting big cost savings. Similarly, electronic CAD links from one organisation to another permit faster response, smaller inventory, and better service to the final consumer.
- *Can IT generate new products?* IT can lead to products that are of higher quality, can be delivered faster, or are cheaper. Similarly, at little extra cost, existing products can be tailored to customer's needs.

Table 4.1 summarises the implications of competitive forces for industry and potential technology impact.

| **Force** | **Implications** | **Potential uses of IT to combat force** |
|---|---|---|
| Threat of new entrants | New capacity, substantial resources, reduced prices or inflation of incumbents' costs | Provide entry barriers |
| Buyers' bargaining power | Prices forced down, high quality, more services, competition encouraged | Buyer selection, switching costs, differentiation, entry barriers |
| Suppliers' bargaining power | Prices raised, reduced quality and services | Selection, threat of backward integration |
| Threat of substitute products or services | Potential return limited, ceiling on prices | Improve price/ performance, redefine products and services |
| Traditional intra-industry rivalry | Competition in price, product, distribution and service | Cost effectiveness, market access, differentiation in products, services, firms |

**Table 4.1 Impact of Competitive Forces**

The use of IT in three generic competitive strategies can be described as follows:

**Strategy 1. Be the Low-cost Producer**

This strategy is appropriate for a standardised product. Significant profit and market-share increases come from driving operating costs significantly below those of the competition. IT offers opportunities in this strategy to:

- permit major reduction in production and clerical staff (this will hit labour costs, lowering cost per unit);
- permit better utilisation of manufacturing facilities by better scheduling, and so on (there will be less fixed-asset expense attached to each unit of production);
- allow significant reduction in inventory, accounts receivable, and so forth (ie reduce interest costs and facilities costs);
- provide better utilisation of materials and lower overall costs by reduction of wastage (better utilisation of lower-grade materials is possible in settings where quality degradation is not an issue);
- permit value-added differentiation to take place in the customer's eyes along one or more aspects of the value chain, thus changing the rules of competition.

**Strategy 2. Produce a Unique, Differentiated Product**

This differentiation can occur along a number of dimensions (such as quality, special design features, availability, and special services that offer end-consumer value). IT offers opportunities in this strategy to:

- differentiate the product by having strong IT components in service, operations, inbound logistics, or outbound logistics (for example, banks, brokerage houses, and credit card operations all use IT-based service differentiation);
- significantly impact the lead time for product development, customisation, and delivery. (In many industries today computer-aided design/computer-aided manufacturing

(CAD/CAM) provides this advantage);

- permit customisation of a product to the customer's specific needs in a way not possible before (eg CAD/CAM in specialised textile, made-to-order operations such as men's suits);
- give a visibly higher and unique level of customer service and need satisfaction that can be built into the end price (eg special-order enquiry status for key items).

**Strategy 3. Identify and Fill the Needs of Specialised Markets**

These markets consist of special geographic regions or a cluster of very specialised end-user needs. Opportunities are provided in this strategy as:

- IT permits better identification of special areas of customer need and various unevennesses in the markets' needs. Here it is possible to analyse company or industry sales databases to spot unusual trends. For instance, greeting card companies describe each card in a number of dimensions and can spot, for example, that three-line verses and red cards with contemporary designs are successful in a particular region and thus take appropriate action;
- the outputs may be IT-intensive products or products whose end features can be modified by IT customisation to local needs.

# 5 Decision Support Systems

## MANAGEMENT DECISION MAKING

The duties of managers generally involve making decisions of one kind or another. In fact, most functions of management could be discussed under the broad heading of *decision making*. Often the manager is oriented towards making decisions about actions rather than towards performing the actions personally; the actions are carried out by others. Thus an effective manager can be viewed as, at least in part, a specialist in the art of decision making.

A decision is a goal-directed item of behaviour made by the individual, in response to a certain need, with the intention of satisfying the motive that the need occasions. It is easy to see that all behaviour involves at least simple decisions. The decision process starts with problem identification and ends with a choice. The rational view of decision making assumes the model of a 'rational man'. In economic thought, for example, to be rational is to select from a group of alternative courses of action that course which maximises output for a given input, or minimises input for a given output.

In systems analysis, decision theory or game theory, to be rational is to select a course of action which has a given set of predicted consequences in terms of some function which, in turn, ranks each set of consequences in order of preference. In both these definitions rationality refers to consistent, value-maximising choice given certain constraints.

Herbert Simon (1977) talks about four phases of the decision-making process. The first phase, *intelligence*, involves searching the environment for conditions calling for decision; the second phase, *design*, involves inventing, developing and analysing possible courses of action; the third phase, *choice*, involves selecting a particular course of action from those available; and the fourth, *review*, involves assessing past choices. These phases are closely related to the stages in problem solving first described by John Dewey:

What is the problem?

What are the alternatives?

Which alternative is best?

In almost every case working definitions of rationality can be expressed by five sequential activities undertaken by the idealised 'rational man':

1) A problem which requires action is identified; and goals, values and objectives related to the problem are classified and organised.
2) All important possible ways of solving the problem or achieving goals and objectives are listed – these are alternative strategies, courses of action, or policies.
3) The important consequences which would follow from each alternative strategy are predicted and the probability of those consequences occurring is estimated.
4) The consequences of each strategy are then compared to the goals and objectives identified above.
5) Finally, a policy or strategy is selected in which consequences most closely match goals and objectives, or the problem is most nearly solved, or most benefit is got from equal cost, or equal benefit at least cost.

## STRUCTURED, UNSTRUCTURED AND SEMISTRUCTURED PROBLEMS

Herbert Simon (1977) describes two types of decisions: programmed and non-programmed. 'Decisions are programmed to the extent that they are repetitive and routine ... Decisions are non-programmed to the extent that they are novel, unstructured and unusually consequential.'

Most real-life management problems are neither completely structured (programmed) nor completely unstructured (non-programmed). Each problem has a structured component and an unstructured component. The mix of the two, however, may vary for different problems. Gorry and Scott Morton (1971) classify them into structured, unstructured and semistructured categories. They also classify information systems by these categories on one dimension and by level of management activity on the other. The result is the framework shown in Table 5.1.

| | **Operational control** | **Management control** | **Strategic planning** |
|---|---|---|---|
| **Structured** | Inventory reorder decisions | Pricing of bids | Acquisition of a company |
| | Production scheduling | Selection of credit line institutions | Addition of new product line |
| **Semistructured** | Selection of vendor | Allocation of advertising budget | Entry into new market |
| **Unstructured** | Hiring of new supervisor | Organisation of a department | New organisation of company |

**Table 5.1 Management Activity**

This classification indicates that structured, semistructured and unstructured decision problems may exist at all levels of management activity. However, Spiegler (1983) talks about the inverse relationship between the categories of problems (or information systems) and the levels of management. That is, strategic planning problems are generally unstructured, and operational control problems are generally structured. This is broadly true as the strategic planning problems are highly complex; operational control problems may be relatively trivial. Nonetheless, many complex problems are amenable to structuring; for example, a complex decision, such as the selection of a new project, taken by the top management, can be handled in a structured manner. Similarly, the decision of a new plant location is taken at the top management level, but there is enough economic theory available to make the problem a highly structured one. However, underlying the highly structured methodology used for project appraisal may be estimates of future cash flows which are little more than intelligent guesses. So there may be unstructured elements hidden in an apparent structure. On the other hand, a highly trivial problem like selecting the colour of the cover page of a progress report may not be amenable to any structure.

Chomsky (1971) distinguishes between the 'perceived structure' and the 'deep structure' of a decision problem. For example, a game of noughts and crosses (tic-tac-toe) has a deep structure. We can specify rules for play that will give the user, whether computer or person, a draw at worst, or, if the opponent blunders, a win. Despite the appearance of structure, however, a five-year-old child just learning to play the game regards each move as an exciting, uncertain challenge. The child cannot tell who is going to win the game if two five-year-olds are playing; sometimes one wins and sometimes the other. They perceive the game to be unstructured.

Similarly, the management problems that appear to be unstructured to us may be merely the result of our insufficient understanding of them. Our experience and deeper understanding of them may eventually help us to see the deep structure. In fact, Chomsky argues that every problem has a deep structure. The perceived structure visible to an individual depends on his level of understanding of the problem. For a novice, every problem is an unstructured one. A time may come when we may be able to describe the underlying structure of every management decision problem. How a problem is to be handled depends on the technical feasibility of the methodology but perhaps also on its economic and political feasibility. It does not make economic sense to spend time and effort researching the complex structures of highly infrequent problems.

## END-USER COMPUTING

The proliferation of microcomputers and their communications interfaces with large computers in the late-1970s and 1980s represents an important development.

Today many managers as end users have a terminal or personal computer on their desk. The end user may be provided with powerful software for accessing data, developing models, and performing information processing directly. This has brought computing directly under the control of the end user and eliminated his dependence on the information systems specialist and the rigidities of predesigned procedures. He may now make ad-hoc queries of information and analyse it in various ways. He may write his own programs or, more often, use ready-made programs stored on the computer, using the computing power of his local PC or the mainframe to which he is connected.

## DECISION SUPPORT SYSTEMS

All information systems in organisations are designed to support decision making. However, early information systems and decision makers operated independently; there was no interaction between the two. The emphasis was on identifying the structure of the problem and programming as much of the decision as possible. The information system then handled the structured (or programmed) component of the decision problem and handed over the results of programmed analysis to the decision maker.

The decision maker received the results of programmed analysis, usually in a prescribed routine, and then used his judgement, providing an unstructured component before arriving at the decision. Because there was no direct interaction between him and the information system, the two stages of the decision process were completely distinct and separate. This is also the basis of the classification, in Mason and Swanson (1981), of information systems into databank, predictive, decision-making and decision-taking systems; here there is talk about the point of articulation between the information system and the decision maker.

However, the extent to which the process is distributed between the two stages depends on the nature of the decision problem; the level of structuring; and the category of information system used. The evolution of end-user computing provides an opportunity to integrate the two stages in an interactive way.

The interactive computer-based systems that provide support for decision making have come to be known as Decision Support Systems (DSS). The key element in these systems is that they support rather than automate the decision process. The decision process is essentially under the control of the decision maker and he uses information and models based on information and models based on information in an interactive way to support his judgement. The essential components of a Decision Support System (see Figure 5.1) are:

- a databank to provide basic facts to the manager relating to the decision;
- a modelbank to provide analytical techniques for the processing of decision alternatives;
- a user interface through which the user interacts and the DSS responds to the commands of the user.

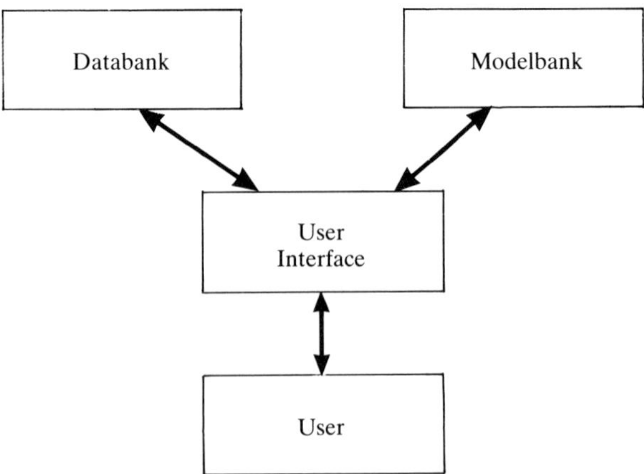


**Figure 5.1 DSS Components**

Sprague and McNurlin (1986) describe the characteristics of decision support systems as:

- tending to be aimed at the less well-structured, underspecified problems that upper-level managers typically face;

- attempting to combine the use of models or analytic techniques with traditional data access and retrieval functions;
- specifically focusing on features that make them easy to use by non-computer people in an interactive mode;
- emphasising flexibility and adaptability to accommodate changes in the environment and decision-making approach of the user.

Some regard decision support systems as an evolutionary development from electronic data processing (EDP) and management information systems (MIS). Others view it as an important sub-set of what MIS have been and will continue to be. Conceptually, DSS are in no way different from MIS. The fundamental development is that the manager can bring the information and analytical power directly under his control. How far the manager can use this facility to his advantage obviously depends on his understanding of the analytical methods.

Alter (1980), on the basis of a study of 56 systems, describes seven types of decision support systems as:

1) **File drawer systems**: These allow immediate access to data items. They are basically mechanised versions of manual filing systems. The purpose of file drawer systems is to provide on-line access to particular data items, eg status information concerning entities ranging from overdue invoices and availability of seats on future aeroplane flights through inventory items, stock portfolios, lots flowing through a shop, etc.

2) **Data analysis systems**: These allow the manipulation of data by means of operations tailored to the task and setting, or operations of a general nature. These are typically used by non-managerial line or staff personnel in analysing files of current or historical data. The portfolio management system is an example of such a system.

3) **Analysis information systems**: These provide access to a series of databases and small models. Their purpose is to

provide management information through the use of a series of decision-oriented databases and small models.

4) **Accounting models**: These calculate the consequences of planned actions on the basis of accounting definitions. They use definitional relationships and formulae to calculate the consequences of particular actions. Cash flow analysis and budget analysis are examples of these models.

5) **Representational models**: These estimate the consequences of actions on the basis of models that are partially non-definitional. They include all simulation models that are not primarily accounting definitions. For example, sales may be calculated on the basis of a model representing the relationships by which price determines sales.

6) **Optimisation models**: These provide guidelines for action by generating the optimal solution consistent with a series of constraints. They are used in studying situations that can be described mathematically as complex relationships whose goals involve combining the pieces to attain a specific objective, such as maximising profit or minimising cost.

7) **Suggestion models**: These perform computational work leading to a specific suggested decision for a fairly structured task. They generate suggested actions on the basis of formulae or mathematical procedures, which can range from decision rules to optimisation methods. In a sense, suggestion systems are even more structured than optimisation systems, since their output is pretty much 'the answer', rather than a way of viewing trade-offs, the importance of constraints, and so on.

## MODELS FOR DECISION SUPPORT

We have identified the three essential components of a decision support system: a databank, a modelbank and a user interface. We have also discussed file systems and database systems for organising databanks; and seen that information systems can be classified into four broad categories: databank information systems, predictive information systems, decision-making information systems, and decision-taking information systems.

Databank information systems are designed to answer questions as to 'what?'. For example, what have been the sales during the last six months?; what have been the production, consumption of materials, expenditure on advertising, expenditure on establishment, etc? Such systems provide factual support for decision making. They depend on the basic data stored in the databank or its organisation and compilation to transform it into the form required by the decision maker. The requirements of such a system are a well organised database and database software called a database management system. Such a system does not use any models of analysis.

Predictive information systems are designed to answer questions as to 'what if?'. What is the expected scenario if a proposed action is implemented? That is, they are expected to provide to the management the expected consequences of various decision alternatives. For example, what is the expected influence on sales if the price of the product is raised from ten pounds to twelve pounds? Or, what is the expected profit of the organisation if the expenditure on advertising is raised from one million pounds to one-and-a-half-million pounds? This type of information system must also have a databank to draw upon the basic data required for generating such predictive information. Indeed, a databank is an essential requirement in all the four types of information system. But the predictive information system also needs a model-bank, or a model to analyse the prediction. For example, a model describing the relationship between the price and sales of a product (which might be based on the past experience of the organisation or laws based on scientific reasoning) may be able to predict the sales value for a given change in price. Such models are called 'descriptive' models. They help to describe what actually exists, or might exist in a given set of conditions, but they carry no connotation of good or bad, optimum or sub-optimum. Input-output models and simulation models fall into this category. The major use of descriptive models is for learning how a given system behaves so that improvements can be made. They do not prescribe any desired or optimum action.

Decision-making and decision-taking information systems are designed to answer questions as to 'what-is-best?'. For example, what is the best allocation of funds to different activities?; what is the optimum reorder level and order quantity of inventory or batch size of production?; what is the best project plan to complete the project in optimum time and at optimum cost?; what is the best price of the products to maximise the company's profits? This type of information system also needs a databank. They also need models of analysis which not only describe the relationships between different parameters but also have clearly defined objectives or goals in the form of an objective function, so that they can measure the expected consequences of different alternatives against that objective function and make a choice of the best alternative. They not only structure the design phase but also the choice phase (in Simon's delineation). Such models are called 'normative' (or 'prescriptive') models. Normative models are used as guides for action; optimisation of the objective function is the prescriptive or normative model for management decision making. The model provides a guide to action. We may not follow the model exactly in any given situation; we may choose instead to follow it only partially or, perhaps, completely disregard it. Still, normative models are quite valuable, since they provide a touchstone. It is only when we make it a rule to follow the prescriptions of the model (of course, when we have developed so much confidence in the model and the assumptions underlying it) that a decision-making information system graduates into a decision-taking information system.

## DECISION CRITERIA

The outcome or consequences of a decision alternative depends on a set of controllable and uncontrollable factors. The controllable or decision factors are the deliberate choices made by the management. The uncontrollable factors are those factors which are outside the control of the management, such as the state of the economy, laws of the land, etc. The outcome measured against the objectives of the organisation is usually referred to as the 'pay-off' of the decision alternative. For example, the objective may be to maximise profits or minimise costs, in which case the pay-off is equal to the profit or the savings in cost. There are situations when the pay-off of the decision alternative can be estimated with reasonable certainty or there might be risks or uncertainty involved in the estimation of pay-off. Depending on how much we know about the states of nature and the business environment, we can consider decision making in connection with:

1 Certainty

2 Risk

3 Uncertainty

4 Conflict.

Decision making under certainty occurs when we can accurately and confidently predict the consequences of each alternative action. For example, the relationship between production and profit can be accurately estimated for a product in short supply, sales being no problem. We can say, if the production is increased by 10,000 items, the profit of the organisation will go up by £50,000 if the prices of raw materials and other inputs are known to be stable. Many decisions in the business organisation fall in this category, such as determining the inventory levels, allocation of resources, production and project plans, etc. In this case, the crucial decision criterion is obvious. The alternative which has the largest pay-off should be selected since there is no logical reason for doing otherwise.

Decision making under risk refers to the condition in which there are a number of possible scenarios or a number of possible outcomes, and the decision maker knows the probability of occurrence for each of the important external factors. In certain business problems, the probabilities of the various factors are known since they are based upon past experience or objective probabilities. An inventory decision problem for optimum stocking of machinery replacement parts is an example of decision making under risk since historical data on parts replaced can be compiled for a certain period of time. Another example is life insurance where insurance rates are based on life expectancy factors. A rational decision criterion to select an alternative is to select the one with the largest expected pay-off. The expected pay-off (EXP) is worked out as follows:

$$\mathrm{EXP} = P_1 r_1 + P_2 r_2 + P_3 r_3 + \cdots + P_n r_n$$

where $P_1, P_2, \ldots, P_n$ are the pay-offs from n possible outcomes and $r_1, r_2, \ldots, r_n$ are the respective probabilities of each of the outcomes. For example, if the profit from the launch of a new product depends on the state of the economy, which cannot be estimated with certainty, the only thing known is that the economy may be damped, moderate or buoyant and the probability of each of these is 0.25, 0.50 and 0.25 respectively. The pay-off to the company in each of these cases may be £50,000, £80,000 and £120,000. Then the expected pay-off from the launch of the new product would be

$$0.25 \times 50{,}000 + 0.50 \times 80{,}000 + 0.25 \times 120{,}000 = £82{,}500$$

The third type of decision criterion deals with decision making under uncertainty. This means that the probabilities of occurrence of various outcomes are unknown. Business problems of this type arise where there is no past experience available for determining the probabilities. Problems associated with a new product, increasing plant capacity, and floating a new stock issue are examples of decision making under uncertainty. Decisions of this type are more complex in nature than with decision making under certainty, and have to depend essentially on subjective considerations.

An optimist may assume the best outcome under each alternative and select the alternative that maximises the pay-off. This criterion is called the maximax (maximum of maximums) criterion. On the other hand, the pessimist may assume the worst outcome under each alternative and choose that alternative which maximises the worst case of outcome. This criterion is called the maximin (maximum of minimums) criterion.

In most practical cases, however, one may not be completely optimistic or completely pessimistic but may be only partially optimistic about the outcome. In such cases a 'coefficient of optimism' can be assigned, depending on the degree of optimism. Here an expected pay-off can be calculated by applying the coefficient of optimism to work out a weighted mean of the best and the worst outcome for each alternative. Note that the coefficient of optimism is a purely subjective assessment. It is like making a subjective assessment of the probabilities of occurrence.

Decision making under conflict is a situation where the firm has only one competitor or a limited number of competitors. The outcome of the firm's actions in such cases are determined, at least to some extent, by the actions of the firm's competitors. Under these competitive conditions, the field of decision theory expands into what is known as 'game theory'. Game theory is useful for determining strategies in various fields: games themselves, war situations, commercial enterprise, etc.

## CORPORATE AND FINANCIAL MODELS

Thomas Naylor (1979) estimated that in 1970 there were fewer than 100 companies actually using corporate models but that in 1979 'a conservative estimate of the number of corporate planning models in use in North America would easily surpass 2000'. He described a corporate planning model as an abstraction of the complex interrelationships among a company's financial, marketing and production activities usually expressed as a set of linear or non-linear differential equations and logical relationships. A simple example of a corporate financial model would be:

Sales revenue = Unit price × Sales volume

Gross profit = Sales revenue − Direct costs

Many financial models are concerned primarily with profit-and-loss and balance sheet accounting. Some examples of these are:

Capital employed = Equity capital + Debt

Operating profit = Gross profit – Depreciation

Net profit = Operating profit – Interest payable – Taxation

Return on capital employed = Operating profit ÷ Capital employed

Capital turnover = Sales ÷ Capital employed

Return on equity = Net profit ÷ Equity capital

Investment appraisal represents another very important area of application. Many organisations today, particularly amongst the smaller categories, still use simple payback approaches to investment. In other words, they require the capital sum invested to be recovered from their profits within a specified time period. Other companies use a simple return-on-investment approach. For example, a machine costing £40,000 generates gross profit of £12,000 per annum over its five-year life. Using the straight line method of depreciation:

Annual depreciation = £40,000 ÷ 5 = £8000

Operating profit = £12,000 – £8000 = £4000

Return on capital employed = £4000 ÷ £40,000 = 10%

During the last 15 years, there has been a considerable growth in the use of DCF (discounted cash flow) methods which recognise that a pound today is worth more than a pound tomorrow.

## DEMAND FORECASTING

Demand forecasting is necessary for any business organisation to plan its activities. In marketing there are a number of decisions that should be based on reliable forecasts of market size and market characteristics; for example, a company that produces and sells household appliances must be able to forecast, by geographical regions and types of consumer, what the demand will be for each of its products. These forecasts can then be used by its marketing department in its plans for advertising, direct sales, and other promotional efforts. In addition, marketing requires forecasts on such things as market share, trends in prices, and new product development. In production a major need for forecasting is in the area of sales by product so that the firm can plan its production schedule and inventories to meet that sales demand at a reasonable cost. The finance department must be able to project cash flows and the rates of various expenses and revenues to keep the company liquid and operating efficiently.

A number of forecasting methodologies are available to the manager, and the choice of individual methodology would depend on the time horizon of the decision involved, the pattern of data available, and the accuracy of forecast desired. The commonly used methods are 'moving average', 'exponential smoothing', the 'Box-Jenkins method', 'multiple regression' and 'econometric models'.

*Moving average* is one of the simplest methods and quite useful for short-term forecasting. This method consists of weighting N of the recently observed values by 1/N. For example, if a regional sales manager were forecasting monthly shipments to a certain geographical region, it might be appropriate to use a moving average involving 12 terms. In forecasting the expected shipments for the next month, each of the values for the past 12 months would be given a weight of 1/12th and that weighted sum would be the forecast. As more observations become available, they can be used in the average, making it a 'moving' one through time.

*Exponential smoothing* is very similar to the moving average method but does not use a constant set of weights for the N most recent observations. Rather, an exponentially decreasing set of weights is used so that the more recent values receive more weight than older values. This notion of giving greater weight to more recent information is one that has strong intuitive appeal for managers and makes sense based on studies of the accuracy of exponential smoothing methods. Additionally, the computational characteristics of this method make it unnecessary to store all of the past values of the data series being forecast. The only data required are the weight that will be applied to the most recent value (often called ALPHA), the most recent forecast and the most recent actual value.

*The Box-Jenkins method* is an autoregressive moving average method. It provides a procedure for determining the number of observations to be included in the model and specifying the weights to be used in that model. The basis on which the parameters are determined is statistical and is done in such a way that the error (the difference between the actual value and the forecast value for any time period) will be a minimum. This methodology provides more accurate forecasts and also provides statistics about the forecast as well as an expected value for the forecast.

In *multiple regression*, the forecast is based not only on past values of items being forecast, but on other variables that are thought to have a relationship with the item being forecast. For example, if a product manager wants to forecast monthly demand for his product line, he might use multiple regression so that his forecast would consider not only past observations of product demand but also such things as his advertising budget, and perhaps the price differential between his own product and competitors' products. In this way, multiple regression allows one to determine the causal relationship between several variables and the item being forecast.

*Econometric models* are more complex and are generally attractive only for highly aggregated data (such as company, industry or national forecasts) or for long-range projections. The basic concept is that a number of equations are developed to represent the major variables in the economy and the relations among them. These equations are then solved simultaneously to obtain a forecast for the key variables such as gross national product, consumer spending, inflation, interest rates and many other macro-economic variables.

A simple regression equation is used to forecast a single dependent variable based on the value and the relations between one or more independent variables. In many situations it is not enough because the item being forecast may depend on a number of variables and they may not be mutually independent. For example, sales may be a function of GNP, price, and advertising. But advertising expenditures also influence the price of the product. Since production and selling costs influence the per-unit price, the price in turn is influenced by the magnitude of sales, which can also influence the level of advertising. We can express these relationships by developing a system of five simultaneous equations that can deal with the interdependence directly:

Sales = f (GNP, price, advertising)

Production cost = f (production and inventory levels)

Selling expenses = f (advertising, other selling expenses)

Price = f (cost, selling expenses, competition)

Advertising = f (sales, profitability, competition)

As with the regression analysis, we must a) determine the functional form of each of the equations, b) estimate in a simultaneous manner the values of their parameters, and c) test for the statistical significance of the results and the validity of the assumptions.

## BREAKEVEN ANALYSIS

Breakeven analysis is an important tool for ascertaining the profitability of a proposed new product. The analysis requires the estimation of cost of production, demand and a suitable price at which the product is proposed to be sold. The cost of production of any product consists of a fixed component and a variable component. Fixed cost is independent of the volume of production once a certain production capacity has been established. The variable cost is that component which varies with the volume of production, and that in fact is proportional to the volume of production. The variable cost is incurred on direct resources that go into the production of the product (ie the materials, direct labour, machinery and equipment, etc). Fixed cost is incurred on the overheads which include the factory overheads, administrative overheads or marketing overheads. The total cost to the organisation is the sum of the total fixed cost and total variable cost and it must be less than the total revenue expected from the sales of the product if it has to be profitable.

Small volumes of production are usually unprofitable as the sales revenue is not able to cover the fixed costs. The product becomes profitable only when the sales volume is enough to cover the fixed costs in addition to the variable costs. The point at which the sales revenue equals the total cost is called the breakeven point for the product. The relation between cost and sales revenue is shown in Figure 5.2.

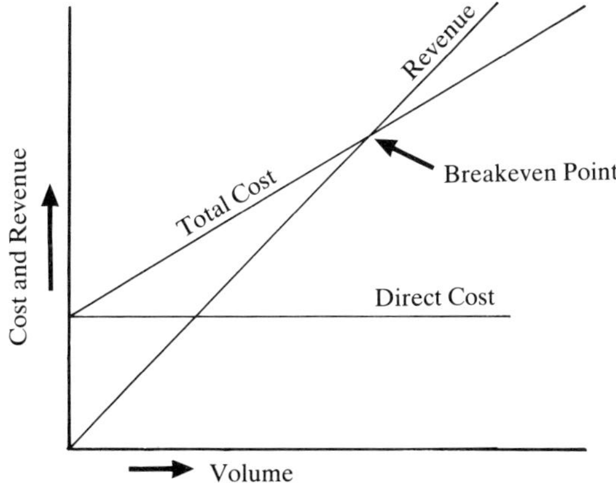


**Figure 5.2 Breakeven Analysis**

Mathematically, the relationships are expressed as:

$$\text{Profit} = \text{Revenue} - \text{Total cost}$$

$$\text{Revenue} = \text{Price per unit} \times \text{units sold}$$

$$\text{Total cost} = \text{Fixed cost} + \text{Variable cost per unit} \times \text{Units produced}$$

At the breakeven point

$$\text{Total cost} = \text{Revenue}$$

ie

$$\text{Fixed cost} + \text{Variable cost per unit} \times \text{Breakeven quantity} = \text{Price per unit} \times \text{Breakeven quantity}$$

or

$$\text{Breakeven quantity} = \frac{\text{Fixed cost}}{\text{Price per unit} - \text{Variable cost per unit}}$$

## INVENTORY CONTROL MODELS

Inventories are maintained in the organisation for raw materials to maintain the continuity of the production process and for finished manufactured goods to maintain continuous supply for sales. Inventories are a dead investment in the organisation as they generate no value and cost a great deal to maintain. The cost of holding inventories includes the cost of capital blocked, space occupied, security, insurance, deterioration in quality, possible obsolescence, etc. While the goods maintained as inventory may be used over a period of time, they have to be replenished in lots for the sake of convenience like purchasing lots for raw materials and batch lots of production for finished goods. If the lots are too big, it leads to increased average inventory leading to increased inventory holding costs. On the other hand, if the lots are too small, much effort and cost is spent in processing orders or machine set-ups.

The objective of inventory models is to find a balance between inventory holding costs and order costs or set-up costs (see Figure 5.3). The optimum lot size is referred to as Economic Order Quantity (EOQ) or Economic Batch Size (EBS).

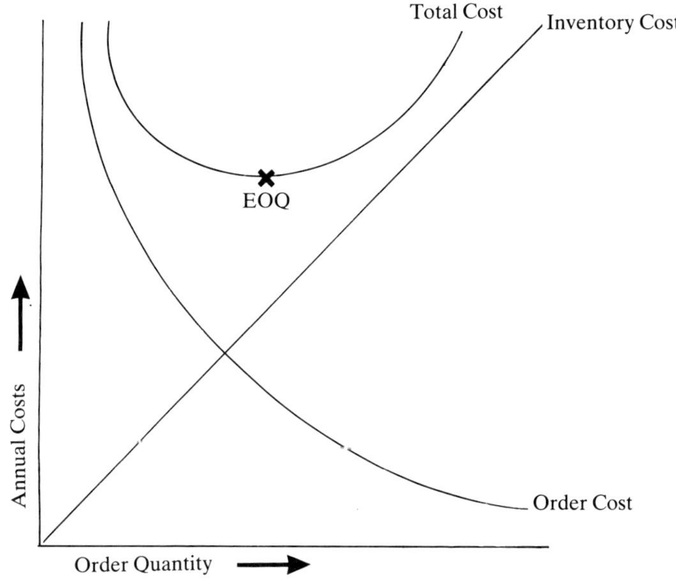


**Figure 5.3**

It can be shown mathematically that

$$EOQ = \sqrt{\frac{2 \times \text{Annual demand} \times \text{Order cost per order}}{\text{Carrying cost per unit per year}}}$$

## RESOURCE ALLOCATION MODELS

Every organisation possesses a limited set of resources. These resources may be manpower resources, material resources and/or machinery and equipment. These resources may be utilised in producing alternative products or performing alternative activities. When there are alternative uses of limited resources, the management is faced with the problem of allocating these resources to alternative activities so as to maximise the pay-off to the organisation. The pay-off is measured in terms of the objectives of the organisation. The objective may be to maximise profit, minimise costs, improve efficiency or maximise welfare.

The management has to maximise the pay-off within the constraints of limited resources or other constraints imposed by the environment. An investment trust officer, for example, tries to maximise the return on invested funds but is constrained by laws and bank policies concerning possible investments. Or a manufacturer, in planning future production, seeks minimum cost while meeting constraints on product demand, production capacity, inventory, employment, and technology.

When the objectives can be well defined in terms of an objective function, and the constraints can be spelled out precisely, the problem can be programmed for optimal solution. When the objective function and the constraints can be spelled as linear relations of concerned variables, the problem is reduced to a 'linear programming' problem. Otherwise it may be a 'non-linear programming' problem. Another variant of the problem – when the problem consists of choosing or not choosing an alternative or a discrete set of alternatives – is called an 'integer programming' problem.

For example, a company may be producing two products 'A' and 'B'. Both may consume certain hours of machine time on each of the machines 'X', 'Y' and 'Z'. The total time available on the machines 'X', 'Y' and 'Z' may be limited to 1500, 1500 and 600 hours respectively. Product 'A' may consume 2 hours on machine 'X', 3 hours on machine 'Y', and one hour on machine 'Z'. Product 'B' may consume respectively 3, 2 and 1 hours. The constraints on machine time for each of the machines can be expressed in the terms of the following inequalities:

$2A + 3B \leqslant 1500$ Machine 'X'

$3A + 2B \leqslant 1500$ Machine 'Y'

$A + B \leqslant 600$ Machine 'Z'

Now, if the contribution to profit calculated as unit selling price minus the variable cost for products 'A' and 'B' are £10 and £12 respectively, the objective function of the company can be stated as

$$\text{Profit} = 10A + 12B$$

where

A = the number of units for product 'A'

B = the number of units for product 'B'

The problem is reduced to maximising 10A + 12B subject to the three constraints stated above. This problem can be solved by the 'simplex method' of linear programming to obtain an answer of

A = 300

B = 300

That is, the profit is maximised when the machine times are allocated in such a way to produce 300 units of product 'A' and 300 units of product 'B'.

Allied to the problem of linear programming are the problems of transportation and assignment. The transportation model deals with the problem of transporting a certain quantity of goods from a set of origins to a set of destinations while minimising the transportation costs. The assignment model deals with assigning origins to destinations, jobs to people, or activities to machines on a one-to-one basis in order to maximise overall efficiency or minimise cost.

## PROJECT PLANNING MODELS

Construction of a new facility is generally a one-time unique activity, unlike the repetitive activities of the production line. A project has a beginning and an end. From the beginning to the end, a series of activities or tasks have to be completed to accomplish the project. All projects consist of a combination of activities to be performed in a desired sequence. The concern of the project management is to ensure the completion of the project on time within the budget outlay making use of a limited set of resources.

A project can be broken down into its smaller components in a series of steps until the level of small manageable activities is achieved. This structural process of decomposition of the project is known as the 'work breakdown structure' of the project (Figure 5.4).

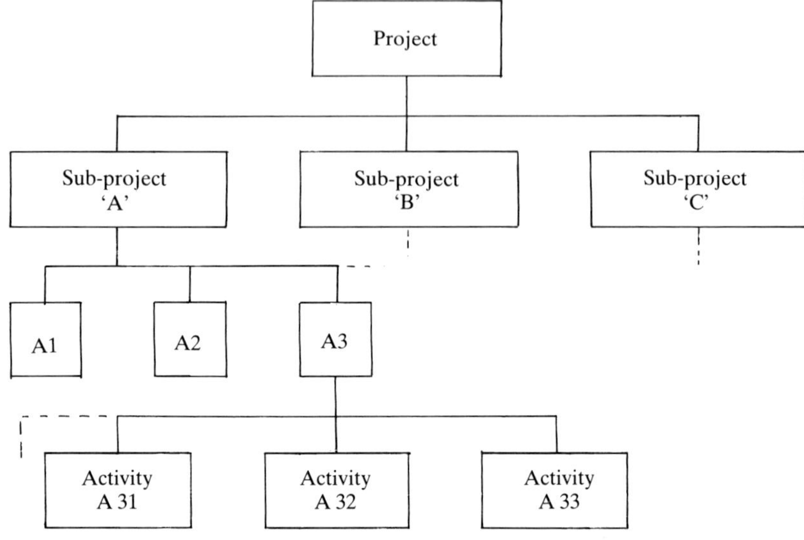


**Figure 5.4**

The work breakdown structure decomposes the project into a series of small manageable steps. The activities are sequentially related to each other. Some of the activities can be carried out in parallel with some other activities; some can be started only after other activities have been completed, ie they have a partial precedence relationship among them. This partial precedence relationship can be represented in the form of a network using such techniques as CPM (Critical Path Method) or PERT (Programme Evaluation and Review Techniques).

There are two methods frequently used for representing activities in the form of a network. The more common method involves an 'activity-on-arrows' diagram. Here the activities are represented in the form of directed arrows, and the interfaces or beginning and completion of activities by 'events' shown by small circles. The other method uses a 'precedence diagram' to indicate activities in rectangular boxes and the precedence relationships between activities by lines connecting them.

In the small network shown in Figure 5.5 there are nine activities, A to I, represented by directional arrows, and eight events, 1 to 8. Two fundamental rules determine the precedence sequence of activities on the network. First, an activity can be started only when its preceding or starting event has been achieved. Second, an event is said to have been achieved only when all the activities leading into the event have been completed. For example, event 6 can be said to have been achieved only when both activities 'D' as well as 'F' have been completed, and activity 'G' can be started only when event 6 has been achieved.

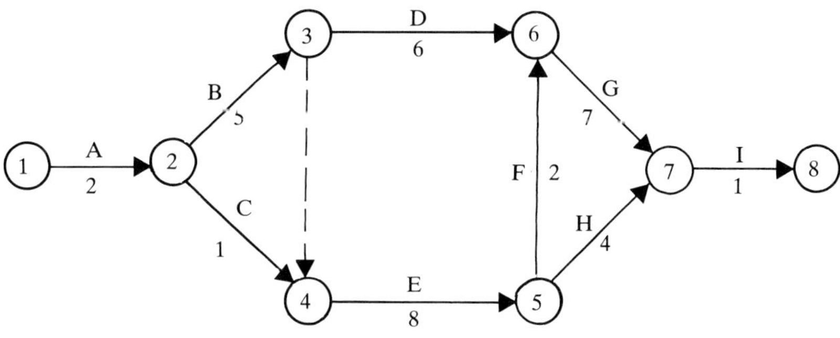


**Figure 5.5**

The dotted line connecting events 3 and 4 is a dummy activity which does not physically exist in the project but is necessary to show the precedence relationship that activity 'E' can be started only after activities 'B' and 'C' have been completed. For each activity there is an estimate of time and resource requirement. The time estimates of activities have been shown below the arrows in the network diagram. CPM assumes deterministic time estimates and hence a single time estimate is enough. But, in PERT, time estimates are assumed to be probabilities and so probabilities are attached to the time estimates of the activities.

## NETWORK REPRESENTATION

The network representation is very useful for determining the estimated completion time of the project and the set of critical activities that determines this completion time. The representation shows the longest path of activities connecting the first event to the last event of the project that determines the project duration; it is called the 'critical path'. All other activities not on the critical path have some 'float' available, ie they can be delayed to some extent without disturbing the completion schedule of the project.

In the network (Figure 5.5), the path connecting activities 'A', 'B', 'E', 'F', 'G', and 'I' constitutes the critical path as this is the longest path of 25 time units. Activity 'D', for example, not on the critical path, can be started as soon as activity 'B' is completed, ie after seven units of time from the beginning of the project, and can be completed as late as 17 units of time. The only activities to be completed after 'D' are activities 'G' and 'I' which take a total of eight units of time and hence the project can still be completed in 25 time units. So, the activity D can be carried out any time from seven to 17 units of time but its duration is only six units; hence it has a float of four time units. As with the activities, the events that are not on the critical path have some 'slack' time available with them.

Production of large products like ships, large transformers, etc can also be treated as projects and analysed using network techniques. In addition to the time analysis, project networks are useful for analysing resource allocation, cost allocation and determining the most cost-effective schedule of activities.

## MONTE-CARLO SIMULATION

Many events in business organisations do not occur in any predictable order. Their occurrence depends on a set of chance causes which can be neither controlled nor precisely determined. Examples of such events are the breakdown of a machine or the arrival of a customer at a bank or airline reservation counter. Such events or processes, known as *stochastic* processes, are unlike deterministic processes where the outcome can be predetermined. Analysis of systems involving stochastic processes cannot be done with the help of any deterministic relationships or models. But, the stochastic processes can be simulated using the Monte-Carlo simulation method. The Monte-Carlo method simulates a stochastic process in a series of four steps:

1 Generates a set of random numbers using a random number generator;

2 Determines the probability distribution the stochastic process has been found to follow in the past;

3 Converts the probability distribution of the stochastic parameter into a cumulative probability distribution;

4 Converts the set of random numbers (using the random number calibrated in the range of 0 to 1 as the cumulative probability) into the set of values of the stochastic parameter on the cumulative probability distribution.

If the stochastic parameters in the system can be simulated, the whole system can be simulated and its behaviour observed over a period of time. For example, a service counter having a random or stochastic arrival of customers and a fixed service time of four minutes can be simulated as shown in Table 5.2 (however, the service time can also be assumed to be stochastic):

| Customer no | Arrival time | Service begins | Service ends |
|---|---|---|---|
| 1 | 9.00 am | 9.00 | 9.04 |
| 2 | 9.02 | 9.04 | 9.08 |
| 3 | 9.05 | 9.08 | 9.12 |
| 4 | 9.10 | 9.12 | 9.16 |
| 5 | 9.17 | 9.17 | 9.21 |
| 6 | 9.25 | 9.25 | 9.29 |
| 7 | 9.26 | 9.29 | 9.33 |
| 8 | 9.31 | 9.33 | 9.37 |
| 9 | 9.39 | 9.39 | 9.43 |
| 10 | 9.40 | 9.43 | 9.47 |

**Table 5.2**

The arrival time of the customers has been generated using the Monte-Carlo method described above. By simulating the system over a period of time, the expected system characteristics (such as the average waiting time of the customers, average idle time of the counter clerk, number of customers served per hour, etc) can be determined. The effect of increasing or decreasing the number of counters or other system parameters like reducing service time by automation, etc can be estimated. Breakdown maintenance of machinery can be simulated in a similar manner to determine the optimum repair crew size, maintenance priorities, etc.

## ELECTRONIC SPREADSHEET

Electronic spreadsheets are a very powerful tool for decision support analysis, whatever the model used. They are available as general-purpose packages on microcomputers. One of the earliest spreadsheet packages was called VisiCalc. SuperCalc and Lotus 1–2–3 are other packages that have sold well in the last few years.

A spreadsheet program is one which presents the user with a set of boxes or cells. The cells are individually identified perhaps in numbered columns and lettered rows (lettered columns and numbered rows are also common). The third cell from the top, four cells to the right of the edge (in the third row and in the fourth column) would, as shown in Figure 5.6, be cell C4. Any cell can be left empty, can contain text, or can contain a numeric value. Any cell can have attached to it a rule. This is most often a formula, and the formula usually refers to the contents of other cells. In a text cell, the maximum length of text would be the rule.

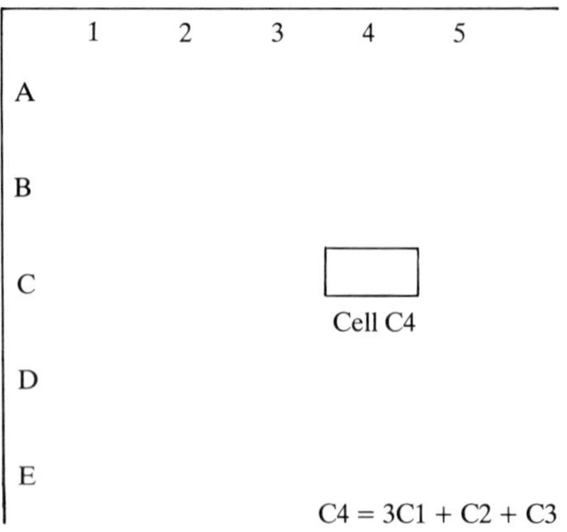


**Figure 5.6**

Consider a simple sales analysis showing the values of sales, month by month, for a range of product groups. It has columns of figures, each referring to a particular month – 12 columns – and a 13th column for the total for the year (see Figure 5.7). Each row would refer to a particular product group. The top row of the cells would contain the month name (with Annual Total in the 13th). The bottom row would be the total sales for that month. There would be a column in front of the first month with the names of the product groups. The formulae which would be set up would be attached to the last column and the lowest row. Assume that the first column (B1 to H1, say) contains the product descriptions, and row A (A2 to A14) has the month names and total.

| | 1 | 2 | 3 | 4 | 5 | 6 | 7 | 8 | 9 | 10 | 11 | 12 | 13 | 14 |
|---|---|---|---|---|---|---|---|---|---|---|---|---|---|---|
| A | | Jan | Feb | Mar | Apr | May | Jun | Jul | Aug | Sep | Oct | Nov | Dec | Tot |
| B | Gp 1 | | | | | | | | | | | | | |
| C | Gp 2 | | | | | | | | | | | | | |
| D | Gp 3 | | | | | | | | | | | | | |
| E | Gp 4 | | | | | | | | | | | | | |
| F | Gp 5 | | | | | | | | | | | | | |
| G | Gp 6 | | | | | | | | | | | | | |
| H | Gp 7 | | | | | | | | | | | | | |
| I | Total | ☐ | | | | | | | | | | | | |

I2 = B2 + C2 + D2 + E2 + F2 + G2 + H2

**Figure 5.7**

The last cell on the second row (B14) would have the formula B2 + B3 + B4 + B5 + B6 + B7 + B8 + B9 + B10 + B11 + B12 + B13. The cell on row C would have C2 + C3 + C4 + . . ., etc, and so on down to row H. The lowest cell in column 2 (I2) would have the formula B2 + C2 + D2 + E2 + F2 + G2 + H2. Now, any value entered into one of the cells B2 to H13 would be automatically added into the value held in the appropriate row and column totals. If a value is changed in a cell, the change is instantly reflected in the totals. Probably the annual total would also be shown in row I column 14, which would have a similar formula to the other rows (B14 + C14 + . . ., etc).

The formulae can be much more complex. They can use Average, Maximum and similar functions, or trigonometric functions. The range is very large. A spreadsheet can include specified cells or groups of cells from another spreadsheet. If the spreadsheet is too large to be shown on a single screen (as most are), the screen can be used as a window and moved about to show any particular area of the sheet. A spreadsheet – or part of it – can be printed out and can be exported to another part of the integrated system for conversion into graphics, or it may be included in a report through word processing.

## INVESTMENT APPRAISAL USING ELECTRONIC SPREADSHEET

We have seen that the electronic spreadsheet is a very powerful tool for decision analysis whatever the model used. We will now illustrate the use of the spreadsheet for investment appraisal using discounted cash flow (DCF) to determine the net present value (NPV) and the internal rate of return (IRR). We have the estimates regarding the cost of investment and expected future cash inflows or gross profit over the economic life of the investment. Every investment has an economic life after which it is too expensive to maintain it, making it uneconomical to operate any longer. The estimates are as follows:

| | |
|---|---|
| Cost of investment | £185,000 |
| Estimated economic life | 4 years |
| Salvage value at the end of 4 years | £20,000 |
| Tax rate | 30% |
| Depreciation method | Straight-line |
| Gross profit before tax | |
| Year 1 | £62,000 |
| Year 2 | £65,000 |
| Year 3 | £65,000 |
| Year 4 | £60,000 |

It is assumed that at the end of four years, the investment can be disposed of at £20,000, its book value at that time. The analysis of costs and benefits is arranged in the form of the spreadsheet as shown (see Figure 5.8). The time periods are entered in columns. There is one column for the present time period (period 0) and one column for each of the time periods over the life of the proposed investment. Row labels identify the various costs and benefits. The spreadsheet is completed by entering the net inflows and outflows in the body of the table and using the proper functions for financial calculations. Labels and data are entered as such in rows 1 to 12.

| A | B | C | D | E | F |
|---|---|---|---|---|---|
| 1 INVESTMENT APPRAISAL DECISION | | | | | |
| 2 | | | | | |
| 3 ASSUMPTIONS: | | | | | |
| 4 Cost of Investment | £185,000 | | | | |
| 5 Life of Investment | 4 | | | | |
| 6 Salvage Value | £20,000 | | | | |
| 7 Depreciation Method: | Straight-line | | | | |
| 8 Interest Rate | 10% | | | | |
| 9 Tax Rate | 30% | | | | |
| 10 | | | Period | | |
| 11 | | 1 | 2 | 3 | 4 |
| 12 Gross Profit before Tax | | £62,000 | £65,000 | £65,000 | £60,000 |
| 13 | | | | | |
| 14 | | | | | |
| 15 TAX CALCULATIONS | | | | | |
| 16 | | | | | |
| 17 Gross Profit before Tax | | £62,000 | £65,000 | £65,000 | £60,000 |
| 18 Taxes | | £18,600 | £19,500 | £19,500 | £18,000 |
| 19 Gross Profit after Tax | | £43,400 | £45,500 | £45,500 | £42,000 |
| 20 Tax Savings on Depreciation | | £12,750 | £12,750 | £12,750 | £12,750 |
| 21 Disposal Value | | | | | £20,000 |
| 22 Net Cash Inflows | | £56,150 | £58,250 | £58,250 | £74,750 |
| 23 | | | | | |
| 24 NPV AND IRR ANALYSIS | | | | | |
| 25 | | | Period | | |
| 26 | 0 | 1 | 2 | 3 | 4 |
| 27 Net Cash Flows | (£185,000) | £56,150 | £58,250 | £58,250. | £74,750 |
| 28 | | | | | |
| 29 Net Present Value £9,005 | | | | | |
| 30 | | | | | |
| 31 Internal Rate of Return 12% | | | | | |

**Figure 5.8**

In the next section of the spreadsheet, the necessary tax calculations are made. In rows 17 to 22, we enter the formulae that refer to the cells in the ASSUMPTIONS section that contain the Gross Profit before Tax. For example, in C17 we enter +C12. In cell C18, we enter C17 * B9, ie the Gross Profit before Tax multiplied by Tax Rate. This formula is repeated in D18, E18 and F18. Gross Profit after Tax in C19 ... F19 is computed by subtracting Taxes from Gross Profit before Tax. In C20 we enter formulae to compute the tax savings on depreciation. Because depreciation reduces net profit (and taxable income), the depreciation in any period results in tax savings as follows:

$$\text{Tax savings on depreciation} = \text{Depreciation for period} \times \text{Tax rate}$$

In this case, straight-line depreciation is used, so we enter the appropriate cell references to effect the following computation:

$$\text{Tax savings on depreciation} = \frac{\text{Cost} - \text{Salvage value}}{\text{Life}} \times \text{Tax rate}$$

Similarly, all the values up to row 27 are computed by entering appropriate formulae. To compute the net present value and the internal rate of return of the investment, we could enter appropriate formulae for them. To make matters easier, the Lotus program provides standard functions which can be referred to by the user to activate the necessary formulae automatically by the program. In cell B29, we can simply enter for the formula + B27 + @NPV (B8, C27 ... F27). @NPV is the name of the function and B8, C27 ... F27 are the parameters of the function which supply the discounting rate and the cash flows to the function. Because the Lotus @NPV function assumes that the first cash flow in the range occurs at the end of period 0 (beginning of period 1) and cell B27 contains a value that occurs at the beginning of Period 0, that cell is not included in the range of cash flows that are discounted by the net present value function.

Similarly, to calculate the internal rate of return of the investment we must enter the formula @IRR (0.05, B27 ... F27) in cell B31. In this instance, the 0.05 is a user-supplied estimate of the internal rate of return. One may enter any rate that is reasonable. The closer the user-supplied estimate is to the actual rate however, the more quickly the result is returned to the spreadsheet.

Alternative proposals can be analysed by just changing the data in the ASSUMPTIONS section. The formulae for the cells in the other sections would remain the same and the actual values of these cells would be computed automatically by the program. The spreadsheet of one alternative can be saved in a file before working on the next alternative. Once the structure of the spreadsheet has been designed, the analysis of various alternatives can be done very quickly.

# 6 Expert Systems

## INTRODUCTION

The use of expert systems as a tool of management is of recent origin. In the past, expert systems were mainly applied to scientific and engineering problems. Early successful applications included medical diagnosis systems such as MYCIN, geological systems such as PROSPECTOR, and design/configuration systems such as XCON. Today expert systems are being applied to a wide range of problems that involve a large number of choices. These problems normally entail a large search space and a relatively slow speed for the particular expert systems. Examples of these systems include factory scheduling applications such as ISIS, and legal reasoning applications such as TAXMAN.

Expert system technology is one of the most successful branches of artificial intelligence (AI). (Other branches of AI include robotics, vision and voice recognition/synthesis.) The problem-solving power of an expert system comes from its stored knowledge of a given domain linked to programming techniques and formalisms. Its knowledge is collected from human experts by experienced AI software engineers, called 'knowledge engineers', and encoded for storage and processing.

Expert systems generally provide the user with a more convenient human-machine interface than do conventional programs, providing an explanation of many different aspects of a problem, and demonstrating how decisions have been derived. Many expert systems allow the user to *ask* why a decision has been made. Such features are expected to increase the cost-effectiveness of software products.

Forecasts of artificial intelligence indicate that sales of AI/expert systems are expected to increase from $150 million in 1984 to approximately $50 billion by the year 2000. In terms of percentage of total computer industry revenue, the share of AI/expert systems would increase from 0.1% in 1984 to about 20% by 2000. This amounts to a general trend in market growth for AI/ES of about 60% annually. Potential for applications of expert systems exists in almost every industrial, commercial and service field. Three major areas already being dramatically affected are manufacturing, military operations, and financial planning.

## FEATURES AND GOALS

The term 'expert systems' suggests mimicry of human experts in a particular field. The ultimate goal of expert system technology is to surpass the performance of human experts. In everyday life, we encounter many people whom we consider experts. They all share an important common characteristic: they must make accurate decisions in environments that are fraught with uncertainty and risks, and they possess the ability to do so as a result of training, experience, and professional practice. The typical characteristics of expertise, in whatever field, can be summarised as follows:

- proficiency at arriving at quick, accurate solutions to problems;
- proficiency at explaining the results to the layperson;
- proficiency at learning from experience;
- proficiency at restructuring knowledge to fit the environment;
- the ability to make exceptions;
- awareness of their limitations.

A solution to a problem is usually the most direct and important benefit we expect from an expert; and this is a prime consideration in any expert system task that we intend to model. It should be remembered that general agreement as to who qualifies as an expert is easier to establish for some fields (eg mathematics, geological exploration) than for others (eg stock trading, economics).

An expert can often explain the results of his/her problem solving to non-experts in terms that they understand. An expert can respond intelligently to enquiries about the results, how they are derived and their implications. Normally, the enquirers can question the expert and receive an explanation.

Experts learn from their own experience, as well as from the experience of others; and they further enhance their knowledge through various means (eg daily practice and trade journals). Experts who do not keep up with their field quickly become obsolete, particularly in the present era of rapid technological development. This ability to maintain a high level of expertise also improves the expert's performance in problem solving.

The expert's effectiveness in problem solving differs from that of a novice in various ways; not least because experts are proficient at restructuring and reorganising knowledge to fit the environment:

- by subdividing their knowledge base and using a critical portion of knowledge so that the search time for the right answer can be reduced;
- by putting the problem in a different perspective using various portions of their knowledge;
- by applying knowledge to the problem at different levels or angles.

When, for example, solving the problem of a malfunctioning computing system, the expert first uses a top-down rough organisation chart of the system's main components to locate the most likely failed parts. The expert then applies the knowledge regarding the schematic of the part to identify the problematic electronic device in the part. The expert's speed and effectiveness in performing these tasks determine his/her proficiency in solving the problem.

It is significant that experts sometimes deviate from established rules. For example, great writers often deviate from orthodox grammar. Experts can perceive rare and unusual events or occurrences and make exceptions from their usual modes of working. For example, an experienced stock analyst will discard a regular analytical pattern regarding a company's stock prices in response to news of the crash of the company's jet in which various company executives were passengers. An expert has the ability to respond in an original way in unanticipated situations.

Experts can assess a problem and determine whether or not it lies within their sphere of expertise. They also know when to refer enquiries to other experts. Experts become less proficient at solving problems when they reach the limit of their expertise. They can bow out gracefully with 'qualified' answers, knowing when to acknowledge their limits.

Expert systems contain two typical features of expertise: the ability to solve problems quickly and accurately, and the ability to explain the results in terms understandable to a non-expert. First-generation expert systems focused on problem-solving performance, with second-generation systems beginning to explore characteristics such as explanation and learning in real-world situations. Current technology exploits detailed knowledge about the structure, function, and design of physical systems. It extends the frontier of computer cognisance into reasoning beyond the rules in the knowledge base.

## STRUCTURE

The major components of an expert system are the knowledge base, the inference engine, the user interface mechanism (including the explanation facility) and data. The major components of conventional programs are data (or the database), code, the interpreter/compiler, and a user interface mechanism (with the interpreter/compiler not obvious to the user).

Expert systems are capable of symbol processing, inferencing, and explaining because of the inference engine and the knowledge base; conventional programs are generally strong in numerical processing and algorithms. In general, the user interface mechanism of the expert system is more extensive than that of a conventional program. Figure 6.1 shows the structure of an expert systems as compared to that of a conventional program.

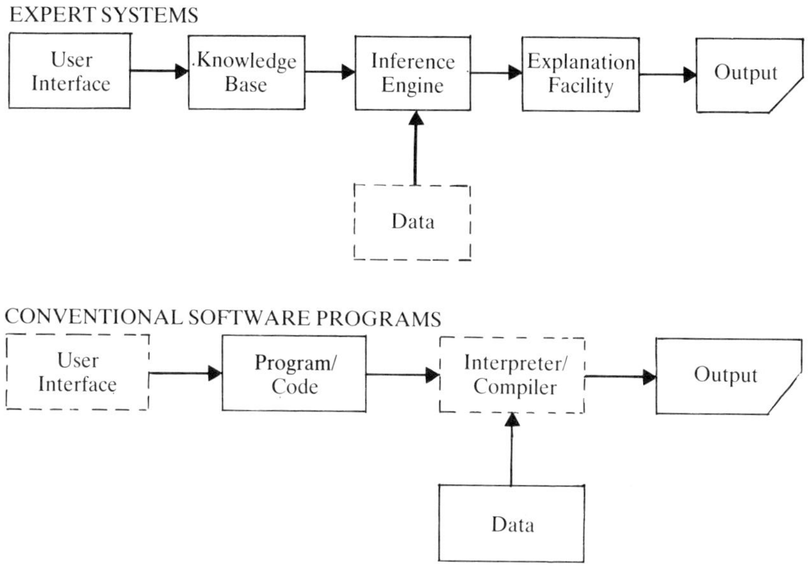

**Figure 6.1**

In an expert system the knowledge base contains facts and heuristics, the inference engine performs interpretation (reasoning) and control of search for solutions, and the user interface provides the user with semi- or full-natural language, or ultimately pictures and verbal responses. One of the features of expert systems is the separation of knowledge from the methods for reasoning using the knowledge. The user often supplies the knowledge with which the system will reason.

Three knowledge representation schemes – rule-based, frame-based and logic-based – are used for expert systems. The simplest way to represent knowledge is in the form of rules. Rules are conditional sentences expressed in the following form:

IF (premise) FACT 1, FACT 2 . . .
THEN (conclusion) FACT 9, FACT 10 . . .

Each rule may be regarded as a modular element of knowledge. The following rules, for example, may be used, for determining the best media for different types of advertising:

rule 1 IF product-category = automobile
  THEN media = television

rule 2 IF (product-category = liquor)
  or (product-category = tobacco)
  THEN media = print

Other rules can be used to determine the most appropriate media outlets:

rule 3 IF (media = television)
  and (age-of-target-market = children)
  THEN specific-outlet = 'Saturday morning cartoons'

rule 4 IF (media = print)
  and (status-of-target-market = middle-income)
  THEN specific-outlet = '*Time* magazine'.

The process of transforming knowledge that exists in a common narrative form into the proper rule syntax of a particular expert system is an important part of the knowledge engineer's skill. When several chunks of knowledge relevant to solving a particular class of problems have been converted to rules in the proper syntax, and these rules are combined with other components, they form a rule-based knowledge base.

Once the knowledge base has been completed, it needs to be accessed by a reasoning mechanism, the inference engine, for the solution of problems. The most common reasoning method in expert systems is the application of the following simple logic rule:

IF A is true, THEN B is true in a statement of 'IF A, THEN B'.

The implication of this simple rule is that:

IF B is not true, THEN A is not true in the same statement.

A simple extension of the rule yields:

Given: IF A, THEN B and
IF B, THEN C

Conclusion: IF A, THEN C

In other words, IF A is true, THEN we can conclude C is also true.

These three simple reasoning principles are used to examine rules, facts and relations in expert systems to solve problems. However, to minimise the reasoning time, search control methods are used to determine where to start the reasoning process and to choose which rule to examine next when several rules are conflicting at the same point. Another common way of representing information in a knowledge base is in terms of frames. A frame is a data structure that is suited to holding information about concrete objects. For example, if the expert system is working in the field of ornithology, it may need to hold information about different kinds of birds. Here the representation can define a 'bird' frame or data structure that contains all we need to know about birds. Then we can define frames for each type of bird. For example, once we have defined a parrot as a bird, the system will automatically know that it has all the attributes defined for the 'bird' frame. We then only need to define those attributes of types of birds that are different from birds in general. This is shown in Figure 6.2.

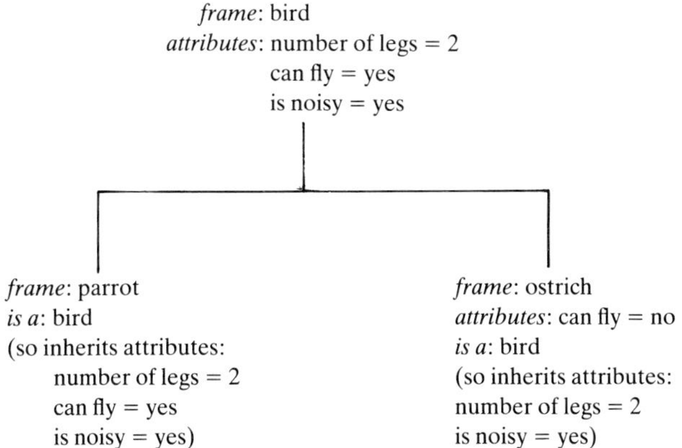


**Figure 6.2**

The expert system's reasoning program, the inference engine, often uses two kinds of reasoning methods: 'backward chaining' and 'forward chaining'. In backward chaining, the expert system is asked a question by the user. It then asks any questions needed in order to answer this top-level query. The inference engine of a forward-chaining system looks at the information it has about the world and makes recommendations based on that information. Backward chaining can be seen as 'input driven' and foward chaining as 'data driven'. For example, a knowledge base might contain the following rule:

IF shivering AND feverish
THEN call doctor

A backward-chaining system would wait for the user to ask if the doctor should be called. It would then answer 'yes' if the user confirmed that he was shivering and feverish. A forward chaining system would wait for the user to assert that he was shivering and feverish, then it would advise that a doctor be called.

The human-machine interface mechanism produces dialogue between the computer and the user. It is the weakest but the most critical element of an expert system because it determines the acceptability of the system to the end user. Major research efforts have been undertaken in natural language interface and voice recognition/synthesis to make expert systems more user-friendly. The current expert system may be equipped with 'menus' of natural language to facilitate its use, and an explanation module to allow the user to challenge and examine the reasoning process underlying the system's answers.

Menus refer to groups of simplified instructional statements that appear on the computer screen and can be selected by the user by pushing designated buttons on a 'mouse' or designated keys on the keyboard. The user does not have to type instructions. A semi- or full-natural language interface is more sophisticated than a menu interface; it allows computer systems to accept inputs and produce outputs in a language closer to a conventional language (such as English). Several expert systems incorporate primitive forms of natural language in their user interface to facilitate knowledge-base development. Explanation modules generate output statements of expert systems in language that can be understood by non-computer-professional users. Most expert systems are equipped with this type of module.

The three aspects of user interface mechanism that affect its efficiency are:

- User modes: client, tutor, and pupil;
- Interface purpose: testing, applications and modifications;
- User groups: domain expert, knowledge engineer, and general public.

'User mode' is defined as how users are going to use the expert system when they interface with it. Three different user modes are associated with an expert system. Users can act as *clients* to obtain answers to problems from the expert system, as *tutors* to increase or improve the knowledge of the expert system, and as *pupils* to harvest the knowledge of the expert system for increasing their skill in a specified subject.

'Interface purpose' is defined as the objective of the user's interacting with the expert system. Interface with the expert system can occur for testing the expert system before it is completely refined, for applying it to the real world situation for consultation on problems, and for modifying it when the experts find the answers are invalid or insufficient.

'User groups' are classified into three categories: domain experts, knowledge engineers, and general public. Domain experts are specialists in a given application field who assist in building the expert system initially, test it, and then apply it to solve problems when it is completely robust.

Knowledge engineers are specialists who obtain knowledge from experts to develop expert systems and then refine the system; they frequently apply the system to real-world problems. The general public does not develop or refine the systems, but benefits by using expert systems. The effectiveness of the human-machine interface for an expert system can be determined once the three aspects are identified.

## DEVELOPMENT

In developing an expert system, expert knowledge of a domain is encoded into computer languages and the system developed is tested and verified by the human experts. The development methodology includes:

1 System requirement specification

2 System architecture and design

3 Knowledge acquisition/representation

4 Reasoning procedures

5 Testing and validation

6 User interface.

The extraction and expression of knowledge are crucial tasks in expert-system development because knowledge is acquired mostly from experts. The selection of experts is crucial for rapid prototyping because the time available for developing a prototype expert system is relatively short. In many cases, identification and selection of the best-qualified experts may take more than one month.

The objective of knowledge extraction/expression is to efficiently and thoroughly extract – from experts – rules, facts, and data useful for the knowledge base. It is necessary to specify how and why the experts approach a problem in a certain way to help solve it, and to encode the expert knowledge to enable it to represent the rules, facts and data to be used in the expert system. The process of knowledge acquisition involves such activities as interviews, content analysis, knowledge organisation and knowledge validation.

### Interviews

The interview is an important way to extract knowledge from experts. Pre-interview planning is critical to the success of the interview because good planning enables the interviewer to extract precise knowledge from the expert within a minimum time span. Expert system projects may rely on collaboration with a single expert, though more complex problems may be broken down into several manageable subproblems to be addressed by a range of specialists.

Concentrated interviews can provide knowledge to fill the information gaps that cannot be filled by scrutiny of books, procedures, manuals and reports. The purpose of the interviews is to document *all* aspects of the expert's problem-solving approaches. Structured experiments during interviews may be required to enable the interviewer to observe the actual process.

**Content Analysis**

The purposes of the content analysis are:

(1) to document the content of the interview;

(2) to select the useful and relevant aspects of the expert's knowledge; and

(3) to prepare and plan for the next interview in which gaps of knowledge can be filled.

Once interviews are completed, knowledge obtained from the expert(s) can be compiled into rules, facts and data that can be assigned to three groups: useful and relevant, superficial and useless, and occasionally harmful if not screened carefully. The useful and relevant knowledge is organised into topic areas that constitute a paper knowledge base or 'map'. By examining the map, gaps can be identified and questions structured around the gaps for subsequent interviews.

**Knowledge Validation**

Knowledge validation is a necessary step to ensure the accuracy of the knowledge base: it is obvious that invalid rules, facts and data may lead to inaccurate decisions or to inappropriate solutions to problems. Such validation can be performed in follow-up interviews.

If an item of knowledge is in doubt, the same set of questions can be repeated in a different format; or the same set of questions can be addressed to other experts. However, if it is impossible to identify the doubtful piece of knowledge, the best approach is to complete the rapid prototyping as soon as possible and to let the experts 'play' with it. This should help them to identify the problematic rules, facts or data. Because most expert systems have a good explanation facility, the experts can often use the prototype, in co-operation with the knowledge engineers, to correct the inaccuracy in the knowledge base.

## EXPERT SYSTEMS TOOLS

Typically, prototypes for expert systems are built, developed and scrapped several times – until the experts are satisfied that their knowledge is represented correctly and the users are happy that the system does what they want. Such cyclic development is necessary because people with expertise usually cannot describe all they know, and take for granted many things that would need to be made explicit in a computer system. They usually need to watch a program doing a task and see clearly what that task involves. So expert systems tools are designed to produce applications quickly: they are good prototyping tools. They also need to represent the knowledge in the expert system comprehensibly since the knowledge engineers must be able to show the experts how their expertise is represented in software.

There are three broad types of software tools used to develop expert systems: shells, toolkits and languages. The use of a language is similar to what happens with programming languages in traditional systems. However, the languages used for expert systems development are different to such traditional languages as COBOL or Pascal. Traditional languages are designed to process numbers, whereas the languages used in expert systems are designed to handle symbols represented by characters or groups of characters. The best known expert systems programming languages are LISP and Prolog.

The idea behind expert systems shells is that a shell should provide everything needed for an expert system apart from the expert knowledge itself. So a shell will provide a standard user interface, a help system and, most importantly, a knowledge representation language (KRL). A KRL is a simple programming language designed to allow knowledge engineers to encode an expert's knowledge. Very often the engineer will write the knowledge base in the KRL syntax using a text editor (as with a traditional programming language). More and more shells now come with a menu-based front-end to the KRL.

Toolkits are a cross between languages and shells. A toolkit consists of one of the expert systems programming languages along with a large library of utilities. These utilities will include several ways of representing knowledge and perhaps several ways of reasoning about it. Most developers, in Europe at least, use shells on personal computers.

## EXPERT SYSTEMS APPLICATIONS

The largest number of expert systems developed so far have been for industrial applications. Other significant areas in which expert systems have been in use are medical diagnosis, scientific research, law and information management. Expert systems developed for industrial applications are involved in design, production planning, production, distribution and field services, and general management. Such systems have had an impact on electronics, computer systems, chemistry, engineering, automatic programming, and geology. Exemplary expert systems in the above areas are XSEL for Computer-aided Design, EL for Simulation, Callisto for PERT/CPM, XPS-E for Production Planning, SRL for production control, DELTA and XCON for customer services.

Expert systems are economically viable when there is a shortage of business experts/specialists, highly priced expert advice, a critical requirement for expert advice, routine detail-dependent decision making or a need to preserve the advice of experts. Opportunities from the use of expert systems in business organisations are presented in the areas of decision support for top executives, strategic planning, future scenario generation, portfolio management, distribution planning, resource planning, personnel planning and management, daily purchase and sale of goods, and facility planning and management. Expert systems are also being used to enhance the capabilities of conventional software packages, to make them more user-friendly, and to render Data Base Management Systems (DBMS) more intelligent.

## EXPERT SYSTEMS EXAMPLES

XCON – also known as R1 – is a widely used and discussed expert system. It was developed at Carnegie-Mellon University for Digital Equipment Corporation (DEC). XCON was used to match the specifications on almost 100,000 customer orders against the parts and equipment shipped by the factory for VAX computer systems; and it is now used to interact with sales, manufacturing, and customer relations departments. XCON contains 4500 rules and is able to perform jobs much faster and more accurately than was possible with earlier methods. For example, a VAX system order that may take a technical editor as long as 20 minutes to process can typically be completed by XCON in less than a minute.

XCON configures VAX systems at a very detailed level based on its task-specific knowledge. It determines necessary modifications on each order, produced diagrams of spatial and logical relationships between hundreds of components in a complete system, and defines cable lengths between components. Rules as well as frames are used to represent knowledge on components.

With the use of XCON, system configuration does not require the experience and skills that were previously essential. Consequently, junior personnel are now capable of performing tasks that were once the province of experts. Such specialists have been transferred to other jobs.

Another expert system, ISIS, creates job-shop schedules. ISIS is a constraint-directed reasoning system which addresses the problem of how to construct accurate, timely, realisable schedules and manage their use in job-shop environments. ISIS constructs schedules by performing a hierarchical, constraint-directed search in the space of alternative schedules. The search is divided into four levels: order selection, capacity analysis, resource analysis and resource assignment. Each level is composed of three phases: a pre-search analysis phase which constructs the problem, a search phase which solves the problem, and a post-search analysis phase which determines the acceptability of the solution.

In each phase, ISIS uses constraints to bound, guide and

analyse the search. Level 1 selects an order to be scheduled according to a prioritisation algorithm based on the category of the order and its due date. It outputs a prioritised list of orders to be scheduled. Level 2 performs analysis of the plant based on current capacity constraints. It determines the earliest start time and latest finish time for each operation of the selected order, as bounded by the order's start and due date. Level 3 selects the resources necessary to produce an order. Pre-search analysis begins by examining the constraints associated with the order to determine the scheduling direction (forward from the start date versus backward from the due date) to determine whether any constraints are missing and should be created (for example, due dates or work-in-process). An iterative search is then performed. Starting with a null schedule, alternative partial schedules are generated either forward from the start date or backward from the due date. Once a set of candidate schedules have been generated, a rule-based post-search analysis examines the candidates to determine if one is acceptable. Level 3 outputs reservation time bounds for each resource required for the operations in the chosen schedule. Level 4 selects the actual reservations for the resources required by the selected operations which minimise the work-in-process time.

The scheduling of ISIS is also reactive. The invalidation of reservations by actions, such as machine breakdowns or other orders taking too long on a machine, results in a minimal rescheduling of only the affected orders, while attempting to maintain previous reservations. ISIS's scheduling is also suggestive. If constraints cannot be met, it attempts to generate a schedule which satisfies as many constraints as possible. For example, if the due date of an order cannot be met by backwards scheduling, it attempts to schedule in the forward direction and suggests an alternative due date. ISIS's knowledge representation language, SRL, can represent an extensive set of constraints and their relaxations. Categories of constraints which ISIS covers include organisational goals (for example, due dates, cost, quality), preferences (for example, for machines), enabling states (for example, resources, previous operations), physical characteristics (for example, accuracy, size), and availability (for example, existing reservations for tools). Due to the conflicting nature of certain constraints (such as cost versus quality), there may not be a schedule which satisfies all of them. Hence, ISIS considers relaxations of such constraints when generating and selecting schedules.

ISIS performs a limited amount of process planning. The constraint set utilised in ISIS includes constraints on the physical features of a product (for example, size and form) and the ability of machines to produce them. During the constraint-directed search, infeasible process routeings are removed by these constraints. As schedules are implemented on the shop floor, unpredicted events are detected by comparing actual to predicted job and resource status. When a deviation is detected, a complete rescheduling is not performed. Instead, only the affected jobs are rescheduled, with an attempt to minimise their deviation from their earlier schedule.

A number of expert systems have been developed for accounting applications. AUDITOR was developed to make diagnostic judgements concerning the adequacy of a firm's allowance for bad debts. The system modelled the judgement of an auditor, using an ES shell. It performed on a level similar to an expert. EDP AUDITOR was developed to assist in the audit of computerised accounting systems. The system modelled the diagnostic judgements of an auditor, using an ES shell. Similarly, AGGREGATE was developed to aid in the design of accounting information systems by developing aggregated financial statements from a set of accounts in order to improve management decision making. The system modelled the aggregation judgement of a management consultant, using Prolog.

ICE is a prototype expert system designed to aid in internal control evaluation. Unlike other accounting-based ESs, ICE includes knowledge about the clients of an audit firm, including information about their management, the industry, and the economy. The system modelled diagnostic judgements of auditors, using LISP.

TICOM is an analytic query tool that incorporates artificial intelligence concepts in knowledge representation and graph simplification in the design, analysis, and evaluation of internal controls.

TAXMAN is a model of facts of certain corporate cases and some concepts from the IRS (the US Inland Revenue Service) that produces the tax consequences of corporate reorganisations. Here use is made of AI (artificial intelligence) concepts in knowledge representation. The model was built using the judgement of a tax attorney.

# 7 Changing Role of Information Systems Management

## GENERAL

Computers were first used in business in the 1950s. They supplanted the earlier unit record equipment and other machines in accounts departments. The well-defined accounting functions were amongst the first candidates for automation. Payroll and financial accounts were common applications for first-generation systems.

The computer was typically located in the finance department and managed by a data processing officer reporting to the financial manager, and an early impact of the computer was felt by clerical staff. A widespread belief at that time was that the computer would cause serious unemployment among clerks, book-keepers, and other white-collar office workers. Unemployment did in fact occur, but some of the displaced people were absorbed into the data-processing function as keypunch operators and control clerks; others found employment in companies that had not yet automated. In one view, computers served more to slow the growth in the numbers of clerical staff than to make them redundant in large quantities.

The 1960s saw a tremendous growth in the computer industry. It was the heyday of batch applications. Huge volumes of data were processed, but only the routine functions were computerised. Most commercial organisations acquired a computer and they were mainly used to produce bills, payroll cheques and periodical reports on sales, production, stocks and accounts receivable. Applications continued to be heavily concentrated in well-defined functions that were once performed manually. At the same time computer applications were also found in inventory control, personnel and manufacturing systems. Firms began to explore the computerisation of processes that were not as well defined as were financial applications. Teleprocessing (TP) was also widely introduced in the late-1960s, though it did not permeate the industry until the 1970s. With the development of on-line teleprocessing systems, airline reservation, credit-card processing and securities tracking systems came into operation.

As computer applications proliferated in the organisation, the staff outside the data processing department became increasingly involved. Stock clerks were required to feed computer information on withdrawals and additions to inventory; shop foremen used computer-generated bills of material explosions and computer-generated production schedules; sales managers used computers to examine the impact of marketing campaigns, and production managers used computers to evaluate the costs of particular processes and products. Data processing was still a highly centralised function working as a virtual service bureau in the organisation. In spite of the rapid growth of non-financial applications, at this time the data processing manager still usually reported to the financial controller.

The 1970s were characterised by the widespread introduction and use of teleprocessing. The continuing drop in hardware costs coupled with increased TP capabilities resulted in the proliferation of sophisticated on-line and real-time applications. Complex management information systems (MIS), whose main function was to provide information for decision making – as opposed to transaction processing systems, which produce a 'product' such as a payroll cheque – were attempted by many large organisations. These systems were frequently developed to provide information for improved decision making and perform functions that were not possible before the advent of the computer.

However, attempts to provide timely and accurate information to improve management effectiveness were not always successful. Data collection problems caused serious inaccuracies. Many managers steadfastly refused to use computer-generated information, even when it was accurate. Long development cycles, lack of tangible system results, and nebulous paybacks often strained the patience of upper management. This resulted in the cancellation of many MIS projects.

Nonetheless, though the complex MIS systems were not always successful, more and more decision-making information became available to management as a by-product of traditional transaction processing systems. This brought about a change in the function of middle management. Managers were expected to learn to use the computer, since much operational data was now readily available. This removed the tedium of manually compiling needed information from mounds of data – but it also removed the control. The middle manager now had to rely more and more on the vicissitudes of computer processing. The data processing function came under tighter performance scrutiny, and a re-evaluation of computer capabilities and limitations caused cancellation of marginal projects and the reduction of overly ambitious plans. Project management controls, standards and efficiency tools were introduced and developed. Ready-made application packages, which reduced development time for many systems, were increasingly available. More attention was paid to end users in order to gain their support and to justify applications.

The increasing spread of computer applications also brought about the geographical dispersal of computing resources. One or more large-scale computers at corporate headquarters processed the bulk of the firm's applications. A central data processing/information systems department directly reporting to the chief executive had a full team of systems analysts, programmers and other software specialists in addition to the operations staff. Terminals at distant locations used to feed the central facility and to access data. A few minicomputers processed some applications independently of the central computer; others worked in conjunction with the corporate mainframe. The older second- or third-generation computers were used to process applications that could not be transferred to the central facility or reprogrammed at a reasonable cost.

Recent years have seen the proliferation of mini and microcomputers and massively increased computing power and control available to end users. High-level languages and inexpensive personal computers that are easy to use and that make few demands on the physical environment have given end users a large measure of control over their own systems. Unfortunately, this has frequently resulted in equipment incompatibilities, lack of standardisation, and the needless duplication of hardware, software and staff. These problems are being addressed through the networking of systems to provide distributed facilities. Networking allows effective resource sharing: systems in the network can 'talk' to each other and transfer data and program files, and the system is brought under central control. In addition, the importance of enforcing standards across the various data processing areas is being recognised. This will serve to place organisational curbs on the promiscuous acquisition and use of computing power by different locations, divisions and departments.

The distribution of computing resources and end-user computing has made new demands on data processing functions. The role of the data processing department and its relationship with other departments is undergoing considerable change. From a service function, it is evolving into a support function.

## CENTRALISATION VERSUS DECENTRALISATION

The data processing function in the 1950s and the early 1960s was usually centralised in the organisation's largest user department, typically the finance department. In highly scientific environments (such as the aerospace industry), the large users were engineering departments – which then acquired the central data processing responsibility. In colleges and universities, it was frequently the central administrative department that controlled this function because of the importance of admissions, registration and student billing systems.

As the number of organisational computer applications grew, the large users, keen to protect their own prerogatives and priorities, often volunteered to do the processing for the other departments. However, different departments were soon acquiring their own computing resources. This led to the decentralised control of the data processing resources, which was accompanied by the emergence of the conglomerates with diverse, sometimes unrelated, business systems coexisting under one corporate umbrella. Each unit had its own processing needs that could not be successfully translated into common application systems. Each unit in the corporation was equipped with its own data-processing hardware, software and staff, which it was loath to surrender. As expenditures on these independent units started mounting, top management began to question the wisdom of so many computers and staffs doing so many things that, on the surface at least, could be combined and performed more economically.

The centralisation-versus-decentralisation debate has been conducted ever since the data processing application grew out of a single functional area in the organisation. Key considerations are the nature of the applications and the size of the data processing function. Sometimes different units in the organisation have totally different hardware and software needs. While the engineering department may need graphics systems for computer-aided design, accounting jobs may be input-output bound. Similarly, for very large organisations, the sheer size of the data processing function sometimes dictates a substantial degree of decentralisation.

Decentralised systems in individual units can often serve the user needs in the best possible way. Direct control over data processing resources may be especially desirable for day-to-day operations of high priority: this can lead to better planning, better understanding of user requirements and the optimal utilisation of resources. On the other hand, fragmentation of resources can lead to under-utilisation of resources, diseconomies of scale, duplication of facilities and staff. Here every installation would require a data processing manager, an applications development team, an operations manager and so on: the benefits of specialisation of staff functions cannot be derived as one person may have to perform several roles – integration of applications across user lines would become impossible, with the result that the overall objectives of the organisation may not be optimally served.

A major advantage of centralisation is the possibility of a larger and more sophisticated data processing provision with specialists in different tasks. It also allows a central training and standards organisation, central project control, and central production and control facilities. Standards can be enforced and wastages can be reduced. Information systems and databases that cross organisational lines and that satisfy overall corporate objectives can be built. The purchase of data processing supplies and equipment can be centrally negotiated and greater flexibility in resource utilisation can be achieved. However, the central specialised organisation may not understand the user functions so clearly and may not be able to resolve individual priorities amicably.

## ORGANISATIONAL PLACEMENT OF DATA PROCESSING

The placement of the data processing function in the organisational structure depends on a number of factors – such as the size of the function, the degree to which it is required to cross organisational lines, who the major user is and the degree to which computer activities influence the main business of the organisation.

The initial data processing facility emerged from within the major user department, often the finance department. As a result, data processing was characteristically a clerical and routine service, involving production of programs for routine clerical operations. There was very little, if any, systems analysis and design. As the scope of the applications grew to affect larger and larger systems, and more skilled people got involved in the data processing activity, data processing came to report to ever higher levels in the organisation. It often began under the financial controller, then moved up to a director of finance working with the controller, until it became a totally separate function reporting directly to an executive director for operations, or to a director of administration.

The major organisational user of data processing services is still one of the most important factors influencing its corporate placement. In highly specialised organisations, where one department is a dominant user of data processing, it may be placed under the manager of that department, but today usage is typically divided between several organisational areas. If data processing is a fairly large activity in the organisation, it usually comprises an independent department on the same organisational level as the departments it serves.

The degree to which data processing systems cross organisational lines is also a powerful factor contributing to the placement of the DP facility. For example, if the inventory system of a manufacturing company affects the production department, which it invariably does, it should be possible to effectively combine the demands of the two departments. In any event, it is necessary to exercise proper control on resource allocation, systems development, and maintenance priorities for the systems serving various users. In organisations where the central business function is directly and critically influenced by the computer function, data processing would normally be placed high in the corporate structure. Examples are airline companies (where the reservation and check-in system plays a key role) and banking and insurance companies (where financial transactions are computerised).

There are conflicting trends in the organisational placement of the data processing facility. On one hand, the development of large, sophisticated systems linked by powerful communications networks calls for control at a high organisational level. On the other hand, distributed processing systems are enabling the development of independent systems at increasingly lower levels. It is unlikely that distributed processing, pervasive as it is becoming, will reduce the need for a high degree of centralised control over expenditures and technology. But increasingly smaller organisational units will be able to develop their own systems. In addition, distributed processing does not reduce the need for uniform, accurate data collection, storage, and manipulation across the company. This cannot be accomplished without substantial standardisation of hardware and software components. Perhaps even more important, the high level of skill required to develop sophisticated systems will probably not be available at every organisational level that operates hardware. A central organisation may still be needed to provide support to users.

## FUNCTIONS AND ROLES IN INFORMATION PROCESSING

Designing and operating information systems is a complex process. The information systems manager is assisted by a team of specialist staff members: systems analysts, programmers, operators, clerks and administrative staff. In fact such staff may have such roles as database administrator, operations research analyst, systems programmer, communications programmer, maintenance programmer, etc. Some of these roles may be combined in a single individual, in the case of a small organisation, but in larger organisations there may be one or more staff members to perform each of these roles and possibly more specialised roles. In order to understand these roles and their place in the internal organisation structure of the information systems department, it is useful to examine the functions performed in the information systems department.

The three main functions performed in the information systems department are:

1 Development of information systems

2 Operation of information systems

3 Technical and support services to the users.

**Development of Information Systems**

The design/development of an information system in the business organisation is generally a *service* function. The information system is developed to cater for the needs of a user or a user department – in such areas as production, finance, marketing and personnel. The user is referred to as the *end user* as distinct from the user in the data processing department.

The objective of system development is to produce a software product which matches the end-user requirements within cost and time constraints. It will also need to meet performance criteria such as ease of use and ease of modification. Other typical performance criteria are such things as accuracy, reliability, efficiency, portability, etc.

The process of system development may involve many stages. It includes an assessment of user needs, a study of the existing system, preparation of an outline of the proposed new system, developing it into a full system specification, constructing programs and databases according to the system specification, etc. The whole process may be carried out by a team of people, with continuous interaction between the system specialists and the users during the process to ensure that the system conforms to user requirements. There are likely to be a number of decision stages during the process, presenting different options according to the costs and benefits of each alternative.

The environment of any enterprise does not remain static for very long; therefore the enterprise itself needs to keep changing. Because of this, the associated systems, whether manual or computer based, also have to change. Some change is very gradual: a slow continuous progression from one state to another. More often, however, a speedy adaptation to new circumstances is necessary and change is rapid.

Change is one reason why a system is considered to have a life cycle (Figure 7.1). Another reason for the life cycle is that all systems go through a series of stages from the original concept to the installation and maintenance of the working system. The classical model of the system life cycle is called the 'waterfall' model. Although many modifications to the waterfall model have been made from time to time (such as the 'V' model, the

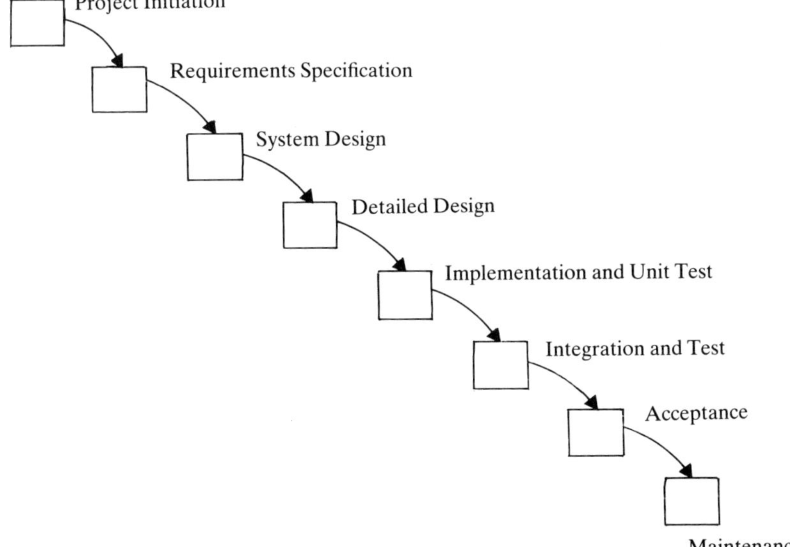


**Figure 7.1 System Life Cycle**

evolutionary model, the transform model and the spiral model) the waterfall model still provides us with a good basis to understand the system development process.

This model describes the system life cycle as a series of chronological and distinct phases. The output from each phase in the development process provides the input to the following phase. The documentation produced by each phase can be defined, produced and approved before proceeding to the next stage, giving a measure of management control over the entire process and the particular phases. This is called 'base lining' (the output of each phase becomes a *baseline* for the following phase).

A software development project is initiated when the customer (or user) enters into a contractual relationship with a developer. The contract would normally specify the system architecture (hardware, software and human tasks); project plans (including resources, costs and timescales); standards; and procedures. The decision to initiate the project is usually made on the basis of a system survey (or feasibility study), essentially an analysis of user requirements with focus on whether an information processing change is technically practical and economically desirable. The user obtains an assessment as to whether or not the information systems organisation can in fact implement a more viable system than the present method of processing the information.

The *requirements specification* describes what the system is to do, how well it should do it, and how this will be demonstrated. The specification includes functional and quality requirements, acceptance test plans, and detailed project plans; and should be sufficiently comprehensive to give the user a clear outline of the system, the benefits it is intended to provide and the approximate cost of development and maintenance. (Although estimates of costs and benefits have already been made in the feasibility study, they are refined at the requirements specification stage.)

The completion of this phase represents the last practical point at which major design and functional requirements changes should take place. It is the last chance for the user to cancel the system entirely. Although systems development *can* be terminated at any point, the personnel and time already invested make such a move difficult for management to justify after the requirements specification has been accepted. Responsibility for completing the general design usually rests with a senior-level systems analyst assisted by one or more less experienced analysts. A significant amount of interaction is required with user personnel and information systems operations. Responsibility for improving requirement specifications and initiating the system design phase rests ultimately with user management.

Frequently, a new system will require hardware upgrades, conversion to a new operating system, or software that must be acquired from outside sources. Special custom-built features may also be needed for TP switching hardware, data-collection terminals and other equipment. These must be identified as early as possible because lead times for their development, delivery, and installation are frequently quite long. In addition, the implementation of the support environment may further extend the lead time.

The *system design* describes how the system will meet the requirements as specified, including the division of hardware and software responsibilities (if relevant), and the high-level software design (ie the division of software responsibilities into subsystems and modules). System design specifies hardware/software functions, the software functional hierarchy, the data hierarchy, interface specifications and subsystem test specifications. The draft user manual is also prepared at this stage. The purpose of this phase is to develop a high-level design of the entire system, including hardware, software and manual subsystems, in sufficient detail to allow program specifications to be written, major procedures to be identified and major hardware components ordered.

The only information in a system design document that is really meaningful to many end-user personnel is the report and display terminal screen layouts. (Most end users can relate to outputs. Even if a person has never worked with display screens or computer-printed reports, they are generally similar to familiar manual documents and forms – which helps the user to understand the computer system.) The key files to be maintained in the system are described at this stage, with attention to their general contents, specific data elements, keys and access methods, estimated volume, etc. The logical design of the database is made up if the system is under the control of a DBMS.

The *detailed design* phase consists of the design of all the modules of the system to a level enabling them to be translated into the coding language. Details of functional specification, data specification, interface specification and module test specifications are prepared. The purpose of this phase of system development is to define all portions of the system to the point where computer programs can be written and processing steps can be implemented. Most detail design activities are begun during the earlier phases but do not result in their ultimate level of detail until the detail design stage. Detail design of individual system components sometimes overlaps succeeding steps in the development process. For example, installation of a subsystem A can proceed concurrently with development of subsystem B and detail design of subsystem C, as long as these subsystems are sufficiently independent to preclude possible system inconsistencies.

During *implementation and unit test* each module is coded in the application programming language, tested in isolation, and debugged until correct. This phase delivers documented tested program modules and test results. Programs are designed and coded from specifications developed during detail design. *Unit testing* is the process of testing individual programs or program modules by running them on suitably designed test data. It is done by the programmer, with occasional assistance from the analyst. An experienced programmer must be able to develop all the test data needed to test an individual program from information provided in the specifications. Sometimes however, test data is developed independently of individual programs and shared by all programmers working on the system.

During *integration and test* the tested individual models are linked together to form the subsystems for subsystems testing, and the subsystems are integrated together to form the final system configuration. At each stage further testing is done and faults are corrected. Testing of the target hardware is done if required. Each system component is tested in series, ie as a member of a system rather than as an individual entity. Generally, test data are processed through the entire system and outputs of programs along the way are compared to expected results. This procedure ensures that individual programs work in concert with other programs. Primary responsibility for system testing rests with the designer. Although the designer is assisted by programmers who write individual programs, only the systems analyst's knowledge of the total system makes it possible to properly plan and execute the system test plan. The system documentation is also completed in this phase and the user manuals are finalised.

During *installation and acceptance* the system is transferred to the customer's site and installed on the target hardware for pre-acceptance testing. The acceptance tests are performed formally. When all testing has been completed and the system performance meets the agreed acceptance criteria, the system is handed over to the customer with total system software, documentation, all test plans and results, update and change control procedures. Training of user personnel is also completed by this time. User staff may be trained in the input preparation, so that they know how to input, correct and analyse data fed into the system. User management also needs training to know how to use the system reports and other outputs. The installation of the system may also involve the conversion of master files and other data from the old system to the new and parallel run testing (ie the new system, is operated in parallel with the old system) before placing the new system into production.

Software as such does not need *maintenance* as hardware does, since it does not deteriorate with time. However, the system continues to need *modification* during its useful life for three reasons:

1 errors found during use need to be corrected;

2 enhancements to system functions are often required;

3 modifications due to outside influences (such as changes in environment, hardware, application, etc) are often needed.

## Buying Prewritten Package Software

Developing a new system can be very expensive and time consuming. Many small companies may prefer to continue with the manual system rather than invest in the development of a new computerised system. However, to use an appropriate application package is one alternative that should always be considered. Perhaps one (or a combination) of the general-purpose packages can meet user needs. But designers are not restricted to evaluating general-purpose packages. There are thousands of specialised packages that are available to organisations. These packages are designed to meet personnel management, accounting, inventory control, billing and countless other needs of specific industries. Unlike the suppliers of general-purpose packages, those who market specialised programs may be willing to make changes in their products to satisfy the unique needs of a prospective customer.

When suitable packages can be located, the *make* or *buy* decision involves trade-offs. The packaged program usually costs less (development costs are shared by many customers), may be implemented in a shorter period of time, and can be tested for errors before a purchase is made. In trying to appeal to many potential users, however, the packaged program may sacrifice processing performance in areas important to a particular organisation. The in-house custom-made program has the possible advantage of greater operating efficiency and the ability to more effectively satisfy the unique needs of users.

Suppliers of application software may be high-street computer shops, hardware manufacturers and suppliers, or software houses and consultancies. Although high-street shops tend to cater mainly for the hobby market, they usually also sell business packages for the hardware which they market. Most commonly, software is purchased from the hardware supplier as part of an initial package comprising hardware and software. In the case of software houses and consultancies, too, software is very frequently obtained as part of a package that also includes hardware. Many software houses and consultancies have arrangements with computer manufacturers whereby they act as agents for the manufacturer, or buy in bulk at a discount. This category of source is particularly geared up to providing facilities for the naive user. In particular, they are usually able to carry out feasibility studies to define the user's requirements, to provide custom-built systems where these are necessary, and to tailor packages to meet the user's needs.

The process of choosing a package to perform a particular function can be described in five stages: specification of requirements, selection, implementation, handover, and live usage. First of all, it is essential to determine the requirements. This may require a detailed investigation of the way in which processes are carried out on the existing system. Without this, it will be impossible to tell whether a particular package would suit the requirements.

It is then a question of contacting suppliers to see whether they have packages available to match the requirements. If there are a number of possible candidates, it is necessary to select the best – from the points of view of cost, compatibility with the specification, support facilities, etc. It is also useful to talk to existing users to find out their experience of the package.

When a package has been purchased it must be installed on the user hardware, staff must be trained in its use, and the system must be tested. Testing will initially be with specially prepared test data, but the system cannot be implemented completely until it has been tested with real data, and the manual aspects have also been tested. If possible a period should be allowed during which the live data is run through the new system at the same time as through the old, so that results can be compared. In some cases this will be impossible, in which case it is even more essential to test the system thoroughly before handover.

It is, however, likely that mistakes will still come to light during live usage. These teething troubles may be in either the computer system or the related manual procedures. Help, when this happens, should be available from the package suppliers.

**Operation of Information Systems**

The operations function essentially relates to the extracting of information in some form for use by the user departments. The activities in operations functions can be categorised into four distinct areas:

- basic processing;
- timesharing;

- information extraction;
- data storage and retrieval.

The primary operations function is of course the basic processing necessary to satisfy systems in operation. Basic processing is most often batch processing, where recurring reports are generated on the basis of some schedule (say, monthly or weekly) or on the basis of cyclical or seasonal variations. An alternative method of processing information is of course on a real-time basis, or on the basis of a request. A basic data file may be processed only when there are a specific number of inquiries, or when someone is interested in a specific item of information.

Timesharing services may be different from other forms of processing services in that often the program is written by the user at the time that the process is being used, or in that the program characteristics are known only to the user because the user originally generated the program. Thus, typically, only the user can tell in a timesharing process exactly the type of resources required for the process. Timesharing services are totally under the control of the user, and are not subject to seasonal or cyclical variation except as determined by the user. The user is capable of initiating the timesharing sequence at a terminal device, so that there is little control exercised by the operations staff.

When a database has been established, it can be made available to all the members of the organisation, even those who may not be directly concerned with the establishment or maintenance of the database. As a result, information extraction is a specific service which the user may exploit, without regard to who developed, or who is a continual user of, the database. The user may extract information through the use of a terminal, or by means of an enquiry card, or by an enquiry being sent to the processing department.

Information may be stored by a specific user for specific retrieval purposes. In this case of data storage and retrieval services, the user is actually responsible for storing this information and for maintaining the database.

**Technical and Support Services**

In addition to the necessary development and operation functions, there are various technical and support services available to the users. There are two principal services of this sort; namely, consulting assistance and specific education. These are both extremely important services because in many instances the user is not totally familiar with the various information processing alternatives that are available. The user need not go through an expensive systems survey, nor implement any type of system, if it can be determined that simple changes to existing systems or a better understanding of the system will in fact improve the operation sufficiently to meet the user's requirements. As a result, these types of organisational services may be quite vital to the user.

Consulting assistance is performed by systems analysts or by technical personnel who participate with the user in brief analysis of user problems. In some cases, users may be interested in obtaining IT components or equipment for their own purpose. If this is within corporate philosophy, then it is still highly desirable for information systems personnel to participate on a consultancy basis in the implementation of systems. Users may also wish to obtain calculating devices, terminals or other components of a total system which can be linked in some form to the central information systems organisation. It is important for the information systems department to participate in such purchases. This will help to ensure that purchasing and contract negotiation meet company requirements and that the standards of the organisation are observed.

One of the principal problems of software development is the poor communication between analysts and users. One of the causes is that neither the systems analyst nor the user has been effectively educated in the discipline of the other party. It is the responsibility of the information systems department to make the necessary education available to their users. User education primarily takes two forms. Firstly, it is necessary to acquaint the user with information system procedures, with the types of facilities that are available within the organisation and how they work. Secondly, the user should be made aware of the systems development process, thereby ensuring that the user can effectively participate in the development process.

## DEVELOPMENT MODELS

In the earliest days of software development, use was made of the basic 'code-and-fix' model. This was basically a trial and error method consisting of repeated iterations of two steps:

1 Write some code;

2 Fix the problems in the code.

After a number of fixes, the code became so poorly structured that subsequent fixes were very expensive. This emphasised the need for a design phase prior to coding.

Use of a 'stage-wise' model stipulates that software be developed in distinct steps: project initiation, requirements specification, etc. However, user managements often did not have a clear understanding of their requirements before the system was implemented. After the implementation, it was often realised that the system was not what they wanted.

The translation of the requirements into the design and the design into the code is rarely a simple progression from one phase to the next. For example, when system design or detailed design is carried out, it may well be found that some of the requirements conflict with others. Similarly, detailed design may show that the system design was incorrect and a different modularisation of the software would be better. Coding and testing also often reveal deficiencies in the requirements, system design and detailed design. Thus two important features in the stage-wise model are:

1 Recognition of the feedback loops between stages; and a guideline to confine the feedback loops to successive stages (to minimise the expensive rework involved in feedback across many stages).

2 Incorporation of prototying in the software life cycle, via a 'build it twice' step running in parallel with requirements analysis and design.

The purpose of developing prototypes is generally to gain knowledge of the main system's requirements definition, design and implementation, and to demonstrate it to the user. The prototype itself is normally intended to be thrown away or possibly employed in user training. The value of the exercise is the learning that takes place while the prototype is being constructed, not the prototype code itself. In some circumstances, however, prototype code can be used in the final system; and in rare cases the prototype itself may be installed as the final system. On the other hand, the development of a prototype may cause the entire project to be abandoned or totally altered.

Even with extensive revision and refinements the waterfall model's basic scheme has encountered some fundamental difficulties. A primary source of difficulty has been the emphasis on fully elaborated documents as completion criteria for early requirements and design phases. For some classes of software, such as compilers or secure operating systems, this is the most effective way to proceed. However, it does not work well for many classes of software, particularly for interactive end-user applications. Furthermore, in areas supported by fourth-generation languages (spreadsheet or small business applications), it may be unnecessary to write elaborate specifications for an application before implementing it.

These concerns led to the formulation of the 'evolutionary development' model (sometimes known as 'incremental development'). The stages in this model consist of expanding increments of an operational software product, with the direction of evolution being determined by operational experience. This approach is well matched to a fourth-generation language application and to situations in which users say, "I can't tell you what I want, but I'll know it when I see it". It gives users a rapid initial operational capability and provides a realistic operational basis for determining subsequent product improvements.

Nonetheless, evolutionary development also has its difficulties. It is often difficult to distinguish it from the old code-and-fix model, whose 'spaghetti' code and lack of planning were the initial motivation for the waterfall model. It is also based on the often-unrealistic assumption that the user's operational system will be flexible enough to accommodate unplanned evolution paths.

Development of tools for the automatic transformation of the specifications into code led to the development of the 'transform' model. Since the modifications are made to the specification, this model bypasses the difficulty of having to modify code that has become poorly structured through repeated reoptimisation. It also avoids the extra time and expense involved in the intermediate design, code and test activities. However, this model has its own characteristic difficulties. Automatic transformation capabilities are only available for small products in a few limited areas: spreadsheets, small fourth-generation language applications, and limited computer science domains.

The 'spiral' model of the software process has been evolving for several years, based on experience with various refinements of the waterfall model as applied to large government software projects. (This model can accommodate most previous models as special cases and further provide guidance as to which combination of previous models best fits a given software situation.) Here the approach is to repeat circles of activities which together form a spiral. Each cycle of the spiral begins by identifying the objectives of the part of the project product being elaborated (performance, functionality, ability to accommodate changes, etc); the alternative means of implementing this portion of the product (design A, design B, reuse, buy, etc); and the constraints imposed on the application of the alternatives (cost, schedule, interface, etc).

An important feature of the spiral, as with most other models, is that each cycle is completed by a review involving the primary people or organisations concerned with the product. This review covers all products developed during the previous cycle, including the plans for the next cycle and the resources required to carry them out. The review's major objective is to ensure that all concerned parties are mutually committed to the approach for the next phase.

## IMPACT OF END-USER COMPUTING

End-user computing is the direct, hands-on use of computers by end users – not indirect use through systems professionals or the data processing staff. End users include executives, managers, professional staff, secretaries, office workers, sales people and others.

One approach is to classify the activities (of information workers) that can be supported by information technology. The classification is based on job procedures and goals rather than on the type of data (for example, numbers versus text) or the business function (production versus accounting). Thus Type I activities tend to consist of a relatively large number of transactions in which each transaction has a relatively low cost or value. Type II activities, on the other hand, handle few transactions but ones of higher value. Type I activities are based on relatively well-defined procedures or processes in which the principal measure of performance is efficiency (units processed per unit of resource spent). Type II activities are not based on defined processes or procedures, and output is measured in terms of the attainment of objectives or goals.

A Type I information worker is told what to accomplish and how to accomplish it. A Type II information worker must understand what the overall goals are; part of the job is to work out how to attain the goals. Type I activities are based primarily on the handling of data, where Type II activities are based on the handling of concepts.

Here the distinction is not the same as between clerical and managerial activities. Managers often do Type I work, and some clerical workers find Type II activities to be a large part of their job responsibilities. Many of the problems that develop in organisations could be described as the use of a Type I approach to a Type II job. Most of the systems in the past were designed to support Type I activities while the way of the future is to apply the rapidly expanding information technology to support Type II activities.

End-user computing takes place mostly at three levels of the organisation: the *department, work group*, and *individual* levels. The types of tasks may include both Type I and Type II activities, although most of the recent emphasis on end-user computing has been on Type II. End-user computing is the most rapidly growing segment of the information systems activity in many organisations. In some organisations it represents as much as 75 per cent of the total workload.

At the department level, end-user computing may be supported by a minicomputer and/or shared microcomputers for specific applications that the information services department cannot support. Here departmental systems supplement the services of the information services department.

Some minicomputers have fourth-generation languages to aid the rapid development of new applications. The work of the department may require a large amount of computing resources for a special application, as is the case with the use of colour graphics; or it may require a fast response that may be expensive or inconvenient for the main computers to provide. The work on the departmental computers is generally confined to the interests of the one department, using data that the department generates.

At work groups level, end-user computing may provide new ways to communicate. A computer message system, for instance, can substantially reduce the number of interrupting telephone calls that a manager receives without lessening the amount or timeliness of the information. Another advantage of such systems is the ability to file the messages electronically, by category, and save for later retrieval. These messages also provide an easy audit trail and historical record. In the near future, similar systems will be used for sending store-and-forward voice messages.

At the individual level, executives, managers and professional staff use personal computers as decision support aids. Managers and professionals will personally make more and more use of computerised data, obtained from both inside and outside the company. When analysing operating problems or developing plans, they will want the ability to access relevant data and to look for patterns in the data that will help to explain the problem or provide a basis for future action. Since a major part of a manager's job involves monitoring work that is being performed by others, personal computing will include a number of aids for monitoring and scheduling. Examples include electronic personal calendars, tickler files, milestone and status reporting tools, and other useful tools for planning and tracking projects. All of these require storing information about the past, the present and the projected future. In addition, there is the need to store not just data but also plans, text and correspondence.

Guiding and supporting end-user computing presents some new challenges for information systems management. There are five areas that need policies and support: hardware, software, data, communications and training. In establishing end-user computing policies, management must tread a fine line between control and support. Control may stifle end-user creativity and experimentation – which is not desirable. However, completely unguided uses of computers might be detrimental and lead to incompatibilities that are wasteful or harmful to the organisation. Furthermore, information systems management needs to keep the future in mind and anticipate what users will want. It is likely that most employees will eventually be direct computer users. Many will do actual programming, in much the same way that people drive their own cars and dial their own telephones.

Issues on software include questions relating to development, ownership and piracy. Traditionally, it has been the practice to separate the development function from the operations function, and operations from users. One of the advantages of this separation is avoidance of potential exposure to fraud or the disclosure of important information to unauthorised persons. Separation of duties is particularly desirable for sensitive applications.

For financial transactions this may mean separating those employees who authorise specific transactions from those who record them and from those who have custody of the results. For instance, a department might want to develop its own application programs for tracking purchases, money, or inventory. In such a case, both the information systems department and the internal audit group will want to investigate the sensitivity of the application. If it is to be developed, operated and used by one or a few individuals, the company may be exposing itself to trouble. Management may want both programming and operation of such applications to be done through the information systems department. In general, sensitive applications should not be written by end users, especially not for running on their personal computers.

Employee-developed applications written in company time usually belong to the company and should be available for common use as a company asset. It may be a good idea to keep copies of user-written applications in a 'software library'. This will provide a central site for back-up as well as for sharing software among users and informing them of software changes. Users should be taught to document their programs properly so that they can be understood and used by others.

Most vendors of software prefer to license, rather than to sell, the use of their copyrighted software. The licence generally applies to use on only one specific machine, so all copies of the package other than authorised back-up copies for that machine are illegal and amount to software piracy. Large corporations have to be concerned about the piracy that is occurring in their organisations because they are the ones most likely to be sued by software houses for permitting this practice.

Data issues relate to integrity, security and privacy of corporate data. Organisations with end users accessing corporate computers employ security features (such as password-protected files, audit trail software, and so on). If users can access corporate data on their own, and if they are allowed to change data, this can be the source of integrity risk. The most likely uses of personal computers will be to extract data from corporate files, store it on the micro, and manipulate it locally. Files that individual end users create are mostly personal files, ie files that other users do not really need to see or use. These files include drafts of memos and reports, personal programs for analysing data, plans still in the formative stage, and so on. These files are the user's responsibility, not the responsibility of the corporate information systems department.

For departmental minis (or work-group multiuser micros), there is more chance that the data entered onto those computers might be of use to others within the corporation. Here the question of integrity does arise: should information systems allow that data to be put onto a corporate computer so that it can be used by others? Most information systems departments do not want to become responsible for the integrity of data over which they have no control, so they do not allow data from user-developed systems to be loaded into corporate files.

Hardware issues relate to incompatibility between different microcomputers, ownership of hardware, and economic justification for the procurement of new hardware. If users are allowed to buy their own personal computers, there may be little compatibility among the different brands of PCs for exchanging data, text or programs. As a result, establishing suitable data communications between a variety of micros and a company's host computers would be a serious problem.

The emergence of the IBM Personal Computer as the ad hoc standard is making some contribution to the compatibility problem. Many companies claim their computers to be IBM PC compatible, but, in reality, they are not fully compatible. For example, the popular IBM operating system PC-DOS was developed by Microsoft but is available only from IBM. The 'open market' version used by the look-alikes is MS-DOS, from Microsoft, which is close to PC-DOS but not identical with it. The arrival of the PS/2 and UNIX operating systems on micros has further complicated the compatibility question.

Since the information systems department works as a service department, all costs incurred on behalf of the users are eventually borne by the user. So, it is logical that they should also be responsible for the economic justification of such costs. However, they may need support from the information systems department in estimating the costs and benefits and identifying the right hardware and software for acquisition. Many of the benefits are really intangible like improved customer service, promoting innovation, and long-term impact of technological upgrading, which need to be considered.

Communication links may be required between the micros and the corporate mainframe or between the micro workstations themselves. Personal computers may provide valuable service as stand-alone devices for spreadsheet analysis, decision support, word processing, graphics and other applications. But they can also serve as powerful and comprehensive workstations when they are interconnected in the corporate network. Communication between the micro and the mainframe may be required to access the corporate mainframe in a time-sharing mode or access corporate data files for the purpose of analysis along with other local data. Management needs to decide not only what data will be allowed to be offloaded from the mainframe to the micro but also what access policies and restrictions should be put on downloaded files. Users may also like to use micros to upload data to a mainframe database. This is, however, subject to the integrity requirements discussed earlier. Communication between the workstations is used to send documents and graphic images between two word processors and here the compatibility problems have to be considered.

Users need to be both educated and trained. They need an understanding of the basic computer concepts as much as hands-on training in the use of specific packages. Companies that started with hands-on training soon realised that they had started at the wrong end. In their impatience to become expert users, they generally tend to underestimate the importance of understanding the fundamental concepts.

Traditional classroom training focuses on the chalk-and-talk method but computer-based training makes it possible to provide a quite different training environment. The training can be on-demand, interactive, specific to the immediate interests of the student, performed where and when the student desires, and (to a great extent) not requiring a human instructor to be active in the process. Multi-media training packages try to combine the benefits of conventional methods with computer-based training and the use of other audio-visual methods such as overhead projectors, video tapes, video disks making use of verbal communication, text, graphics and computer control.

Users need training in computers and data processing concepts, hands-on skills, refresher aids, help in overcoming difficulties in advanced use, and models of analysis. Computers and data processing concepts include file and database structure, file creation, back-up, and maintenance; methods of data organisation, access modes, storage, retrieval, reorganisation, etc, as a part of general computer literacy – learning how things are done in data processing.

Hands-on skills include the use of equipment and its utilities, switching on and off, operating system command; the use of application packages; and the use of other electronic facilities available. Since many end users will not be using each computer application every day, they are likely to forget how to perform certain operations. Refresher aids can be provided through computer-based tutorials, help screens, etc. Managerial users using decision support models need to understand the underlying assumptions as well as the concepts used in building the model, or else they may use them incorrectly. Modelling packages often have a 'parameter screen' or assumption lists that act as an assumption review, as well as a device for controlling the package.

# 8 Planning for Information Technology

## INTRODUCTION

Information technology is playing an ever increasing role in modern organisations. While an increasingly large number of organisations have introduced information technology in one way or another, the technology itself has been expanding rapidly. The older technologies of batch processing and automated accounting have reached a stage of maturity in most organisations, and the newer technologies of process control, computer-aided engineering/manufacture and office automation are at varying stages of absorption in different organisations. The rapid evolution and spread of information systems technologies has created a new set of managerial challenges. Starting from small data processing sections in the accounting departments, information technology has led to the creation of new departments with massive recruiting of staff, major investments in computer hardware and software, and the installation of systems that have profoundly affected how the firm operates in the modern competitive environment.

The introduction of a new technology in the organisation passes through the stages of investment, learning and adaptation, rationalisation and maturity. The first stage is the exploratory stage when the new technologies are identified and their potential for the organisation examined. This stage may involve a pilot study or project to see the impact of the technology on the organisation's productivity and assess its costs and benefits to the organisation.

After the introduction of the technology, the stage of experimentation and learning begins. During experimentation, the user develops new insights into the potential and limitations. Often the implications turn out to be quite different from those expected. Gradually the technology is adapted and absorbed. Then the process of rationalisation or management control begins.

Once the applications are reasonably understood, efforts are made to develop appropriate tools and controls. Now the focus shifts from stimulating awareness and experimentation to the efficient utilisation of the application, and the development of controls to maintain them over long periods of time. Formal standards, cost-benefit studies, and user charge-out mechanisms come into force. Once the technology has passed through the gamut of organisational learning, with technological skills, user awareness and management controls in place, the stage of maturity is reached. At any one time various information system technologies may be at different evolutionary stages in the same organisation.

Information technology has affected different industries in different ways. In some industries, it has enabled a massive transformation of the various operational aspects of the production chain. Embedding technology in the product, computer-aided design and manufacturing (CAD/CAM), multifaceted automation, the demand for increased quality, etc, have all changed the industry's modes of competition as industry leaders put great pressure on competitors to meet new standards. In other industries, the new technology has more strongly affected marketing and distribution. New channels of distribution have been set up, prior methods have become outmoded, new customer service features introduced, new promotion and market research methods developed, etc.

In the airlines industry, with highly evolved reservation systems, some of the large airlines have been able to offer new services such as 'frequent flyer' programmes and joint incentive programmes for hotels, car rental agencies and other airlines. Operations management, focusing on such aspects as seat allocation, crew scheduling, maintenance, etc, has also become highly sophisticated – and reliant on computer-based systems. The smaller airlines have come under severe competitive pressure to provide comparable services as well as to improve the cost effectiveness of their operations.

The banking industry has made equally aggressive use of information technology to provide new products and services for their customers. Large banks, particularly, are able to provide a wide variety of services tailored to the individual needs of various types of customers. The defence industries have been deeply affected on the manufacturing side with the use of CAD/CAM, robotics and embedded technology. Retailing operations also have been significantly altered by the technology, though not yet to the same extent as airlines or banks. Display management, computer-assisted cosmetics analysis and point-of-sales terminals have seen significant effects on their marketing strategies.

In some industries, information technology has played a predominantly operational role; while, for others, its impact has been on marketing. In many of these environments, industry leaders have aggressively transformed the rules of competition and put followers under great pressure. For some organisations, IT activities represent an area of great strategic importance; for other organisations, they play a cost-effective and useful role but one distinctly supportive in nature. In some industries, IT plays a strategic operational role in companies' day-to-day operations and its applications have reached a mature stage so that future development applications do not offer the same pay-off.

In yet other industries, while today's existing IT applications are not critical to the firm in meeting its goals, the enthusiasm for the new systems applications portfolio has great significance for the future. An understanding of these issues is critical to developing an appropriate organisational IT strategy. Industries can be classified in four distinct IT environments: strategic, turnaround, factory and support.

The *strategic* environment includes those companies for whom smooth functioning of the IT activity is critical to their operation on a daily basis, and whose applications under development are also critical to their future competitive success. Banks, insurance companies and heavy-equipment manufacturing companies usually fall into this category. Such companies not only require considerable IT planning but also a close organisational relationship between IT and senior management. In some of these firms, the head of the information systems function is a member of the board of directors.

In the *turnaround* environment, the firm may receive considerable support from IT operations, but it is not critically dependent on this support to achieve either short-term or long-term objectives. However, the applications under development are vital for the firm to reach its strategic goals. A rapidly growing manufacturing firm is likely to fall into this category. The information technology embedded in its factories and accounting processes, though important, is not absolutely vital to their effectiveness. However, the rapid growth of the firm's domestic and international presence – in number of products, number of sites, number of staff and so on – would rapidly make the existing systems obsolete. In such circumstances, planning for information systems with suitable organisational placement of IT is absolutely necessary.

In the *factory* environment, firms are heavily dependent on cost-effective, totally-reliable IT operational support. The development of information systems is however limited to the maintenance of existing systems; and their future applications portfolio, though important in its own right, is not fundamental to the firm's ability to compete. Some manufacturing, airline and retailing firms may fit into this category. In these organisations, even a one-hour disruption of existing systems has severe operational consequences on the performance of the business unit.

In *support* environments, information systems play only a support function. Their operations are not fundamentally dependent on the smooth functioning of the IT systems, nor is the applications portfolio essential to the strategic needs of the company. Such organisations may have fairly large IT budgets and may be obtaining a good return on investment. Here IT is installed at a significantly lower organisational level and the commitment to planning – particularly at the senior management level – is quite low. A large number of organisations fall into this category.

## ISSUES IN IT PLANNING

Planning for IT usage in the organisation presents challenges which are different from those in planning for routine production; such challenges are necessarily related to the nature of the technology. Here the first issue of concern to the planners is the rapid growth of the technology. Rapid technical developments have thereby offered new and profitable IT applications.

Coping with these changes, and using them for the best advantage to the organisation, requires a continuous interaction between IT staff and user management. Changes significant to the company need to be identified on a regular basis and plans developed to manage them. Potential users should be made aware of the implications (including the problems) of the new technologies. They may then identify, in their areas of responsibility, profitable new applications that would not necessarily occur to the IT staff.

As the technology changes, planning becomes increasingly important to avoid proliferation of incompatible systems. Also, because the lead times for acquiring and updating equipment are often long, integration of new equipment into a company's existing technical and administrative configuration frequently extends implementation schedules by as much as four years.

Another major issue that confronts the IT planners is the scarcity of trained technical resources (such as systems analysts and programmers, as well as managers). This is compounded by the need for long training cycles to keep such staff fully effective.

The proliferation of IT productivity tools and software tools has, to some extent, controlled the explosive requirement for programmers: the availability of these personnel has traditionally lagged behind the needs of the proliferating applications in organisations. An increasing number of US firms have looked overseas for English-speaking technical personnel to meet staff shortages. This has further aggravated the problems in 'donor' countries.

Scarcity of IT middle management personnel, particularly in the area of development, is a significant constraint. The inability of companies to train sufficient project leaders and supervisors has significantly restrained IT development. This has sometimes caused significant reductions in many application portfolios and the undertaking of unduly high-risk projects because of inadequate human resources.

There is an increasing trend towards the design of integrated systems, though physically distributed around integrated corporate databases. Obviously, such integrated systems cannot be implemented in a single phase, but the individual phases have to be implemented with a long-term perspective. Such a long-term view of the evolution of applications is critical to the appropriate selection of both the contents of databases and the protocols for updating them to adequately support the systems using them.

The relationships of the IT plans to the overall corporate plans of the organisation are becoming increasingly important as the IT systems play an increasingly significant and strategic role in the achievement of corporate goals. In many organisations new marketing programmes, new product design and introduction/implementation of organisational strategies increasingly depend on the development of effective IT support.

It is important to understand these points of dependency. The validation of the corporate plans with respect to the supportive IT plans needs to be ensured at an early stage so that the resolution of the problems can be achieved while alternatives are still available. This linkage is more important in organisations where the IT products are integral to elements of the corporate strategy than for those organisations where IT plays an important but distinctly support function.

## PLANNING FOR STAGES OF GROWTH

Richard Nolan and Cyrus Gibson (1974) observed that organisations go through four stages in the introduction and assimilation of new technology:

1. Early successes: The first stage involves the initial use of new technology. While some stumbling generally occurs, early successes lead to increased interest and experimentation.
2. Proliferation: Based on the early successes, interest grows

rapidly as new products and/or services based on the technology come to the marketplace. These are tried out in a variety of application systems. This proliferation stage is the key learning period, both for users and others.

3. Control of proliferation: Eventually it becomes apparent that the proliferation must be controlled. Management begins to feel that the costs of using the new technology are too high; that the variety of approaches generates waste. The integration of systems is attempted but proves difficult and suppliers begin efforts toward standardisation.

4. Mature use: At this stage, the use of the particular new technology might be considered mature. The stage has been set for introducing still other new technology, wherein the pattern is repeated. In fact, different forms of technology can simultaneously be at different stages in the same organisation.

McFarlan and McKenney (1983) discuss a somewhat modified version of the four stages. They consider:

1. Identification and initial investment.
2. Experimentation and learning.
3. Management control.
4. Widespread technology transfer.

Each of these four phases poses a quite different planning challenge. During the first phase, the basic focus of planning is oriented towards both technology and human resource acquisition. Key planning problems include identification of an appropriate technology for study, site preparation, development of staff skills, and development of the first pilot applications using this technology. Here short-term technical problem resolution is critical and experience limited, so any long-term strategic thinking about the implications of the technology is precluded: those involved usually do not yet have a strong enough background in the technology and its implications for the company to think long term. As the organisation gains experience, selection of appropriate applications for the technology becomes more informed, and the company enters the second phase.

During the second phase (learning and adaptation), the basic aim of planning is to develop the potential users' awareness of the new technology, and to communicate the type of problems it can help solve. Planning in this phase has a heavy strategic focus. Both user and developer lack familiarity with the technology and its implications. Hence planning at this stage does not have the same predictive value as planning for technology in a later phase.

The planning of projects may focus on the required numbers of staff and on the skills that are needed, on the equipment to be acquired, and on the generation of appropriate financial data. However, what may emerge from the projects may be quite different from that planned. It is critical during this phase to attract the interest of some potential users and to enlarge their understanding of the technology. Success here leads to later requests for service. Planning during this phase involves a programme of planned technological innovations, encouraging users to build upon past experience and encouraging organisational receptivity to change.

During the third phase (management control), planning must aim to rationalise the broad range of experimental operations. While technological learning and adaptation planning has a long-range perspective, planning for management control is dominated by short-term (one- to two-year) efficiency and organisation considerations. These include solving application problems, upgrading staff to acceptable knowledge levels, reorganising to develop and implement further projects, and efficiently utilising the new technology. During this phase, the aim is to set appropriate limits on the types of applications that make sense, and to ensure they are implemented cost-efficiently. At this time, planning has a much stronger management and operational control flavour and a relatively weak strategic planning thrust.

During the last phase (widespread technology transfer), the maturity of technology leads to a wider spectrum of systems applications within the organisation. With organisational learning essentially complete and a technology base with appropriate controls in place, it is appropriate to look more seriously into the future and to plot longer-term trends. It is important that planning based on business and technology has not become too rigid. Unexpected quirks in the evolution of technology, as in the business, are still possible.

Given the current dynamic state of IT, all four planning phases are likely to co-exist in a typical organisation. Planning for batch processing systems, for example, may be in phase 4 while electronic mail may be in phase 2 in the same company. This suggests that uniformity and consistency in planning protocols are inappropriate because the organisation's familiarity with particular technologies varies.

## METHODS OF PLANNING

### Critical Success Factors Method (CSF)

The Critical Success Factors (CSF) method developed by John Rockart (1979) focuses on individual managers and their current information needs. The CSF method is used to help companies identify the information systems that they need to develop. For each executive, critical success factors are the few key areas of the job where things must go right for the organisation to flourish. There are usually fewer than ten of these factors that any one executive should monitor. Further, they are very time dependent, so they should be re-examined as often as necessary to keep abreast of the current business climate. These key areas should receive constant attention from executives, yet it is found that most managers have not explicitly identified them. Rockart identifies four *sources* for these factors. One source is the industry that the business is in. Each industry has CSFs that are relevant to any company in it. The second source is the company itself, and its situation within the industry. Actions by a few dominant companies in an industry will most likely provide one or more CSFs for small companies in that industry. Further, several companies may have the same CSFs but, at the same time, have different priorities for these factors.

The third source of CSFs is the environment, such as consumer trends, the economy, and political factors in the company's market environment. For example, prior to 1973, virtually no chief executive in the United States would have listed 'energy supply availability' as a CSF. Following the oil embargo, however, many executives began monitoring this factor very closely. The fourth source is temporal organisational factors – areas of company activity that normally do not warrant concern but which are currently unacceptable and need attention. A case of far too much or far too little inventory may classify as a CSF.

In addition to these four sources, Rockart has highlighted two *types* of CSFs. One he calls 'monitoring' – that is, keeping abreast of ongoing operations. The second he calls 'building' – tracking progress of 'programmes for change' initiated by the executive. The higher the executive in the organisation, the more 'building' CSFs are usually on his/her list. Rockart sees CSFs varying from organisation to organisation, from time period to time period, and from manager to manager.

One way to use the CSF method is to list the corporate objectives and goals for the year. These are then used to determine which factors are critical for accomplishing the objectives. Then two or three prime measures for each factor are determined. Discovering the measures is the most time-consuming portion of this stage. Some measures – the ones that use hard factual data – are the ones most quickly identified. Others use 'softer' measures, such as opinions, perceptions and hunches; these require more analysis to uncover their appropriate sources.

Rockart and Crescenzi (1983) suggest a three-phase methodology for systems planning and development, each phase using a key technique to accomplish a sub-objective of the entire process. The three phases are:

1. Linking to business;
2. Developing well-understood system priorities;
3. Prototype systems development.

The objective of the first phase is to tie the systems plans closely to the business plans. Again the key technique is critical success factors. The objective of the second phase is to identify the required systems and establish a priority scheme for their development. A by-product of this process is that managers develop the confidence that the system will accomplish the intended objectives. The key technique for this phase is the use of decision scenarios to identify recurring decisions and the questions that the managers ask of themselves and others while making these decisions.

The scenarios are then used to identify which items of information could be provided by the proposed new information systems and which could not. The technique helps to provide insight into what the new information systems could do for the company and the types of information that should be carried in the systems.

The objective of the third phase is to develop the systems that will begin reaping the intended benefits. The key technique is prototyping, so that benefits can begin early and system performance assessed and refined along the way.

### Business Systems Planning

Another popular planning methodology is Business Systems Planning (BSP), developed and marketed by IBM. The basic philosophy of BSP is that data is a corporate resource. As such, it should be managed from an overall organisational viewpoint, so that it can best serve the organisation's objectives and support its decision-making activities. The goal of BSP is to discover a stable information architecture that supports all of the processes of the business. Once the basic data needs of a business process (such as purchasing) have been identified, and as long as that process remains basically the same, the information framework will be stable. BSP also uses this information framework as a basis for future information systems planning.

The BSP Guide published by IBM describes 14 steps in the method, two of which are preparatory to the actual study and one of which involves possible follow-up activities.

1. **Gaining commitment**: BSP begins by requiring a commitment from management – either corporate or division management, depending on the breadth of the study. The top executive of the organisation is normally the 'study

sponsor'. All final study recommendations are presented to the sponsor for review and approval to proceed. The study also requires the commitment of one top executive to serve as team leader who selects other executives to join the team and then directs the team's activities. It will be the team's responsibility to determine the information needs of the organisation and recommend future information system actions.

2. **Preparing for the study**: Preparations for the BSP study are usually handled by the team leader (with outside help, if necessary). These preparations involve creating the study schedule, making out the list of executives to be interviewed, gathering reference materials, locating and equipping a meeting room and so on.
3. **Starting the study**: At the initial meeting of the team, the objectives of the study are presented by the sponsor. The team leader reviews any preparations already made, as well as the study schedule. To establish the technical environment, an overview of the company's information systems is presented by the chief information systems executives.
4. **Defining business processes**: In this step the team identifies and describes all the processes of the business, such as product development, marketing, purchasing and receiving. They are identified independently of the current organisational units responsible for them, so that future organisational changes will not affect the list of processes. This step also identifies the processes that are key to the success of the business.
5. **Defining business data**: Next, the team groups all of the data used in the company into logical categories, called data classes. A data class is information about anything that needs to be tracked, such as customers, vendors, parts, machines, work orders, contracts and so on. A company generally has 30 to 60 data classes; the BSP guide describes several approaches for classifying these.
6. **Defining an information architecture**: The information

architecture of the organisation shows the relationship between data classes, processes and information systems. BSP delineates a procedure for defining information systems in terms of the data they create, manage and use to support related business processes. The creation, as well as the use, of data is important, because the creator of the data should also maintain it. Data created in one system and used in another is identified so that subsystems can be identified either as 'create' subsystems or 'usage' subsystems. The team analyses these subsystems to see which must be placed before others can be implemented.

7. **Analysing current systems support**: Now that the team members have studied the business, its activities and its data, they turn their attention to the company information systems – both current and planned. From this study the team can discover which processes receive no formal information systems support, which receive some support, where possible redundant systems exist and where shared information systems are possible.

8. **Interviewing executives**: Next the team interviews ten to 20 executives within the top three levels of the organisation. The purposes of these interviews are (1) to verify the organisational assumptions made and the processes/data classes developed thus far, (2) to determine the information needed by these executives, and (3) to uncover their problems and priorities. Each interview lasts two to four hours.

9. **Defining findings and conclusions**: By this stage, the study team has amassed a huge amount of material: research and organisational information, interview summaries, relationships of processes and data classes, organisational structure and so forth. These must be organised and summarised in order to be useful for determining the corporate information architecture. First the team assesses the business problems and opportunities discovered in the interviews. For each problem stated by the executives, the team considers the importance attached to that problem, the processes causing the problem, other processes that are

affected and possible solutions. Finally, the team lists the root causes and end effects of these problems.

Using this list, the team determines if a problem lies in an existing information system, is caused because no information system exists, or is not an information systems problem at all. Some problems can have both organisational and systems solutions. The need for better market information, for example, could require establishment of a market research group as well as creation of a supporting information system.

10. **Determining architecture priorities**: In this step the team decides the order in which subsystems are to be developed. This is based primarily on what would be most useful to the executives and, secondly on traditional evaluation criteria (such as cost, development time). The highest priority systems or subsystems are then described in considerable detail for evaluation by the study sponsor.
11. **Reviewing information resource management**: Having analysed the business processes and the data used to perform them, the team then studies the company's information systems management policies in order to identify the changes implied by the study recommendations. BSP recommends quite an in-depth study of the planning and control aspects of the information systems function. The study looks at the function's objectives, personnel, finances, facilities, applications, data and users. Implementation of the study team's recommendations may require some fundamental changes in information systems management practices. For example, a move to distributed processing could require new funding, cost charge-back, control and training policies, to name a few. The team lists such implied changes as they study the department.
12. **Developing recommendations and an action plan**: This step produces the final set of recommendations and an action plan for implementing them. The recommendations from the BSP study fall into three areas:
    - an information resource architecture, including the subsystems that make it up;

- information systems management recommendations, specifically the management, planning and control of data;
- the sequence in which the systems are to be developed.

The action plan describes the costs, potential benefits and schedules for the recommended projects. Generally, several concurrent projects are recommended.

13. **Reporting results**: In reporting the results of its study, the team hopes to gain approval from the study sponsor to proceed with its recommendations and action plan. The presentation is both verbal and written, with the verbal overview for top executives lasting no more than one hour.
14. **Overview of follow-up activities**: The BSP manual stresses the importance of various people, including users, assuming responsibility for implementing the team's recommendations, and it recommends a steering committee to oversee the information resource architecture. The manual also describes various aspects of activities such as implementing changes, maintaining and refining the architecture and developing the first system.

The BSP methodology requires a major initial commitment of time and effort to launch a systems plan. Once the initial framework has been developed, future planning and development are facilitated.

### Investment Strategy Analysis

Investment strategy analysis to support information systems planning is based on traditional techniques of portfolio planning and investment analysis. Five major types of information systems applications in use have been identified:

1. Institutional procedures – the processing of internal transactions, as represented by conventional data processing systems;
2. Profession support systems, such as engineering support, managerial decision-making support and similar activities;
3. Physical automation;

4. Systems that serve users outside the company, such as customers and suppliers;
5. Systems providing basic technical infrastructure to permit the development and use of the above applications, such as telecommunication networks, database standards, and other systems software.

A two-dimensional table can be created with the five types of systems on one dimension and the main functional users (such as research and development, manufacturing, marketing, and other service and support functions) on the other. This can help the manager to analyse the current portfolio of expenditures and then decide where they should be made in order to align the information systems investment with the business strategy.

**Scenario Approach to Planning**

The scenario approach to planning is gaining popularity in socioeconomic planning and corporate planning. It is based on generating various alternatives on planning strategies as well as environmental factors and simulating these alternatives on the computer using decision support systems. Enzer (1984) describes how strategies for introducing new information systems might be developed using a scenario approach. Scenarios are built on the basis of projections of different aspects of technology and the business environment.

The scenarios help to identify some problem areas that could arise if some factors change, such as the amount and type of competition or changes in wage rates. Once these scenarios have been generated, managers choose several that could happen. The 'most likely' scenario is selected as the basis for long-range plans. Scenarios also provide alternative plans to fall back on, should it be necessary. This is the role of the other scenarios that are less likely but still feasible. They identify the leading edges of changes that management should monitor.

The selected scenario of the future is used to develop a phased schedule for achieving the desired ends. Projects required to implement the scenario are divided into phases, and the commitment to proceed is given for the next phase of each project over time. This concept is employed to highlight unexpected changes in the overall situation that might require a reassessment of the continued feasibility of the scenario.

The future is always uncertain and plans may have to be continually changed. Companies are being acquired and merged. There are changes in the business environment due to foreign competition and new government regulations. Changes in the technology may accelerate. Mid-course corrections are part of the scenario process. As scenarios of the future are regenerated at later points in time, they will certainly show new pictures of the future. That is the time for management to assess the changes, to determine if plans must be modified, and to decide if a new approach is needed.

# 9 User Involvement in System Development

## INTRODUCTION

Formal user involvement is necessary at all stages of development to ensure that the resulting system conforms to the user requirements and meets the necessary quality standards. One project management methodology gaining increasing attention prescribes three distinct components of the project management organisation:

- the project board;
- project management (project and stage managers);
- the project assurance team.

The project board consists of three senior management roles (each representing major project interests): the executive role, the senior user role, and the senior technical role. The executive role provides overall project guidance, and assesses the project continuously from a financial and senior management point of view. The senior user role represents end users (of the system or of the major products which the project will deliver). The senior technical role represents those who have responsibility for technical implementation and for operations.

At the operational level, project management is carried out by the project manager and the stage managers. While the project manager is responsible for the whole project, the stage managers are responsible for the individual stages of the project. Those two roles may in practice be performed by separate individuals or by the same individual, depending on the size of the project and the skills available.

The project assurance team consists of three technical and administrative roles: the business assurance co-ordinator, to maintain administrative controls against schedules and budget; the technical assurance co-ordinator, to maintain technical assurance controls and monitor technical integrity; and the user assurance co-ordinator, to maintain user assurance controls and to represent the user's interests.

The project board assumes overall control, provides overall guidance and direction to the project throughout the project. It authorises the project initiation and the project closure, appoints individuals to the roles in the project board, project management and project assurance team, defines their responsibilities and objectives, and reviews and approves project plans from time to time. Each of the roles in the project board (ie the executive role, the senior user role, and the senior technical role) may be performed by one or more individuals. The executive role is to perform the top executive function to ensure that the project is completed within the cost and timescales, and achieves the expected benefits.

The project board provides direction to the entire project management staff, authorises expenditure, and commits resources to the project. It represents the top management of the organisation in the project and has a good understanding of IT concepts and the overall IT strategy of the organisation.

The senior user role represents the interests of all user departments affected by the project. It specifies user requirements and commits user resources to the project on behalf of all the users. It approves user education plans, briefs and advises user management on all project matters and supervises the work of the user assurance co-ordinator. Individuals performing the senior user role are expected to have extensive management knowledge of affected user functions, information technology from the user's point of view and the way users will operate the new system.

The senior technical role represents the interest of the

development and operations organisations or the technical management of the project. It specifies objectives for technical activities such as system design, development, and testing; assigns technical resources; and reviews and approves the technical plans of the project from time to time. The senior technical role demands extensive IT management experience, and a good understanding of the affected user functions and overall IT strategy of the organisation.

The project manager and the stage managers perform all managerial activities under the overall direction and control of the project board to ensure the production of all required project products to the required standard of quality, and within specified constraints of time and cost. The three roles of the project assurance team closely match the three roles in the project board. The business assurance co-ordinator acts as the focal point for administrative controls to plan, monitor and report on all business assurance aspects of the project. He/she helps the project manager in preparing the resource plans to match the project technical plans, monitors programmes and costs against the project's business case, and contributes to the project evaluation review.

The technical assurance co-ordinator is responsible for planning, monitoring and reporting on all technical assurance aspects of the project. He/she helps the project manager to prepare the technical plans to match the project resource plans, monitors technical progress against plans and advises on the technical impact of all modifications in plans and achievements. The user assurance co-ordinator represents the users on a day-to-day basis and is responsible for monitoring, and reporting on, the user assurance aspects of the project. He/she ensures that the user requirements have been taken care of in full, monitors all reports to user management and any user problems that arise during system development.

## PRODUCTS OF SYSTEM DEVELOPMENT

A system development project involves the production of a set of products. The products which are required to satisfy the needs of the end user are called the 'business products'. These are the products required by the customers. Additional products are needed to build and support business products. These are called 'development products'. Other products needed are 'management and control products'. The project can be broken down into its various products in a number of stages very much like an organisation structure, each step breaking down the product into its various components. At the top of this structure chart is a simple box which represents everything to be produced by a project. At each successive level of the chart, the system is represented in greater detail. The Production Breakdown Structure (PBS) contains a box for each type of product. Boxes below these 'product boxes' represent components of products; boxes above the 'product boxes' represent groups or categories of product. Each product is described by its purpose, derivation, composition, standards for format and presentation, and the quality criteria which apply to it. A typical product breakdown structure for a system development project is shown in the linked diagrams (Figures 9.1 to 9.4).

The products which involve users of the system are now described.

The Survey of the Current System identifies the facilities offered by the current system, and its limitations on the basis of the investigations carried out by interview and questionnaire with the relevant user departments. Users and maintenance teams provide input to the survey. Users and an independent, experienced analyst join the review team.

The Requirements Specification specifies the users' requirements, including any constraints and future enhancements, so that possible solutions can be identified. Relevant users provide full information about their requirements. Relevant users, and an independent, experienced analyst from another team join the review team.

The Logical System Design provides a detailed logical structure of the option selected by the user which will be used as input to the system build strategy, the physical system design, and the testing strategies. Relevant users join the review team.

The Acceptance Criteria provide a means of establishing, by specific criteria, whether the completed system is acceptable to

System
Management Products
2
Interface Products
3
Development Products
4
Implementation Products
5
Handover Products
Post Handover Products
Operational Products
6
Maintenance Products
7
Quality Products
8
System Audit Results

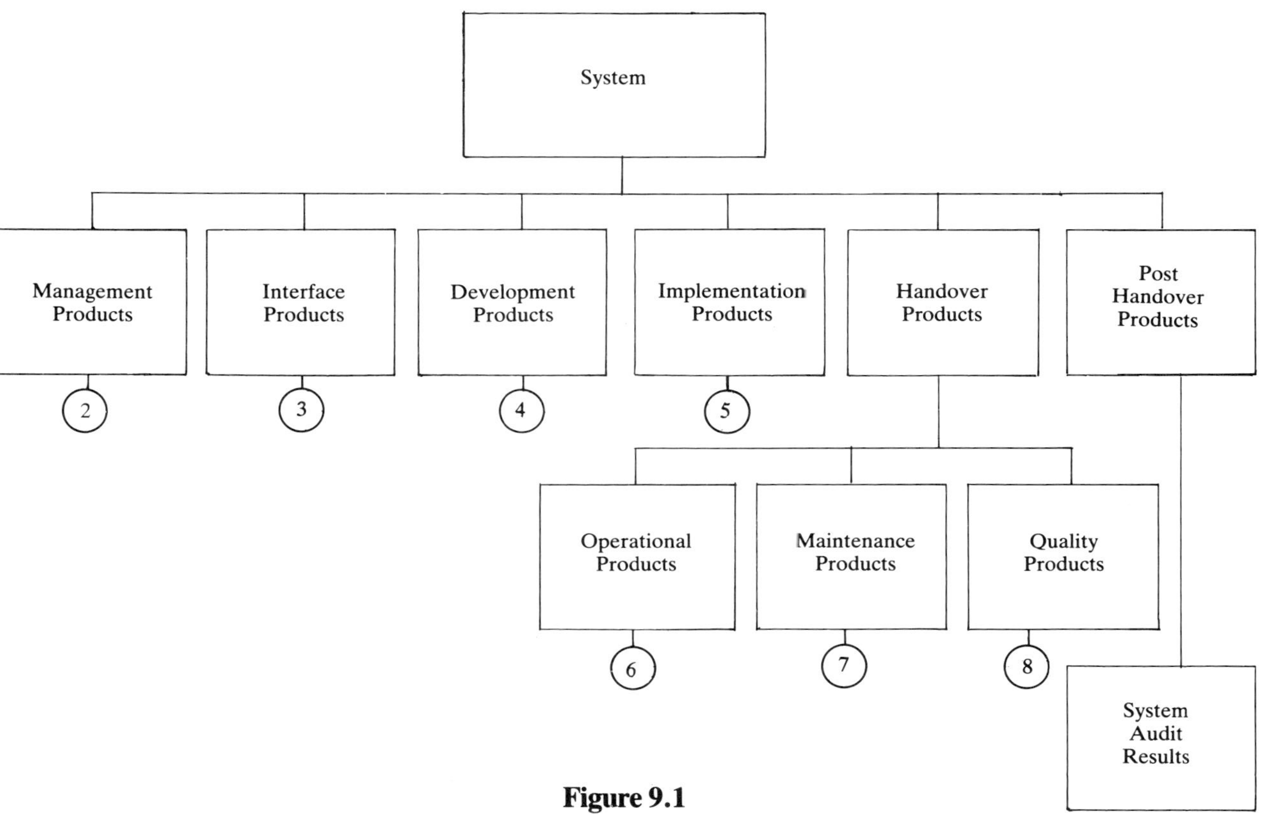

**Figure 9.1**

2
Management Products
Mgt Guide
Project Plan
Mgt Guide
Stage Plans
Mgt Guide
Checkpoint Reports
Mgt Guide
Highlight Reports
Mgt Guide
Off-spec Reports
3
Interface Products
Info For Risk Assessment
Info For Capacity Management
Products to Co-ordinate Other Projects
4
Development Products
Survey of Current System
Project Initiation Document
Installation & Conversion Strategy
Education Strategy
System Build Strategy
Possible Solutions & Recommendation

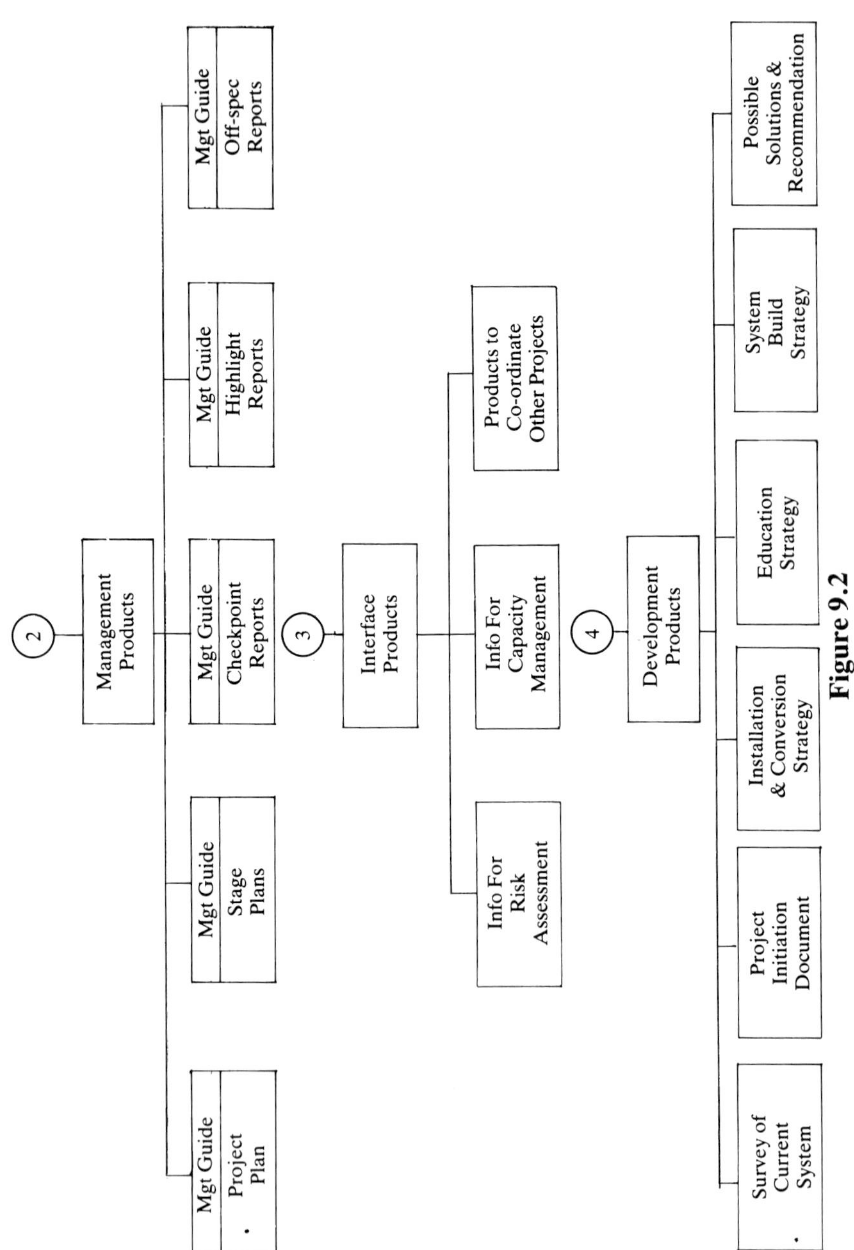

**Figure 9.2**

5
Implementation Products
Installation Guide
Release Package
6
Operational Products
Conversion Run Results
Installation Run Results
Operating Environment
User Guide
Operations Guide
Trained Staff
Hardware Resources
Support Software
Computer Stationery
Manual Stationery

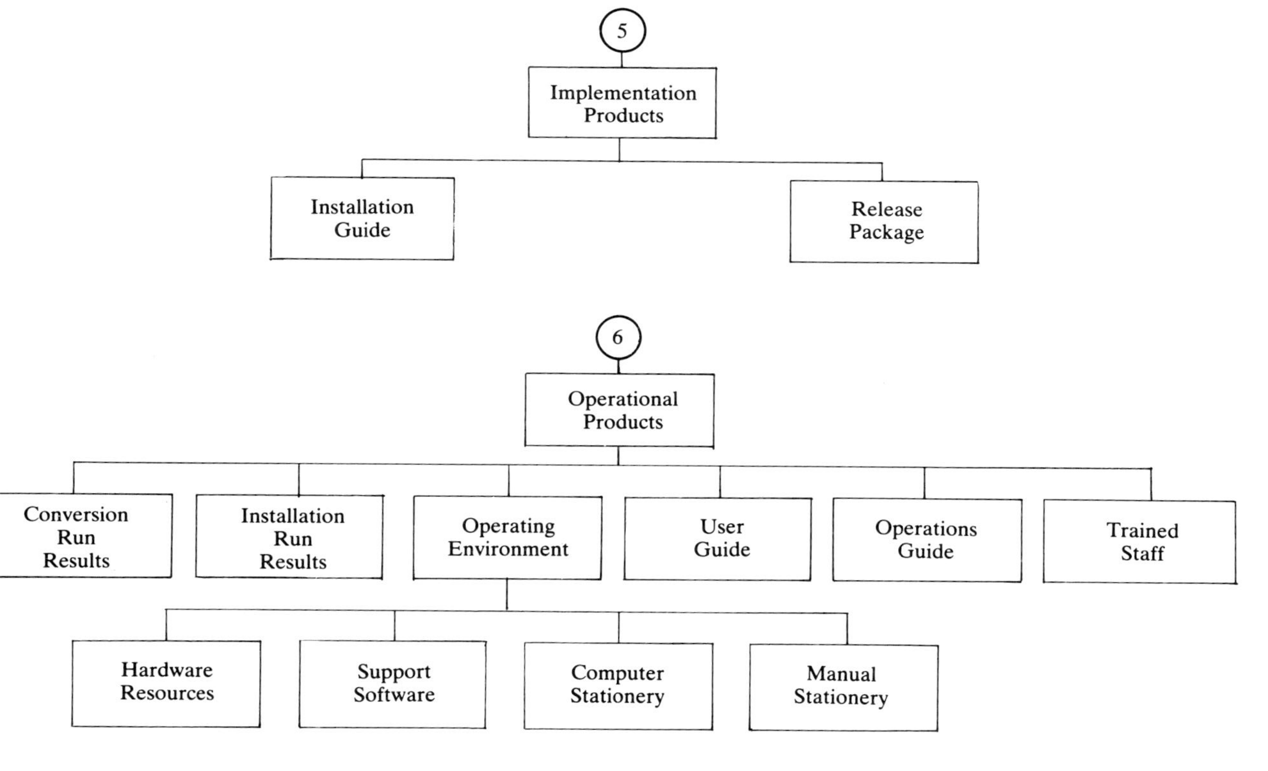

**Figure 9.3**

7
Maintenance Products
Logical Design
Physical Design
Program Design
Programs
Unit Test Products
System Test Products
Acceptance Test Products
Education Guide
Strategy
Specn
Data
Results
Strategy
Specn
Data
Results
Strategy
Specn
Data
Results

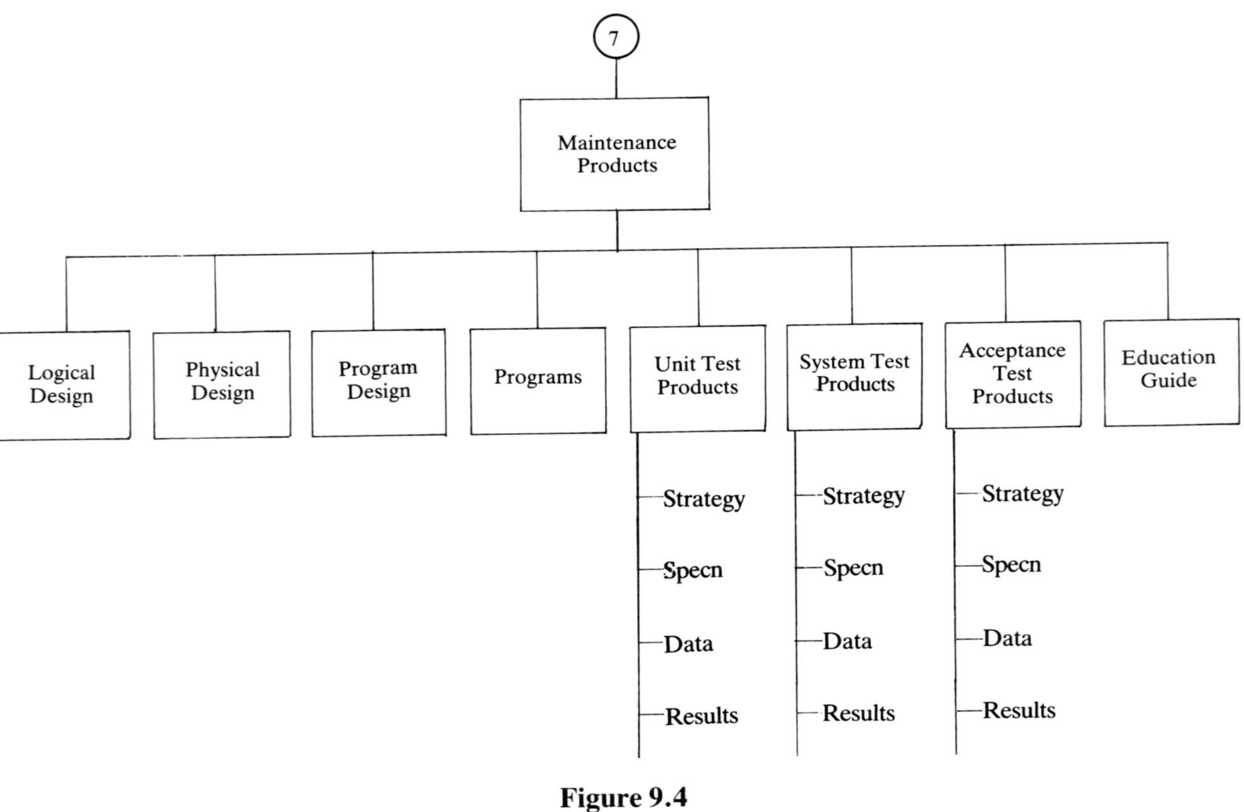

**Figure 9.4**

users and to operations staff. Relevant users and operations staff agree criteria, and join the review team.

The Installation and Conversion Strategy defines the approach to be taken in installing the system in its operational environment. Users, operations staff, DP staff, and representatives from other staff groups affected by the system provide information. Users and operations staff join the review team.

The Education Strategy identifies the staff training that will provide the skills required to manage, use, control, operate and maintain the new system. The strategy covers the training necessary to familiarise existing staff with the new system; and addresses future training needs, spanning the operational life of the system. Representatives of management, users, operations, and systems and programming departments provide information. A representative from each group joins the review team.

The Physical System Design defines an operationally viable system which meets the Requirements Specification and is consistent with the Logical System Design. Users agree any changes in requirements necessary to produce an effective design. Users also agree any operations/management rules to which procedures will be subject. Users and operations representatives join the review team.

The System Build Strategy defines in detail how the system is to be built in technical terms; the order in which programs, jobs and subsystems are to be developed and linked together to form the total system. Representatives of users and operations staff join the review team.

The Unit Test Strategy applies to the testing of individual programs produced as specified in the system design. It defines the types and stringency of the unit testing to be undertaken. Representatives of users and operations staff join the review team.

The System Test Strategy applies to the system after the integration of units. It defines the types of test to be carried out at the system testing stage. Representatives of users and operations staff join the review team.

The System Test Results show the outcome of the system tests, including retesting carried out after any necessary corrective action has been taken. Once satisfactory results have been obtained, the system can be installed in the new environment. Representative user and operations staff join the review team.

The Acceptance Test Strategy defines the types of testing to be undertaken at the acceptance testing stage. Representatives of users and operations staff join the review team.

The Acceptance Test Data are created to enable the system to be tested in accordance with the Acceptance Test Strategy. Representatives of users and operations staff join the review team.

The Acceptance Test Results show the outcome of the acceptance tests, including retesting carried out after any necessary corrective action has been taken. Once satisfactory results have been obtained, system development is complete. Representatives of users and operations staff join the review team.

Train Staff involves training to manage, use, control, operate, and maintain the new system. These trained staff will contribute to the organisation and running of Acceptance Tests. Management identifies those staff who require training, and assesses the capabilities of these staff following training.

The Release Package provides a machine-readable version of the programs which have been subjected to successful system testing, and which can now be installed in the new environment. Users and a representative of the operations staff join the review team.

The Education Guide includes instructions on how to use any educational software that has been developed. It is used in the training of relevant staff to manage, use, control, operate, and maintain the new system. A representative of each audience joins the review team.

The User Guide acts both as a training document and as a reference manual. It describes to users, present and future, how to use the system. Users discuss documentation needs and join the review team.

The Installation Run Results provide evidence that the software has been run successfully on the installed system, and functions as expected. Users and a representative of the operations staff join the review team.

The Possible Solutions and Recommendation report on a number of possible solutions which would satisfy the user requirements. Each alternative presents a high-level system design, and is evaluated from the business and technical aspects. Solutions are evaluated and one solution is proposed as the optimum solution. Users and an independent, experienced analyst join the review team, and comment on the acceptability of the recommendation.

The Conversion Run Results provide evidence that the necessary manual and machine-readable data has been converted as required. Users and an experienced, independent software engineer join the review team.

## PRODUCTS OF PROTOTYPING

Prototyping is used in a wide range of situations for a variety of purposes. The common factor is the development of an initial version of one or more products, where this version is less than complete, and is intended as a basis for further work. The prototype is part of a trial or an experiment and is used to refine and agree the user requirements, or to evaluate alternative design solutions. It may be used to assist non-technical users to formulate their requirements by giving them some practical feedback ("Is it what you mean?"). It may also be used to test the method of interaction between the user and the system (the user interface), or to assess the system performance. A project is described in terms of the products which it is required to build and deliver. This is no less true for a project which is required to build and deliver a prototype of some sort.

The products of prototyping are defined in terms of the requirements which those products have to satisfy, their relationship to other products (inside and outside the project), and the quality criteria against which they will be judged. At least three products can be defined for each prototyping exercise: first, a prototype specification which sets out the objectives of the prototyping exercise, and the bounds and constraints which apply to it; second, the prototype itself, making it clear whether the prototype is to evolve during future development, or whether it is a 'throwaway' for demonstration only; and third, the prototype assessment which records the results of the prototyping exercise, in terms of the knowledge gained and its success in meeting its objectives. The products of prototyping, as with any other products, undergo a quality review commensurate with their size and importance. Where the prototype is designed to assist the refinement of user requirements, it is essential for user representatives to attend the review.

# 10 Information System Standards

## AIMS AND ORGANISATIONS

The British Standards Institution (BSI) lists the broad aims of standardisation as:

(a) Provision of means of communication amongst all interested parties;

(b) Promotion of economy in human effort, materials and energy in the production and exchange of goods (through variety reduction);

(c) Protection of consumer interests through adequate and consistent quality of goods and services (by defining those features and characteristics that govern their ability to satisfy given needs);

(d) Promotion of the quality of life: safety, health and the protection of environment (definition of what is acceptable as a reasonable level of risk in the foreseeable use or even misuse of a product, process or service);

(e) Promotion of trade by removal of barriers caused by differences in national practices.

Standards relating to information technology and systems are required for hardware devices, software and communications as well as application systems. A number of organisations at international, national and industry level are engaged in the formulation of standards for IT. Standards are required at the international level because they are essential to permit data flow across national boundaries. Examples of this type of standard are character codes, standards covering international data communications over telephone lines, and standards for the physical formats of magnetic tape records. Standards are required at the national level to, for example, identify places and objects of national significance amongst a host of other standards. The ANSI numeric codes for the counties and states of the USA and the Brussels tariff codes for commodities are examples of this type of standard.

The main organisations actively engaged in developing and promoting standards at an international, regional or national level can be grouped into seven categories:

- international standards bodies, such as ISO and CCITT;
- national standards bodies, such as BSI and ANSI;
- manufacturer associations, such as ECMA in Europe and CBEMA in the US;
- professional associations, such as the BCS, ACM, IEEE, DPMA, etc;
- political bodies, such as national governments and the EEC;
- computer manufacturers;
- computer user organisations.

The International Standards Organization (ISO) with its administrative headquarters in Geneva is an association of about 80 of the world's national standards bodies. Each national standards body can choose whether to participate in any specific area of the ISO's standardisation activities. The bodies most active in the field of computing include the UK's British Standards Institution (BSI), France's Association Francaise de Normalisation (AFNOR), Germany's Deutsches Instut fur Normen (DIN), the Canadian Standards Association (CSA) and the USA's American National Standards Institute (ANSI). Other interested organisations, such as CCITT and ECMA, are represented in ISO.

The work of the ISO is undertaken by many dozens of Technical Committees. TC97 is the Technical Committee concerned with computing and information processing. Each committee is divided up into several subcommittees, and each subcommittee in turn may generate several Working Groups to study specific aspects of a topic and develop recommendations. Recommendations are formulated as a Draft Proposal, which is presented to the appropriate Technical Committee for review and comment. When agreement is reached within the Technical Committee, the Draft Proposal becomes a Draft International Standard and is voted on by the full membership of ISO. If the Draft International Standard achieves 75% approval, it becomes an International Standard. Thereafter, it is reviewed (and possibly revised) every five years.

Comité Consultatif International de Télégraphie et Téléphonie (CCITT), also having headquarters in Geneva, is one of the four permanent organisations of the International Telecommunications Union (ITU), which originated in the early days of telegraphy in 1865 and now has about 150 member countries. The work of the organisation is carried out by Study Groups, which prepare recommendations that are presented to a Plenary Assembly of CCITT every four years. Its basic aim is to study technical, operating and tariff issues relating to telecommunications and to develop recommendations on them. CCITT works closely with ISO and, via that organisation, with the various national standards bodies. The CCITT Study Groups most relevant to computer communications are:

- Special Study Group A, which is concerned with data transmission, including modems and interfaces;
- Special Study Group 1D, which is concerned with digital transmission channels and systems;
- Joint Working Party ALP, which is concerned with transmission codes;
- Joint Working Party NRD, which is concerned with new data networks.

The British Standards Institution (BSI) generally draws on members from trade, industry and professional associations, and government and other national and technical and scientific organisations. In the computing field, the BSI relies heavily on the computer industry and large-scale computer users to help it carry out its duties. The BSI has a committee structure; the committee responsible for data processing standards being DPS. The committees of the BSI may propose standards, but usually seek international agreement before issuing the corresponding British Standard.

This pattern is typical of most national standards bodies, with the notable exception of the US. In the US, the American National Standards Institute (ANSI) is the main organisation (but by no means the only one) fostering the development of standards for American industry. Members of the ANSI are typically companies who have something to gain from the development of standards in their particular industry, and who are prepared to contribute manpower and expertise to it. Standards for the computer industry are the responsibility of ANSI project X3. This project is financed by the principal trade organisation in the computing field, the Computer and Business Equipment Manufacturers' Association (CBEMA).

The various working groups (committees, task forces) within ANSI are derived in equal measure from the computer industry, the computer user community, and the general public (often taking the form of government agencies). When a working group has developed a draft standard, it is made available for review by the general public both inside and outside the US. Eventually the standard is approved as a standard by the ANSI executive board.

The European Computer Manufacturers' Association (ECMA) provides a forum in which many technical issues of standardisation between manufacturers have been worked out. It works closely with ISO and with the various national standards organisations, where it comes into contact with computer users and their representative organisations. It has published more than 50 standards relating to the design and use of computer equipment. The Computer and Business Equipment Manufacturers' Association (CBEMA) is the American equivalent of ECMA and it too takes a close interest in standards development activity. Professional associations also take a close interest in the standards scene.

The British Computer Society (BCS) is regularly involved in

the standards development activities of the British Standards Institution. In the US, the American Federation of Information Processing Societies (AFIPS) is an umbrella organisation to which individual professional associations such as the Association for Computing Machinery (ACM) and the Data Processing Management Association (DPMA) belong. Bodies such as the BCS and AFIPS in turn are members of the International Federation for Information Processing (IFIP), the corresponding international body.

Computing and telecommunications have attracted substantial political interest in recent years. This is due to the increasing recognition among national governments of the social (and hence political) impact of information technology. In the UK, the Department of Trade and Industry (DTI) has shown considerable interest in the issue of standards development in recent years. Structured Systems Analysis and Design Methodology (SSADM) is the DTI standard for systems analysis and design methodology. It is now in the process of finalising the standard for management of IT systems. It is working on a methodology called PROMPT. A consultative document commissioned by the DTI from the UK National Computing Centre (NCC) in 1977 reported that computing is now going through the stage that railways went through in the middle of the nineteenth century, when it was realised that localised developments were being inhibited by the paramount need for standardisation on a global scale. Having identified this need, however, the NCC document went on to report that standards development was not keeping pace with developments in the computer industry. It recommended a programme to generate public awareness and use of existing standards, and to accelerate the standards development process generally.

The European Economic Community (EEC) has undoubtedly been one of the main forces behind standardisation efforts in Europe, resolving as far back as 1947 to promote joint action on standards and applications and in public procurement policy in order to foster more efficient and economical use of resources. In 1976 the EEC adopted a programme to develop standards, procurement and other policies relating to data processing, with the aim of maximising the range of choice open to the user, and the market opportunities open to suppliers of computing equipment and services. It created a Standards Working Group to develop an effective standardisation policy, and to liaise with telecommunications authorities to establish a competitive EEC-wide market for supply contracts for telecommunications equipment.

The first priorities identified within the EEC's standards programme were the development of a standard programming language for real-time systems, and a solution to the problems of software portability. One of the main motivations behind the EEC's actions was its concern about the dominant role of American and Japanese agglomerates in the informatics industry (in particular, IBM) and the ability of the major manufacturers to shape and delimit the market for many different types of computing hardware through control of the standards, interfaces and software that bear on information systems as a whole.

A considerable number of organisations in the US take an active interest in the field of computing standards. The National Bureau of Standards (NBS) is an organisation within the US Department of Commerce that develops standards for use by US Government agencies. Standards developed by the NBS are known as Federal Information Processing Standards (FIPS). The US Department of Defense (DoD) is yet another US government agency active in the standards field. There is considerable interaction between these various bodies and the ANSI. However, ANSI, FIPS and DoD standards are by no means necessarily the same. Despite the tendency towards unilateral standardisation on the part of the US as a whole, there is no single national body in the US with sufficient clout to co-ordinate standards development activity and to achieve harmonisation of standards at a national level.

Computer user organisations have started to make their voices heard in the standards field quite recently, mainly in the areas of telecommunications and computer networking. Large corporations have recognised the potential benefits of 'Open Systems Interconnection' (OSI), a standard for communication between computer systems. Most large-scale users of computing and communications systems nowadays have a vested interest in the development of appropriate national and international standards, particularly the multinational corporations with subsidiary operations in several different countries.

The main benefits perceived by such organisations are inter- and intra-company compatibility of management information, reductions in costs through the ability to share common systems and systems development resources, and the ability to be independent of particular computer and communications suppliers. In the UK, the increasing concern among user corporations has led to the formation in recent years of ITUSA – the Information Technology User Standards Association – specially to expedite standards development in areas where lack of acceptable standards is holding up the effective use of information technology in British industry. ITUSA itself has since given birth to a subsidiary organisation USFIT – the User Standards Forum for Information Technology – which provides individuals (as opposed to corporations) with a voice in standards development. USFIT is funded by ITUSA, but has its own constitution. It establishes Shadow Groups to monitor the activities of 'official' standards organisations, and to alert ITUSA if user interests are being ignored or overridden in standards development.

The major computer manufacturers also contribute to international standardisation efforts, although their efforts in this field have generally been lacking in commitment, and in many cases actively counter-productive. IBM in particular has generally not been a prime mover in efforts to bring about international and industry standards. Indeed, it has often reacted against such efforts, often mounting strong counter-standardisation campaigns, claiming as justification significant 'improvements' on the official standards. Its own proprietary standards for hardware, software and communications now effectively constitute another de facto international standard.

Many software houses have been established as a result of the demand for applications software from the huge IBM customer base; for example, systems using the IBM-PC compatible DOS operating system, while whole industries have grown up specialising in conversion to and from IBM standards. IBM has been in constant war with plug-compatible manufacturers (PCMs), who avoid the huge investment in research and development and in original design of products and their interfaces, and thereby are in a position to undercut IBM. To make life difficult for the PCMs, IBM has frequently modified its own product standards, and as a result there has evolved the specialised mini-industry of 'IBM-watching': monitoring and publishing expensive reports on IBM product and market plans and strategies.

Apart from the perceived threat from the PCMs, an equally strong reason for IBM's reluctance to participate in industry-wide standardisation activity has been that any form of industry-wide standards, even among the recognised major manufacturers, allows existing customers to select equipment from alternative suppliers. Protection of its existing customer base from competition has long been a central element of IBM's marketing strategy.

The EEC's interest in standardisation has been greatly spurred by concern about the dominant role of IBM in the computer industry, so much so that it now actively pursues a strategy of using standards as a means of giving European computer and communications companies a competitive edge in the marketplace. It is interesting to note, however, that IBM's dominant position in standards does not extend to the telecommunications field. Whereas computing has evolved in an essentially free-enterprise environment, telecommunications has always been subject to government control. In the telecommunications field, CCITT is still probably the most influential body. IBM was forced to discuss, and work towards, agreed industry standards for open systems interconnection.

## SOME BSI STANDARDS

Amongst the existing BSI standards, there are standards on data representation and interchange codes, data layout on disks and tapes, keyboard layout, line and character spacing, ribbons and spools, control of computer operations, safety, etc. In the field of computer software there are standards on operating systems and programming languages, including database languages like NDL and SQL. In communications there are standards on interface systems, local area networks, messages, and open systems interconnection. In computer graphics, there are standards called computer graphics metafile (CGM) and graphics kernel system (GKS). Similarly, there are standards on computer peripherals such as printers, disk cartridges, disk packs, magnetic character recognition, optical character recognition, microfiche, microfilm, etc.

The BSI standard on Open Systems Interconnection was issued in 1988 and is based on the similar ISO standard of 1984. It relates to the interconnection of computing systems not only for the transmission of data between systems but also for the exchange of information to achieve co-operation amongst systems to work jointly on a common problem or task. This involves a broad range of activities like interprocess communication, data representation, data storage, process and resource management, integrity and security, and progress support.

There are many items and concepts not defined at national or international level – such as systems development methodologies, requirements and design specification techniques, program and system documentation formats, project reporting procedures, coding techniques and so on. These will inevitably vary from one installation to another and it is the responsibility of the information systems management to define them for the installation concerned.

## ORGANISATIONAL STANDARDS

The areas in which an organisation needs to evolve its own standards on information systems include:

- **systems development standards**, including a methodology for the controlled development of information systems; controls built into the methodology, particularly in terms of project justification and authorisation, resource allocation, project reporting, monitoring and control, user involvement and post-implementation reviews;
- **systems operation and maintenance standards**, including procedures for accepting systems into production; procedures for the control of production systems, including data back-up and recovery procedures, program change control procedures and emergency 'fix' procedures;

- **documentation standards**, including file/data structure documentation, system and program specifications, user documentation and operations documentation; forms for project proposal, justification and approval, and for computer systems design;
- **naming standards** for assigning names to systems, programs, modules, files, data items and so on;
- **security and privacy standards** for protection of corporations' computing assets including programs and data as well as hardware against accidental or malicious damage.

## QUALITY ASSURANCE

The function of quality assurance is closely related to the function of standards. Quality assurance is particularly concerned with systems development standards. The concept of software quality presupposes the existence of standards against which software is to be measured. However, the quality of software depends on many different characteristics, such as readability, comprehensibility, maintainability, reliability, portability, efficiency, etc. Not all of these characteristics will apply to every piece of software, or have the same relative importance for the organisation. The question of which quality standards should apply at an installation is therefore often peculiar to the organisation concerned. Invariably, the question will involve consideration of economic factors.

In practice, the most important single criterion for software quality in today's economic climate is that of maintainability. Any standards aimed at reducing the high costs of maintenance will almost certainly be cost-effective. Two particular areas of concern for quality assurance are the use of programming languages and systems development methodologies.

Standards for programming languages need to define the set of programming languages available for systems development at the installation; and which features within each language are to be used and which not. Today there are thousands of programming languages available, each with its own adherents who are only too happy to advertise the merits of their particular favourite. The dangers of a proliferation of languages within an installation are very real.

Programmers need to be trained in most if not all the languages used. Project and operations management also need at least a working knowledge of the languages concerned, to be able to control program development activity. Quality assurance personnel, as well as auditors reviewing information systems, also need to be able to review program code.

If each program were to be written in a different language, the result would be chaos. However, an installation that frequently uses software houses and consultants to perform well-defined, short-term pieces of work could very well find itself saddled with a wide variety of languages to support unless it defines standards for the programming languages to be used, and enforces these standards through strong management. For each language used at the installation, there will normally be syntactic and semantic standards to be developed, defining which language constructs are to be avoided. This may be necessary to ensure future compatibility and for portability of software. The question of portability also requires an awareness of international standards activity.

While standards bodies spend a great deal of time and effort in defining the best possible mix of features to be associated with a particular language, the average installation is usually not so much concerned with what the detailed standard features of a language are, as how, by following a standard, it can easily convert applications from one machine or operating system to another, or upgrade from one compiler to another. In addition, there will be standards that are not language-dependent, concerning items such as readability and complexity of data and control flow.

Another area of concern for quality assurance is the systems development methodology, particularly the early stages of development concerned with requirements definition and system design. Errors made at the requirements stage are notoriously expensive to remedy if not caught early. Where specific requirements tools (eg specification languages) are not used, it may be advisable to develop standards in the form of guidelines for specifying requirements. Meaningful design standards are very difficult to evolve, simply because so much of the design process is an intuitive and personal matter.

Standards are also required to ensure the designing-in of adequate error detection, isolation and (where feasible) correction procedures, and facilities for the generation of adequate diagnostic information when errors occur. And there is a need for standards relating to the tools and techniques used to support standards enforcement. There are two categories of such techniques, manual and automatic. Manual techniques cover such things as structured walkthroughs and inspection, which basically consist of formalised methods of reviewing a design or a piece of code by people other than the author of the design or code under review. Automatic techniques cover a wide variety of tools, ranging from code reformatters (to aid readability), through to analysers of varying degrees of complexity that can enforce syntactic and semantic standards in a language and more esoteric tools such as automated correctness provers and symbolic executers.

## STANDARDS DOCUMENTS

It is important to plan from the beginning for an awareness programme for information systems standards, so that they quickly gain acceptance and recognition. Apart from providing training in standards, standards documents are ready reference material for users to follow standards. Some of the key standards documents needed are now described.

**Corporate Information Systems Guide** – This is an overview document at the apex of the standards documentation structure. The guide should describe the corporate IT environment, explain policies, goals, objectives and modus operandi of the corporate information systems function and provide pointers to all other information systems standards documentation. This guide is helpful to the users of corporate computing facilities (microcomputer as well as mainframe), business line managers, consultants and contractors; in short to anyone who needs a brief, comprehensive overview of the way in which information technology is used in the organisation. It promotes a common goal and identity among all information systems staff; and uniformity of decision making among supervisory staff, through awareness of goals, policies and objectives.

The guide ensures that user management is aware of the facilities available within the information systems department, so that there is less tendency for users to go out and buy separate microcomputers. It ensures common understanding of the respective roles and responsibilities of the information systems department and user departments in the acquisition and use of information technology in the organisation.

**Systems Development Methodology** – A systems development methodology (SDM) is an approved general framework for developing computer-based systems at an installation. The goal for an SDM is to ensure that systems development takes place in a controlled manner and in accordance with corporate policy and objectives. It guides the corporate management (both user and information systems) along the path of least time, cost and risk in the development of computer-based systems. It ensures that common business solutions are chosen to common business requirements throughout the corporation. It also ensures the commitment and involvement of all parties involved in the development process. It is useful to develop the project management and systems skills of staff. A standard SDM documentation provides easily usable reference for the conduct of a project.

**Microcomputer User's Guide** – This is a useful reference document for user management, for those user staff developing their own business applications to run on the microcomputer, and also to those user staff running business applications on a microcomputer, whether developed by the user or by the information systems department. It should provide information on standard hardware and software packages and their capabilities; and guidelines on the most cost-effective way of performing commonly required tasks. It should specify standards for security and privacy of data and other standards of relevance to the microcomputer user. The *Microcomputer User's Guide* is also the manual of all services available to the microcomputer user from the information systems department. It may specify the standard for microcomputer equipment and configuration, and procedures for obtaining standard equipment and software. Facilities for installation, maintenance and support, training, applications development and operation may be outlined.

**Programming Language Guide** – This guide is aimed at the systems development staff, and defines the policy for use of the language, ie the circumstances and/or types of system for which the language is to be used and which features of the language are to be avoided. There may be one such guide for each language used in the organisation. Adherence to standards in the use of programming languages simplifies the task of maintenance of systems, improves operational efficiency of systems, and ensures that the knowledge and expertise of staff already experienced in the language are made available to other members of staff.

**Computer Centre Operations Guide** – This is a guide for all professional members of staff within the computer centre, defining detailed procedures for the provision of support and services to the users. The aim of this guide is to provide greater efficiency in operation of the computer centre, through well defined procedures for processing user requests for support and services.

# 11 Security, Integrity and Privacy

## INTRODUCTION TO COMPUTER SECURITY

The inability or failure of computer-based systems to perform the particular functions or provide the particular services for which they were intended, may be regarded as a loss of security. The large number of possible causes of loss of security can be divided into two basic categories: *accidental* threats and *deliberate* threats. Some possible accidental threats are flood, lightning, human error and component failure. Examples of deliberate threats are arson, theft and fraud. Accidental threats may have their origins in shortcomings of system design, manufacture or maintenance, or in errors and omissions in operation due to the lack of adequate training and/or supervision of operating staff. Loss of security due to threats such as storm or flood can be prevented by taking the proper precautions or made more likely by complacency or lack of forethought. Deliberate threats, on the other hand, involve human activities of employees, authorised visitors, unauthorised intruders, hackers, virus makers, etc. The selection of appropriate countermeasures very much depends on what sort of person poses the deliberate threat.

## PHYSICAL SECURITY

The physical environment bears directly on the security of a computer system. Proper consideration of factors such as location and building design/construction is vital, especially at the planning stage. Physical security and administrative controls are often the only means of protecting IT resources. Many factors contribute to adequate physical security, and they tend to conflict with each other. The need to control access and provision of emergency exit routes is one such example.

Weather and its consequences are the most important natural risk for most locations. Wind, rain, snow and ice have obvious and often dramatic effects. Few sites are immune from the possibility of extreme weather conditions. Floods commonly follow heavy rainfall, but can be avoided by selecting a well drained site on high ground. Storm damage is commonplace from high winds, especially in areas subject to tropical storms. Lightning rarely causes structural damage to properly protected modern buildings, but it may affect electric power supplies to the site. There may be interruptions to the supply, or surges and transients which the equipment cannot tolerate. Communication lines can also be affected by lightning. Terminals may be damaged or destroyed unless the lines are protected. Ground stability is vital, but often overlooked. Earthquakes and ground tremors are fairly common everywhere, though most frequent in the earthquake zones. Landslip is very common, often associated with movement of ground water. Landslip often blocks roads, rendering the site inaccessible. The slippage may rupture services such as water or gas pipes.

The site may collapse, common on cliff-top locations and valley sides. Activities in the neighbourhood environment such as building works or heavy industry may cause risks such as vibrations from pile driving, or dust from cement silos. The chemical industries often involve hazardous processes or toxic substances. Sociopolitical risks are particularly difficult to deal with. Vandals, demonstrators, rioters, terrorists can all take actions that may disrupt operations, or even destroy the installations. An unobtrusive site in a good neighbourhood is a good first line of defence against these risks.

The building housing the installation makes a very important contribution to its security. It provides accommodation for the computer system, personnel and ancillary services. Failures or shortcomings in the design will affect the installation in all sorts of ways. Conventional construction techniques and materials should be used. This eliminates unknown risks from new untried methods. Many modern materials produce toxic fumes in a fire, and some assist the spread of flames. The structure should be fire-resistant. Sound construction can eliminate many problems. The layout and design should so far as possible eliminate hiding places. A smooth exterior is desirable to minimise the possibility of concealing explosive or incendiary devices.

If the building is shared then proper segregation is needed. The computer area should be separated from other activities by fire- and flood-resistant walls or ceilings. These must extend through any floor voids and false ceilings. Wherever possible, all facilities should be located above ground level to avoid danger from flooding, back-up sewers, or fire-fighting measures. Underground areas must be provided with floor drains, pumps or other protection. In multi-storey buildings the floor above the computer must protect against spillage, or other water leakage. The routes for services such as gas and water need selecting with care, and header tanks for heating systems should be eliminated from the computer area. Water pipes and other services in false ceilings should be avoided. The number of doors, windows, ventilation inlets and outlets should be limited. It is an advantage to have a perimeter fence or even a low wall that is clear of the walls of the building. This is better than having the building fronting directly onto the street or other public places. The existence or location of the computer installation should not be obvious or made apparent to outsiders. Direction signs and descriptive nameplates are best avoided, except for 'Way Out' and 'Emergency Exit' signs.

The imposition of any sort of access control might be taken to imply a lack of trust and might be resented by staff. Management should explain clearly the need for a system, how it is to be used, and what penalties will follow non-compliance. The selected system should cause minimum inconvenience consistent with the level of security needed. Normal entry and exit should be through properly controlled and monitored access points.

Ideally, records should be maintained of who was present at all times, so that there is a proper audit log. Security guards and mechanical locks are the conventional methods of restricting access, though electronic systems are now increasingly popular. Card locks, using optical or magnetic encoding to record identification, are inserted into a slot alongside the controlled door to release the door latch. Systems can be arranged so that different cards are allowed access at different periods. The facilities can be programmed so that individual cards are given access to particular sets of doors, possibly at different times. Modern systems use microprocessors to allow programming of quite complex arrangements, and lost or mislaid cards can be cancelled. Individuals can be given temporary access to special areas, without the need to modify the card in any way.

Card keys can be combined with identification badges, including photographs and other details. An advantage here is that the key looks less like a key. The casual finder might think it is only a badge. Pass-back of cards is less of a problem when the card is also a badge that must be worn. Follow-through is a problem in any unmanned system, and turnstiles can help to overcome this. Doors can be linked to an alarm that sounds if the door is not closed promptly.

However, electronic locks can be bypassed as effectively as mechanical ones. They do not monitor presence within the controlled areas. The best systems are able to log all usage, such monitoring being programmed to disclose unauthorised or irregular out-of-hours activity.

Card systems and mechanical locks are not tolerable for use more than a few times a day. A system which overcomes the problem of inconvenience is one in which the operation of the security device (lock, barrier, alarm, etc) is controlled electronically. A transmitter is carried by those authorised to enter any of the protected areas. When someone approaches a controlled area, the electronic system automatically checks whether the would-be entrant is authorised to enter that particular area, and the system then releases the door lock.

## UNINTERRUPTIBLE POWER SUPPLY

Reliable power supplies are essential to efficient computer operation. Supplies need to be continuous, since computers can usually only tolerate failures of millisecond duration. It is also necessary to prevent transient variation, and to maintain voltage and frequency within specified limits. Parity errors, hardware malfunction, and loss or corruption of data are among the consequences of unreliable supplies. An alternative power supply is required if long interruptions to the power supply are expected. An engine-driven generator provides a solution to the problem. Following a power failure, the generator is started up, the computer is disconnected from the public supply, and is then connected to the standby generator. Recovery operations may then be necessary to correct data and files damaged by the supply failure. If advance warning of power loss is received, the computer can be powered down at a suitable processing break-point to prevent damage to files. When the public supply is restored, the computer is powered up at that break-point and connected to the public supply. An engine-driven generator can be used as a standby supply; in fact it can be used for running the computer directly if maintenance is continuously available.

An Uninterruptible Power Supply (UPS) system maintains the quality of the power supply and will continue to supply power for a predetermined period, following a failure of the public supply. This period (usually from five minutes to several hours) should be sufficient to enable a controlled shutdown of computer operations to take place. The system consists of a battery charger (static rectifier), batteries, and a static invertor. If long power failures are a problem, then a back-up engine-driven generator should also be installed to provide AC power to the UPS system after a power failure. The UPS system in this case will keep the computer running. Meanwhile, the generator set will be automatically started up to replace the public supply before the UPS batteries are exhausted.

## AIR CONDITIONING

Small computers are often installed in ordinary offices. Larger machines dissipate so much heat that ventilation is needed simply to maintain tolerable summer working conditions for staff. For mainframes, the manufacturer stipulates the environment required. Humidity and temperature must be controlled, and a dust-free atmosphere maintained. This can be achieved only with air conditioning plants. Typical conditions are a temperature of 21°C ± 2°C (70°F ± 3°F) and relative humidity of 50% ± 5%. If no magnetic media devices are installed these conditions may be relaxed. Usually the air conditioned space is maintained at a slight positive pressure, so that any leaks are clean air passing outwards, rather than dirty air passing inwards. The air that is lost and the air conditioning cooling plant have to remove the waste heat from the computer. If the plant should fail, then the room temperature will quickly rise, putting the equipment at risk. Variations in conditions can lead to overheating of components, moisture precipitation (especially if the equipment is switched off) and to build-up of excess static electricity. Too dry an atmosphere may cause curling of cards and magnetic tape. Stationery may distort in extreme conditions and be unusable.

## SOFTWARE FAILURE

Computer software includes both applications programs and systems software. Most important of all from the security point of view is the operating system, which controls and monitors the entire workload of the installation. Computer programs are never perfect. Faults may be introduced into programs at any stage of development. During specification, the analyst may omit to specify what a program should do under certain circumstances, and the programmer may omit to ask. As implemented, the program may either do the wrong thing or do nothing at all. During design, the processing algorithms chosen to do a particular job may be wrong, in that they fail to reflect real life. During implementation, through carelessness, misunderstanding or lack of testing, the programmer may not code what is required. During maintenance, while enhancing the program or correcting known faults in it, new faults may be introduced as unexpected side-effects. The larger and more complex a program is, the more faults it is likely to have. A large program can be very difficult to maintain, since on average correcting a fault may cause more problems than it cures. Software failure can be minimised by following suitable control procedures during development and maintenance.

It has been estimated that three-quarters of all software errors arise from design – and only one quarter from development. Those errors which do arise from development are mostly removed before installation of the system. Only about half of the design errors are removed before installation and the remainder do not come to light until after the system is live and running. To assure proper quality of software, rigorous verification and validation tests have to be carried out on the software. The test procedure should be concerned with checking that:

- the data is vetted and processed properly;
- the invalid data routines function as intended, and that correct files and reports are produced;
- restart and recovery procedures work properly;
- all error messages are unambiguous and can be properly actioned;
- incorrect responses by operators are detected and appropriate actions taken;
- terminations are correctly carried out, and files are not left unclosed, undated, unlabelled, etc;
- label checking procedures are complete and accurate;
- data files passed to or from other applications are correct in content and structure, etc.

## HARDWARE FAILURE

A fault may develop in any component of the hardware system; in, for example:

- the central processor and its main memory;
- auxiliary input-output processors and channels;
- peripheral devices and their control units;
- storage media: disk packs and tapes;
- data-communications processors and controllers;
- communications lines, terminals, modems, multiplexers, concentrators, etc;
- environmental equipment: air conditioning, power supplies, etc.

Some components are more reliable than others. A central processor, for example, is protected in a clean, controlled computer room, and is regularly maintained. It is likely to be far less prone to error than a communications line, which is buried in the ground and is subject to electrical interference, corrosion and vibration. However, it should be remembered that reliability is a complicated concept.

The most obvious characteristic of a reliable system is that, most of the time, it is available and operating normally. That is to say, it does not break down very often and, when it does, it can be repaired quickly. Availability can be measured by two engineering parameters:

- mean time before failure (MTBF);
- mean time to repair (MTTR).

Availability is the proportion of the total time (scheduled for operation) that the system is actually available for normal service, ie

Availability = (MTBF)/(MTBF+MTTR)

The phrase 'mean time between failures' is sometimes used, and this includes the time to repair. A quoted availability figure should be treated with care. It may represent frequent interruptions of short duration or infrequent failures which may take a long time to repair. Thus, an average of one three-minute break in every hour gives an availability of 95%, but so does an average of one full day per month (of 20 working days). The same availability represents two quite different patterns of behaviour. Which is more acceptable depends on the requirements of the users.

A simple way to improve the reliability of a computer system is to duplicate the components which are likely to fail. Examples of duplication are leased communication lines backed up by public switched network facilities; reserve terminals in some important offices; duplicated communications controllers or front-end processors; spare tape and disk drives, printers, card-readers, etc; twin central processors; and spare channels.

It is clearly wasteful to keep hardware sitting idle, waiting for a failure in the main system which may happen only rarely, and one would like to find some employment for the spare equipment during normal operation, when it is not required for back-up. There are two possible approaches to this: the duplex system; and the dual system. In a duplex arrangement, the primary system is capable of handling the full workload and runs on its own. The spare system is a complete copy of the primary system, and when required, it can take over all of its work. While the primary system is operating normally, the spare need not be idle. It can be handling a variety of jobs, such as program development and testing, and other low-priority batch work; file maintenance and reorganisation, general housekeeping for the primary system, file dumping and checking; off-line printing, etc. In a dual arrangement, the two halves of the system work in close co-operation with one another, normally sharing the processing load. The spare capacity can be used to meet unusual peak volumes of work, or to provide better response time or throughput. When one component fails, its twin immediately takes over the full load, although perhaps at reduced performance.

## FALLBACK AND RECOVERY

No systems design is complete, from a security point of view, unless it adequately covers aspects of recovery and contingency planning to ensure a rapid and successful return to normal processing after a system failure. The systems design must consider all possible types of eventuality which might cause the system to fail, and produce appropriate countermeasures. These may apply only to new applications or may be adopted as new standard procedures to improve security of all systems.

A good systems design has the qualities of high availability, graceful degradation, fail-safe, and rapid recovery capability. Rather than have the failure of one component cause the complete collapse of the processing equipment, it is often preferable for the system to remain available though operating with a reduced level of service, ie to degrade gracefully. When the system fails it should not lead to any threat to security, ie it does not go out of control (and cause interaction with other systems) or leave the system open to abuse. Whenever the system fails, and whatever the cause, it must always be possible to recover from the situation – and speed in recovery is essential.

If the possible consequences of a failure are serious, it is necessary to prepare contingency plans for immediate and effective action in appropriate circumstances. Each organisation must identify for itself which contingencies could have serious consequences – in terms of financial loss, damage to good will, bad publicity, etc – and must plan accordingly. The contingency plans must take into consideration the value of computer assets, data and documentation; the importance of the various computer applications, and the maximum delays that could be tolerated; and the ease with which the organisation could revert to manual procedure where necessary. The critical factor in recovery from a disaster may be the speed of repair or replacement of computer accommodation and related services. Whilst new or existing equipment can often be installed, tested and operational within a few weeks, accommodation may be a problem. Consequently, several organisations have prepared their own temporary 'emergency centre' where normal computing can be resumed quickly. Power supplies, air conditioning, fire protection, communication lines and other support services are provided as necessary.

## NEED FOR SYSTEM CONTROLS

One of the most important aspects of security in the computer environment is data control. Data control embraces all those procedures, both manual and programmed, which are specified within a system for the purpose of checking the accuracy and reliability of that system and the data handled by it. Controls must be adequate to ensure that any malfunction in the system or inadequacy in the data presented to, held, or produced by the system will be reported for remedial action. Incorrect statistics in a stock control program could result in investment in redundant stock. Errors in order processing could have a significant effect on customer relations. Most errors are not generated by the machine but by the people involved in the system. No matter how efficient the computer, human beings will continue to make mistakes, and it is this factor which must be given due consideration when designing an information system.

Administrative controls are necessary to ensure an adequate reporting system, appropriate segregation of duties and an acceptable standard of discipline and efficiency within the information systems department. Procedural controls need to be exercised at all stages of system development. These are particularly important from the point of view of data control in respect of documentation, testing procedures, implementation, and file creation. The weakest points in most systems lie in the manual procedures required to prepare computer data, and to action computer output. Controls are needed to ensure the security of the system, and to provide adequate checks on the manual operations of both user and computer staff. Computer procedures may require programmed controls to check the acceptability of input data and files, the correct functioning of program instructions, hardware operation and data handling, and to detect any accidental or deliberate misuse of data or malpractice within the system. The ultimate responsibility for all aspects of system control lies with user and information systems management. Higher management must specify the overall requirements for controls within a particular system and define clear boundaries of responsibility.

Controls cost money. Development costs are higher, testing more complex, and operating costs may rise due to additional clerical and computer procedures. The problem is to balance these costs against possible penalty costs of processing corrupt information. In the absence of suitable reconciliation procedures, computer output may be produced showing incorrect information and actions may be taken on the assumption that the output is valid. Lack of controls may result in system failure, or the production of results which are so obviously faulty that they cannot be used. Non-receipt of expected results, or delay in their receipt, cost the user in obtaining essential information by alternative means. The failure to produce valid and timely results not only has immediate cost implications to the user, but may also cause other subsequent costs arising from action taken in the absence of the required information, eg a failure of the sales forecast may result in excessive stock-out or gross over-ordering. Any error which reaches the user undetected, or any failure to provide the promised output, inevitably causes some loss of faith.

Repeated trouble with a computer system causes users to react in a costly defensive manner. In the extreme case, the customer will revert to his previous manual system and, usually unknown to senior management, will by-pass the computer results. A data error will not necessarily cause a run failure or an output which is evidently erroneous. Corruption may occur in data which is not immediately output. Alternatively, a corruption may only be noticed at the time of a later check, by which time further processing may have taken place, and recovery is either costly or impossible. Faults are rarely diagnosed by the user.

Generally the occurrence of an error will be reported, or the user may only voice fears that the information he is receiving is suspect. It is usually left to the information systems department to investigate the cause. Faults may be diagnosed as due to programming bugs, corrupt data or procedural failures. Program amendments must be specified, written and tested, and the availability of good documentation will reduce these costs. Data errors and procedural failures must be corrected, and measures taken to ensure that the same failures do not recur.

## BATCH SYSTEM CONTROLS

The input to a batch processing system must be accurate, complete, and properly authorised. Many user-oriented problems arising from a computer application occur as a result of human failure rather than that of the computer itself, and for this reason great emphasis should be placed on the control of data input. The use of a properly designed input document promotes the accuracy and completeness of data by minimising omissions, ensuring proper authorisation and providing accountability, an audit trail, and a means of recovery in the event of system failure. The form itself should make use of preprinted information for repetitive data such as document type, transaction code, etc. It should also have appropriate areas for the entry of written authorisation, control totals, cross-checking balances, retention dates and a preprinted document sequence number. Access to source documents and blank input forms should be strictly limited to authorised persons who require such documents to perform their required tasks, and access to the information contained therein will also be limited to those with a 'need to know'. The actual storage location will also be chosen with due regard to potential hazards. Access to 'accountable documents' (such as cheques) should be most strictly controlled.

After source documents have been raised and given proper authorisation, it is necessary to undertake certain tasks before the data is ready for input. These tasks consist of transaction identification, user review of input data, batching, logging and transmission. At each of these stages, the accuracy and completeness of data has to be ensured by the user department. Batch serial numbers are allocated to batches in order to provide accountability of data, to record the receipt of data and for logging purposes. The batch size should be so chosen as to facilitate the process of reconciliation and error tracing. The physical size of batches will also be governed by the requirement of transportability between the user and the information systems department. Data should be batched as close to its point of origin as possible in order to establish control over the origination of source data. Batching also gives security against loss of individual transactions, and the insertion of unauthorised (possibly fraudulent) documents. Manual control logs will be kept for the recording of batches as they pass between stages of transportation and/or authorisation in order to maintain accountability and to identify any items which go missing.

Whilst computer hardware has now reached a high level of reliability, it is possible that during the processing of files and the manipulation of data within the computer, errors may occur regardless of the accuracy of the input data and the machine reliability. It is therefore essential that the applications systems include suitable detection and control systems. Control totals are passed between jobs and between steps in jobs during the production process. In this way the entire system can be balanced, a balance can be achieved between systems, and other files can be balanced and reconciled.

Whenever the user does not specify a particular course of action, then a standardised default action will be carried out at the appropriate point in the process. In order to ensure the integrity of input, the applications system is designed to expect a particular type of input and to detect any deviation or omission from this expectation.

Whenever a particular program control is overriden or bypassed, an exception report is produced so that the matter can be investigated and any necessary corrective action taken. Controls are built into the system design so that errors which are detected at the processing stage result in the rejection of the transaction and that procedures are defined which ensure that errors are corrected and that the transactions are resubmitted. This is so designed as to prevent data loss or the failure to process some transactions. Equally the system should prevent the same corrections from being re-entered twice.

Data output control is performed by the user as well as by the information systems department. The user must check each report to verify that all expected output has been received and that the output appears to be normal in its size and appearance. He will then record its arrival and his acceptance. Checks on the data itself can be made both by sampling random pieces of information and by detailed cross-checking of various files to ensure the data integrity.

## REAL-TIME SYSTEM CONTROLS

An on-line computing system permits data to be entered directly into the system through a terminal, and output to be made available directly where it is needed. The intermediate stages of data conversion are largely avoided. Data may be entered through the keyboard of an interactive terminal. Transactions may be entered at random, one at a time and in any order. Any one transaction may be quite independent of any other transaction and there need not necessarily be any logical relationship whatsoever between different transactions.

Examples of some on-line systems are: seat reservations, sales order entry and processing, stock control (receipts and withdrawals), production monitoring, account enquiry, goods despatch, point-of-sale data collection, rents and rates payments, hospital information, credit information, banking systems, computer-aided design, process or traffic control and statistical analysis.

Controls should ensure that all transactions are correctly entered at the terminals, correctly transmitted, and correctly processed. It is also necessary to provide fallback and recovery procedures to be used during emergencies, which will arise from time to time, so that disruption of the normal method of working will not have disastrous consequences and so that the business of the organisation can continue. Controls must also be maintained throughout recovery.

The design of the terminal and the type of terminal can have a significant effect on error rates. It may be easier for the operator if the dialogue tends to be built into the hardware of the terminal rather than into the software, but this reduces flexibility. VDUs have facilities to help the operator to compose the message on the screen accurately and quickly. A form can be displayed on the screen. This assists the operator because it reminds him of what information he has to enter, and because he has to enter the variable information only (eg the quantity of each product).

Menu techniques are also employed where the operator is asked to select from the options displayed on the screen. Sometimes it is possible to control groups of messages which are input randomly over a period of time to compensate for the batch controls exercised in the batch processing system. Perhaps every hour, or once a day, or every 100 transactions, the computer can report a summary of what has happened. This can be checked against a summary which has been separately accumulated locally, or a physical check can be made. This is useful in situations involving cash transactions or receipts into (and withdrawals from) stock, eg a cash receipting terminal may accumulate totals.

## UNAUTHORISED ACCESS

A remote terminal without proper safeguards, can provide a would-be penetrator of the system with the opportunity of spending a great deal of unsupervised time in searching computer files for information which could be of use to him in conducting criminal or malicious activities. The first step in protecting the system from illegal terminal use is to supply physical security measures. Access to terminals should be restricted to authorised users by using some means of 'key'. This should be a mechanical lock and key or a more sophisticated electronically controlled device such as a badge-reader or card-reader with the option of further identification checks such as keyboard-entry code numbers or passwords.

Data security and authorisation of access are best organised in a two-dimensional matrix, dividing users into several levels of security classification and dividing data into various functional sections. This method ensures that a user in one department of the organisation cannot have unauthorised access to files belonging to other departments, even if he is given the highest security classification within his own department. Within any one department, each user will be given a security classification which will restrict his access to data which he has a 'need to know'.

With remote terminals, the prime security method is the password, backed up at the log-in time by the insertion of some personal identification device. For less sensitive areas, passwords alone are used. Passwords should be changed frequently in order to thwart attempts made at obtaining them. The communication of a password to a user must also be secure. The passwords currently in use, and the lists of available and future passwords held in the computer system must themselves be secure. The password files should be accessible only to those persons in positions of highest security, ie the computer manager, security officer or auditor.

## COMMUNICATION LINE SECURITY

In data communications, the first step in establishing an effective and secure link is to identify the terminal devices. The communications protocol between devices will include terminal identification data, and this will be checked against the device allocation table held by the operating system. This will guard against wrong connections, masquerading, or illegal connection of devices as a deliberate attempt to commit a breach of security. The terminal identification is held in the circuitry of the terminal which should be tamper-proof, and yet allowing necessary maintenance to be carried out. With a legitimate user, accessing authorised information by means of an appropriately authorised terminal, the danger of information being lost, copied or corrupted during its transmission, still remains. The most likely place for an intruder to penetrate the communications network is near to the terminal equipment and the internal telephone exchange. It is at these points that lines are usually identified so that ease of interception is afforded. Assuming that access can be gained, a wire-tap could be fitted and lie undetected for some considerable time. In this area we must rely on physical security measures to prevent the tap being placed.

## AUDIT OF COMPUTER SYSTEMS

Adequate records should exist throughout the system covering all personnel involved and showing a visible trail of all activity of the entire system. An audit trail should permit identification of an item of data throughout the system. It should record the origin of the item, who entered it, which device was used, and the time and date the item was created, accessed, amended or deleted.

Many large, modern operating systems incorporate a system journal which is very carefully protected to maintain its integrity. Such a journal can be employed for security purposes. Details about all application transactions can be recorded in the journal for subsequent processing and analysis. Similar facilities exist in good database and file management software, but these may be less tamper-proof than the ones in operating systems. Operating system logs and database log files often include elaborate recovery mechanisms, so that, in the event of a failure or error, there is minimum loss of data. In real-time systems the audit or inspection department often has on-line monitoring facilities so that activity on the system is subject to continuous surveillance. Any 'sensitive' error or unauthorised activity can be detected as it happens. Appropriate action can be initiated at once. This kind of control is common in banking systems.

It is possible for a system to have an embedded audit module for the use of the auditor which will enable him to extract data as it is being processed by the system. Another technique is to tag a transaction for subsequent reporting as it passes through the system processes. The auditor may consider such facilities to be perfectly adequate if he is not concerned about the possibility of his program being tampered with or data not being presented to him.

## PRIVACY AND DATA PROTECTION

Individuals tend to think that certain kinds of information about them ought to be kept private. Patient records, other medical data and salary information are typical examples. There is public concern about the possible misuse of large files of data about individuals. Some people are worried that a profile about an individual might be constructed from data drawn from several sources, using computers to co-ordinate it. Various countries have data protection laws to regulate the use of personal information. These control the kinds of data that can be collected and held and the ways it can be processed or disclosed. The regulations usually specify security and confidentiality requirements that the user of data must uphold.

The debate about computers and personal information began in the late-1960s. Information about individuals may be sensitive and there is increasing concern about the way that computer systems might be used to handle personal information. The growing size and power of computers gave rise to fears about possible abuse. Privacy has been defined as the claim of individuals, groups or institutions to determine for themselves when, how and to what extent information about them is communicated to others. Another definition also describes it as the individual's ability to control the circulation of information relating to himself. Data protection is concerned with regulating the ways in which data about individuals is collected, stored and used. It is also concerned with the quality of the data, its relevance to the business activity and the ways in which it might be disclosed. This involves various ethical questions.

## NEED FOR DATA PROTECTION LEGISLATION

Two international agreements recognise the concerns about handling of personal information. They are:

- the OECD (Organization for Economic Cooperation and Development) guidelines governing the protection of privacy and transborder flows of personal data;
- the Council of Europe Convention for the protection of individuals with regard to automatic processing of personal data.

About 30 countries have laws concerning the handling of personal information. Sometimes the law covers all files of information, including paper records and not just computer files.

The first legislation on data protection was passed in the German State of Hesse, and the first national legislation was introduced in Sweden. Although the UK Data Protection Act came on to the Statute Book only in 1984, it had been under discussion for a long time. The policy of the present UK Government was set out in 1982, and this policy has been broadly followed in the ensuing legislation. The reasons for introducing legislation were stated to be to limit the possibility of individuals being harmed by the abuse of computerised personal data, and to enable the UK to ratify the Council of Europe Convention.

Countries where data protection is in force are understandably reluctant to send their data abroad to places where their own restrictions may be flouted. This would defeat the whole object of the legislation. To prevent such evasion of national laws many countries have a clause forbidding the export of personal or sensitive data without the consent of the Data Protection Registrar (or equivalent).

The number of cases of reported misuse is very small, and in most of those the misuse could have occurred equally well with manual files. Nevertheless the scope for abuse of computer files is greater than that of manual files due to the speed and versatility of the computer. Data collected for one purpose can more readily be adapted for use for another or can be collated with data from another source. The individual therefore regards the power of the computer with some misgiving. Although the incidence of reported abuse has been small, legislation is intended to limit the undoubted potential for misuse.

## SCOPE OF UK DATA PROTECTION ACT

The UK Data Protection Act (1984) refers to data that is, or has been, processed on a computer. It is further restricted to personal data, which is data that refers to an identifiable living individual. Personal data shall not be used, disclosed or sent abroad except in accordance with the registered particulars. Every computer bureau handling personal data shall be registered. The person about whom data is being held (the data subject) is entitled to be told what that data is. A data user shall abide by the principles enunciated in the Act.

Disclosure, where this implies misuse of the data, has two categories. First there is the deliberate passing on of data by the data user or by a bureau to a third party not declared in the registration particulars. Disclosure of this type can also mean passing on exempt data to a third party where such passing on invalidates the exemption from the Act. 'Unauthorised disclosure' is the second category and this applies when data is passed on through carelessness or poor discipline without the consent of the data user or bureau. Obviously, the data user should ensure that the declaration he makes to the Registrar covers all possible uses or disclosures of the data that he intends to make. If not, the particulars should be amended or the relevant disclosure should not be made. Unauthorised disclosure is rather more difficult to prevent due to its unpredictable nature.

All staff handling data must be aware of the legislation and their responsibilities under it. These staff should be aware of the limits set on the use of the data, which should correspond with the particulars to be registered. The security systems should ensure that all possible precautions against loss of data have been made.

# 12 Human Response

## THE INDIVIDUAL IN THE ORGANISATION

The individual in the organisation has been the subject of study ever since the industrial revolution and particularly since the 1920s. The revolt of the individual against the highly repetitive nature of operations on the production assembly line focused attention on human needs in the organisation. Behavioural researchers found that financial reward was not the only thing that the individual expected: there are many other factors. Psychological studies of the individual have focused on motivation, judgement, perception, learning, remembering, imagination and personality. Every person is unique but has characteristics shared with others. The perceived differences and similarities provide knowledge about how persons behave, both alone and in association with others.

The spectrum of human needs is very important for organisations. Unless an organisation is helping an individual to satisfy particular needs, the individual is not motivated, is underachieving and may leave. If the organisation frustrates the person, recalcitrance or, at worst, sabotage may result. Typically, a person makes sacrifices for the organisation, but expects adequate compensation.

Human needs can be grouped into two broad categories – 'biological' and 'social'. *Biological* needs are common to all persons; everyone needs food, water, oxygen, protection from extremes of weather, etc. *Social* needs vary greatly from person to person. Satisfying them is not usually necessary for a person's physical survival, but they are always principal influences upon a person's actions. They include the desire for power, for companionship, and for love and affection. A person's need for social experiences can be very strong and critical to the individual's functional effectiveness. Individual needs also change with time. Some may vanish altogether and others appear, gradually or with dramatic rapidity and the progress of an individual toward the satisfaction of any need is likely to be erratic. Even as one is working toward a particular objective, needs may change and the individual may move in another direction. Shifts in personal objectives can derive from the ever-shifting influences on the individual.

## MASLOW AND McGREGOR

One of the best known theories of motivation is the 'hierarchy of needs' theory put forward by the psychologist Abraham Maslow. He saw human needs in the form of a hierarchy, and concluded that when one set of needs was satisfied, this kind of need ceased to be a motivator. The basic needs identified by Maslow, in an ascending order of importance, are:

1 **Physiological needs:** These are the basic needs for sustaining human life itself – food, water, warmth, shelter, sleep, and sexual satisfaction. Maslow took the position that until these needs are satisfied to the degree necessary to maintain life, other needs will not motivate people.

2 **Security or safety needs:** These are the needs to be free from physical danger and the fear of loss of a job, property, food, or shelter.

3 **Affiliation or acceptance needs:** Since people are social beings, they need to belong, to be accepted by others.

4 **Esteem needs:** According to Maslow, once people begin to satisfy their need to belong, they tend to want to be held in esteem both by themselves and by others. This kind of need produces such satisfactions as power, prestige, status, and self-confidence.

5 **Need for self-actualisation:** Maslow regards this as the highest need in his hierarchy. It is the desire to become what one is

capable of becoming – to maximise one's potential and to accomplish something.

Each individual has a unique set of needs, but there is enough similarity among many needs to enable persons to exploit organisations for satisfaction. Persons of similar backgrounds, for example, may have similar wants, needs and desires. Many successful organisations are based on this fact.

As the individuals in an organisation work to accomplish their objectives and the broader objectives of the organisation itself, the interactions among these persons will influence their future individual objectives. This influence will eventually alter the form, direction, or intensity of the individuals' objectives. The same interactions also exert influence in the opposite direction; ie the individuals will alter the organisational objectives.

Organisations, and the individuals within them, are continually changing. A person's needs and the objectives that they lead toward are crucial to the organisation. Organisations exist because persons need them – to do things that they need to do or want to do, and that they either could not do so well or could not do at all in isolation. The effectiveness of any organisation is ultimately determined by the degree to which it helps its members to achieve these individual objectives. Unless the people responsible for managing an organisation understand the importance of individual objectives, the organisation cannot be accurately understood, nor operated at its full potential.

According to McGregor, most managerial principles have been derived from a negative set of assumptions about human beings. These assumptions are:

1 The average human being has an inherent dislike of work and will avoid it if he can.

2 Because of this human characteristic of dislike of work, most people must be coerced, controlled, directed or threatened with punishment to get them to put forth adequate effort toward the achievement of organisational objectives.

3 The average human being prefers to be directed, wishes to avoid responsibility, has relatively little ambition, and wants security above all.

McGregor saw it as providing an explanation for some behaviour patterns in industry. To a large extent the McGregor explanation was a self-fulfilling analysis. Organisations have been greatly influenced by concepts of standardisation and mass-production. Skilled jobs have been subdivided into many smaller parts. Individual performance on these minute tasks have been programmed, with initiative and discretion reduced. This process, extending over decades, has caused many individuals to feel alienated from their work. Employees have inevitably responded with boredom and recalcitrance, encouraged to work in ways that are sometimes detrimental to organisational efficiency. Management, faced with these circumstances, may be tempted to impose yet more restrictions. A vicious circle is set up and managers are encouraged to regard workers as indolent, without ambition, and resistant to change and responsibility.

As a consequence of such considerations, McGregor moves to a further theory. This proclaimed that:

1 The expenditure of physical and mental effort in work is as natural as play or rest.

2 External control and the threat of punishment are not the only means for bringing about effort toward organisational objectives.

3 Commitment to objectives is a result of the rewards associated with their achievement.

4 The average human being learns, under proper conditions, not only to accept but to seek responsibility.

5 The capacity to exercise a relatively high degree of imagination, ingenuity, and creativity in the solution of human problems is widely, not narrowly, distributed in the population.

6 Under conditions of modern industrial life, the intellectual potentialities of the average human being are only partially utilised.

## SATISFIERS AND DISSATISFIERS

Herzberg studied white collar employees and managers to determine those things that caused them to be satisfied and dissatisfied. He obtained very consistent results. One interesting conclusion of Herzberg's studies was that satisfaction and dissatisfaction appear to be unrelated, ie satisfaction is not simply the absence of dissatisfaction. One may feel no dissatisfaction and yet not be satisfied.

Five factors were identified that most often contribute to employee dissatisfaction. These included perceived fairness of company policy, pay, working conditions, relations with one's supervisor, and relations with co-workers. These were labelled as 'hygiene' factors. To satisfy or motivate employees, it was found, a different set of factors was needed. These satisfiers included achievement, recognition, the work itself, responsibility and advancement. The satisfiers or motivators centred around the higher-level needs on Maslow's hierarchy: esteem and self-actualisation.

### Job Enrichment

Herzberg recommended job enrichment as a means to making a job more satisfying. He saw the key to job satisfaction in increasing a person's freedom. Each person should be given additional authority, greater opportunity to use talents and some control over the job itself. Job enrichment should be distinguished from job enlargement. Job enlargement attempts to make a job more varied by removing the dullness associated with performing repetitive operations. In job enrichment, the attempt is to build into jobs a higher sense of challenge and achievement. A job may be enriched by variety, but it also may be enriched by:

1 giving workers more freedom in deciding about such things as work methods, sequence, and pace, or the acceptance or rejection of materials;

2 encouraging participation of subordinates and interaction between workers;

3 giving workers a feeling of personal responsibility for their tasks;

4 taking steps to make sure that workers can see how their tasks contribute to a finished product and the welfare of an enterprise;

5 giving people feedback on their job performance, preferably before their supervisors get it;

6 involving workers in analysis and change of physical aspects of the work environment, such as layout of office or plant, temperature, lighting, and cleanliness.

However, the motivating factors vary with people and situations. What is challenging to one may not be challenging to another. Research has shown that workers with few skills want such factors as job security, pay, benefits, less restrictive plant rules, and more sympathetic and understanding supervisors. As we move up the ladder in an enterprise, we find that other factors become increasingly important.

One of the most interesting approaches to motivation is the quality of working life (QWL) factors. These represent a systems approach to job design and a promising development in the broad area of job enrichment, combined with a grounding in the sociotechnical systems approach to management. QWL is not only a very broad approach to job enrichment but also an interdisciplinary field of enquiry and action combining industrial and organisational psychology and sociology, industrial engineering, organisation theory and development, motivation and leadership theory, and industrial relations.

## MOTIVATION FACTORS OF DP PROFESSIONALS

Couger and Zawacki (1980) conducted a survey of the motivation factors of data processing professionals: analysts, programmer/analysts, and programmers. They used the method of Job Diagnostic Survey developed by Hackman and Oldham in the mid-1970s. The Hackman/Oldham model identifies the three 'critical psychological states' associated with a high level of internal motivation, satisfaction, and quality of performance. These psychological states are: experienced meaningfulness of work, experienced responsibility for the outcomes, and knowledge of actual results. The existence of these psychological states in a job should lead to low absenteeism and turnover, and high levels of internal motivation, satisfaction, and quality of performance.

The jobs of data processing professionals were evaluated as

compared to other jobs on the basis of five job characteristics or core job dimensions. These five characteristics used were: skill variety, task identity, task significance, autonomy and feedback. Skill variety is defined as the degree to which a job requires a variety of different activities and involves the use of a number of different skills and talents of the employee. Task identity is defined as the degree to which the job requires the completion of a 'whole' and identifiable piece of work, ie doing a job from beginning to end with a visible outcome. Task significance is the degree to which the job has a substantial impact on the lives or work of other people – whether in the immediate organisation or in the external environment. Autonomy is the degree to which the job provides substantial freedom, independence and discretion to the employee in scheduling his/her work and in determining the procedures to be used in carrying it out. Feedback is the degree to which carrying out the work activities required by the job results in the employee obtaining information about the effectiveness of his/her performance.

The survey indicated that the job of the analyst rated higher than that of other professionals in all the job characteristics except autonomy, which was rated marginally lower. On the other hand, the job of the programmer was rated lower than other professionals on all counts except feedback. The evaluation of critical psychological states showed that the job of analyst scores higher for experienced meaningfulness but lower on account of experienced responsibility and knowledge of results as compared to other professionals. The job of the programmer rated lower on all three critical psychological states. The rating on 'knowledge of results' was lower mainly due to lack of feedback from the supervisor. The feedback from the job itself was approximately the same as for other professionals.

Job satisfaction was measured in terms of general satisfaction, satisfaction with co-workers, and satisfaction with supervisors. The survey indicated that general satisfaction is higher in the cases of both analysts and programmers as compared to other professionals. However, the satisfaction with co-workers as well as satisfaction with supervision was found to be lower for both analysts and programmers than for other professionals.

Couger and Zawacki conducted a similar survey on more than 800 data processing managers. The job of data processing manager obtained higher rating for all the five job characteristics as compared to analysts and programmers as well as compared to other managers. The ratings were significantly higher on skill variety, task identity, task significance and autonomy, and marginally higher for feedback from job. The job of data processing manager rated higher on the critical psychological states of experienced meaningfulness and experienced responsibility but rated lower on the knowledge of results. The feedback from the job is rated higher than the feedback from managers. The results of the survey on satisfaction levels indicated that general satisfaction is higher than other managers but satisfaction with supervision is lower.

## IMPACT OF IT ON WORK

Information technology has led to a phenomenal growth in 'information work' in organisations. Traditionally occupations were classified as 'white-collar' and 'blue-collar'. White-collar workers ('office workers') dealt with information rather than with things. With the development of information technology, information work is no longer confined to the office. As robots are introduced into the factory, the shop-floor operators themselves become information workers, since they need to know how to operate sophisticated equipment. The proportion of information workers to the total workforce has increased from about 42% in 1960 to well over 50% today. One estimate is that more than 70% of working hours, for a wide cross-section of modern employees, is spent on what may be called information work.

Office work, generated by specialisation in a bureaucracy, can be complex, especially in large organisations. To get virtually anything accomplished, numerous steps must be completed. If there are professional specialists involved, work must travel from desk to desk. For each organisation there is a characteristic number of information transactions which are necessary to a task or objective. For example, a number of co-ordinating steps are necessary within the organisation to take care of a single customer's request. Intraorganisational communications expand enormously with the size of organisations. Well-structured ordered tasks can be automated in the office but to deal with unstructured and unpredictable office work is still a principal challenge to information technology. The emerging social and industrial system based on the use of IT has been dubbed the 'post-industrial' society, a further step in the evolutionary process of social change. The emerging society based on information technology is also depicted as a 'service' society. A society based on services, like other types of society, is concerned with the creation of wealth by the capabilities of its people. The role of information technology is totally subordinated to this objective. An abundant supply of low-cost agricultural and industrial products is already secure. Agricultural and industrial employment is declining rapidly because of the high levels of efficiency attained in those sectors.

The service society is characterised by incessant investigation of how to create new and superior services. Wealth is extracted from high value-added benefits in the delivery of high-quality services *on a global scale*. Its primary resource is knowledge. The institutions of a service society are shaped by questions of the ownership and control of knowledge.

Paul Strassman forecasts the following changes in the sociology of work in the transition from the industrial culture to one based on service:

1 Simple jobs based on common skills will be replaced by jobs demanding individual competence. Industrialisation requires interchangeable parts. People must also fit this pattern, because total predictability is a prerequisite for running a clerical operation which processes standard tasks. Interchangeability of human operators in handling data-processing equipment is achieved by making each job simple and replicable, and by requiring only skills that represent the lowest common denominator in knowledge. One ends up demanding hardly any skills at all. The essence of the service economy, however, lies in customised responses and in adaptive handling of a client's wishes. A broad range of adaptive behaviour thus becomes a prerequisite for delivering services without referring every new question to another specialist.

2 Standardised jobs will be replaced by jobs with variety. Industrial-age organisations define information jobs in terms of the procedures which are followed. People are assigned to minutely subdivided repetitive jobs. Service-age organisations, however, define information jobs in terms of the employee's relationship to clients. Organisation decentralisation and market segmentation further strengthen the view that work is best accomplished by assigning people to jobs designed around customers, within flexible boundaries, defined by market needs rather than by the administrative processes. Variety on the job comes from the fact that precisely the same situation will hardly ever be encountered twice.

3 Isolated tasks will be replaced by jobs with a sense of task completion. Industrial-age organisations design jobs in terms of discrete clerical procedures. The flow of work tends to be routed to specialists. There are 'dedicated' computers and specially assigned peripheral devices that process the workload in standardised batches. This leads to an isolation of tasks and a loss of sensitivity to the individual customer's identity in the process of handling transactions. Service-age organisations, however, are designed to assure high-quality completion of a client's administrative work, even under adverse conditions. The flow of work is channelled to people who understand both how the client operates and how the internal organisation can respond. There are specialised computers designed to handle each subset of the administrative workload. Even more important, there are computers that integrate all of the part into a meaningful whole. This leads to the visibility of all work done by an employee for a particular client.

4 Immutable jobs with a finite scope will be replaced by jobs with opportunity for learning and change. Industrial-age organisations define jobs in terms of the factory process. Inflexibility in industrial design is applied to the way in which jobs are assigned to people. There is no way of changing the scope of a person's activity except by physically moving him to another assignment. The design of computerised jobs has largely followed the patterns learned from factories. Data-

processing operations were initially organised around a disciplined, sequential and totally predetermined handling of punched cards. As data-processing operations grew in scope, their managers drew rigid lines between the roles of data preparation, equipment operations, programming, systems analysis, and administration. The same attitude spread to wherever remote computer terminals were installed. If any learning took place, it was accomplished by sending personnel to formal courses where they acquired specific qualifications so they could leave one position and assume another. According to industrial-age principles, even training was treated as a predetermined factory process in which people without knowledge were fed in at the start of the course and qualified employees came out at the end. Service-age organisations, however, design jobs so that people do not need to be reclassified or physically moved if they wish to upgrade their roles or their earning capacity. Work is viewed much more as a co-operative team effort, where the entire team progresses by expanding its influence in a constantly changing and evolving competitive environment.

5 Jobs with entirely predetermined options will be replaced by jobs with autonomy for discretionary decisions. Industrial-age organisations thrive on standard procedure manuals, printed forms, and elaborate systems to ensure that several approval signatures are secured before any important action is taken. Service-age organisations, however, will thrive on worker initiatives. They too will have standard procedure manuals, printed forms, and elaborate security systems for quality control. They will focus on servicing customers and obtaining the highest possible commitment from their people in support of their enterprise's objectives. Standards of performance will be defined externally, as seen from the standpoint of the customer, rather than internally, in terms of some expert's opinion of what expected behaviour is.

6 Socially unrelated jobs will be replaced by jobs where social support comes from fellow-workers. Industrial-age organisations isolate workers by means of job design. Only experts, whether they are industrial engineers or systems analysts, have sufficient knowledge about the entire operation to

define a worker's relationship with others. A worker has little to say to his associates about the content of work, except perhaps to complain about it. Service-age organisations, however, emphasise work teams as the nucleus of job design. Groups are assigned well-defined missions and are left to allocate work among their members. The objective of each team is to achieve as much self-sufficiency in coping with information technology as resources permit. Therefore, experts such as systems analysts, programmers, or communications specialists are brought in as consultants and teachers rather than decision makers. A great deal of social interaction is necessary among team members because each individual must be flexible enough to cover another person's learning time. People become much more dependent, not only on each other, but also on external assistance.

# Glossary

**Acoustic coupler** — A device which uses sound signals to link a digital computer system to an analogue telephone connection (see *Modem*).

**Acoustic hood** — A device placed over a printer to reduce its noise.

**Ada** — A high-level language based on structured software engineering principles; named after computer pioneer Countess Ada Lovelace.

**Algorithm** — A set of rules or defined procedures which perform a particular task; a mathematical formula or program procedure.

**Analogue** — A way of representing numerical values by a continuously changing physical quantity, such as electrical wave-form currents or the hands of a non-digital watch.

**Analyst workbench** — A graphics-based system that helps in carrying out the analysis, design and documentation tasks in the front-end of the software development life cycle.

**Applications generator** Software which automatically generates program code from requirements specifications and designs.

**Applications software** Programs that carry out the computer functions needed to perform user application tasks, rather than activities oriented to controlling the system's resources (see *Systems software*).

**Architecture** 1. The blueprint design which defines how the components within a computer system are interrelated.

2. The design of a network showing how the computing and telecommunications capabilities fit together and information flows through them.

3. The internal structure of a computer, such as the number of bits in a basic word length and the set of instructions available to be programmed.

**Artificial Intelligence (AI)** The study of how computing can be applied to carry out intellectual, communication and sensory activities in ways that are characteristic of human beings and other animals.

**Assembler** 1. A low-level programming language (also called an *assembly* language) similar in structure to machine code but using mnemonic instructions and meaningful symbolic addresses that are easier to work with.

2. Software that translates a low-level language into machine-readable code.

**Availability** The percentage of time an information system provides a useful service.

**Back-up** 1. Information copied from a computer system regularly and stored separately from current data so that it can be used to reconstitute data to a recent state if the current information is corrupted or destroyed.

2. A computer installation which could be used to run the workload of a system that is out of action for some reason.

3. Duplicate *standby* systems components, like processors, which can be switched to live operation if the existing unit fails.

**Bandwidth** Measurement of the information transmission capacity of a telecommunications link (see *Narrowband*, *Wideband*).

**BASIC** Relatively easy to learn and use high-level programming language that has been particularly popular on personal computers.

**Batch processing** Applications processed sequentially using batched, not on-line, input, with allowance made for applications' priorities in scheduling the sequence of processing.

**Baud** Measurement of data transmission speed, equivalent to bits per second.

**Benchmark** A test to measure the performance of a system for a predefined workload.

**Binary** A representational system that can be in one of two states; the binary digits 0 and 1 are used to process, store and transmit data in digital information systems.

**Bit** A single binary digit that takes the value 0 or 1; abbreviation of *bi*nary digi*t*.

**Board** A sheet of plastic on which many chips are interconnected to perform particular computing functions (also called *Printed circuit board*).

**Bug** An error, say in a computer program.

**Bureau** A computer services company that offers access, at commercial rates, to its own computing capabilities, such as processors, storage and software packages.

**Bus** The part of a computer system's architecture that defines how information is exchanged internally between systems units and how connections are made to external input, output and storage.

**Business analyst** A professional with expertise in business applications *and* the systems analysis and design techniques needed for specifying and developing computer-based information systems.

**Byte** A group of 8 bits widely used as the length of a coded *character* in computer systems (some architectures have different character bit-lengths).

**C** — A structured programming language used for many systems software and applications developments.

**Capacity management** — The function of analysing the computing resources needed to satisfy a given workload, monitoring actual performance and planning for future workload requirements.

**Central Processing Unit (CPU)** — The main processing control unit in traditional computer architectures (see *Von Neumann architecture*).

**Chip** — A piece of material, about the size of a fingernail, that contains many integrated circuits used for computer processors and main memory (see *Silicon*).

**Circuit switching** — Linking systems and devices in a network by directly connecting transmission circuits via switching centres or exchanges to the traditional public telephone network.

**COBOL** — High-level language widely used for commercial applications.

**Compiler** — Software which translates a high-level language into machine code (see *Interpreter*).

**Configuration** — 1. The hardware elements that comprise a complete system.

2. All software and hardware elements that comprise the complete version of an information system at a particular phase of its life cycle.

**Configuration management** The control of various versions of a system that may be in existence at any one time, say in various development, test and operational phases.

**Conformance testing** Tests to ensure a system meets a given standard.

**Connectivity** The ability to link systems together flexibly and efficiently (see *Open systems*).

**Contract staff** IT professionals employed for a fixed contract period, rather than as permanent employees.

**Cost-benefit analyses** Systematic evaluations of the likely costs and benefits of an investment, used to assist making a decision about whether to proceed with a project, how much to invest, etc (see *Feasibility studies*).

**Critical path analysis** A technique used for managing projects involving the co-ordination of many activities and tasks (see *Gantt charts, PERT*).

**Cursor** Pointer on a VDU screen which indicates the current point of activity.

**Cybernetics** The study of control and communication in organisations, machines, people and animals.

**Daisywheel** A printer mechanism with character printheads at the end of spokes (or petals) around a central hub, which produces letter-quality output.

**Data** Raw facts that can be converted into useful information stored, processed and transmitted by computer-based systems.

**Data centre** A centre containing major corporate computing resources, such as mainframes and large amounts of data storage.

**Data flow diagram** A design diagram that shows relationships between an information system's data, processes and relevant external factors.

**Data model** The analysis and specification of the theoretical organisation, structure and relationships of data in an information system.

**Data preparation** The conversion of data from paper documents into computerised digital form.

**Data processing** Computer-based information processing typified by the administrative, accounting and commercial applications of traditional mainframe-based systems.

**Database** Computerised information organised and structured to optimise its ability to be shared among many users, applications and locations efficiently and reliably.

**Database administrator** An IT job function responsible for co-ordinating the administration and control of a database management system.

| | |
|---|---|
| **Debug** | To search for and eliminate errors, particularly in software. |
| **Decision support system** | An IT application which provides access to information and modelling aids to help users make decisions. |
| **Desktop Publishing (DTP)** | The application, from ordinary office desks, of personal computers and workstations to carry out the editing, design layout and other functions involved in printing and publishing newsletters, magazines, newspapers, etc. |
| **Discounted cash flow** | A cost-benefit analysis technique that investigates how long it will take for benefits received to pay for an investment, anticipating and making allowance for falling value of money over time, due to factors like inflation. |
| **Disk** | A disk-shaped data storage medium, coated with magnetic material which is used to represent binary digits (see *Floppy disk, Hard disk*). |
| **Diskette** | see *Floppy disk*. |
| **Distributed processing** | An information system where computer processing capabilities are in many locations; also known as *distributed computing* or *distributed data processing*. |
| **Dot matrix** | A printer mechanism where characters are formed as a matrix of tiny dots by small rods. |
| **Dumb terminal** | A terminal which does not incorp- |

orate any of its own computer processing capability and can operate only when linked on-line to a computer.

**Editor** Software which enables users to edit information stored in a computer, say in desk top publishing and word processing applications.

**Electronic Data Interchange (EDI)** An information system where documents and other information are transmitted electronically between different organisations.

**Electronic funds transfer** An information system that carries out financial transactions, like payments, by purely electronic means.

**Electronic mail** The transmission of messages and other communications by purely electronic means, typically in office automation applications.

**Electronic point-of-sale** A computer-based system used to record sales at the place where a retail transaction takes place, such as a supermarket checkout.

**Emulation** Making one system behave like another, say in predicting the performance of a new computer system before it has been implemented.

**End user** A term often used by IT professionals to refer to the person who uses the final computer-based service or product.

**Enterprise model** A model of the structure and interaction of a complete organisation or business.

| | |
|---|---|
| **Entity-relation database** | A database technique that manages many objects, like documents and program code, in addition to data items. |
| **Ergonomics** | The study of the interaction between people and machines to improve overall efficiency, effectiveness, comfort and safety; can be used synonymously with human factors engineering, but is often associated more with the physical aspects of equipment design. |
| **Ethernet** | A form of local area network. |
| **Expert system** | An application based on a technique that seeks to follow the reasoning processes of human experts, rather than the machine-oriented logic of other programming methods; a form of *Artificial Intelligence.* |
| **Facilities management** | A service which gives an outside supplier management control over all, or part, of an organisation's computing capabilities or IT function, such as running a data centre. |
| **Facsimile communication** | Electronic transmission of the image of a document. |
| **Fax** | Abbreviation of facsimile. |
| **Feasibility study** | The investigation of conditions under which an investment is justified and the detailed requirements for projects that are given the go-ahead. |

**Field** The basic structural element in a file (see *Record*).

**Fifth-generation systems** Computer architectures that apply a range of advanced (by 1980s standards) hardware, software and user interface techniques to make systems more intelligent, cost-effective and easy to use.

**File** Information organised into an interrelated set of records.

**File management** The data management technique based on having separate files for different functions, rather than a common database that integrates and shares data needed for a variety of functions.

**Firmware** Software stored in a fixed form, typically on ROM chips (see *Hardwired*).

**Flexible manufacturing** An IT application that enables production processes to be altered quickly and efficiently by changing software controlling many machine tools and numerical control machines.

**Floppy disk** Disk storage made of thin flexible material contained in cardboard jacket, and which usually holds less data than a hard disk.

**Flowchart** A graphical representation of the structure and logical interactions of a system, such as a program; generally applied to non-structured design diagrams.

**Formal organisation** — The organisational structures and interactions defined by official rules and procedures (see *Informal organisation*).

**FORTRAN** — A high-level language used for scientific applications.

**Fourth-generation language** — Programming languages and application development aids designed for users who understand the application, rather than for software specialists.

**Front-end processor** — A system which removes some of the processing load from a central computer, typically by handling some processing and co-ordination at the interfaces between communications lines and the main computing system.

**Gantt charts** — A graphical representation of the various sub-tasks that need to be performed to complete a project; used in project management techniques like critical path analysis and PERT.

**Garbage In/Garbage Out (GIGO)** — A warning that incorrect input to a computer system will produce incorrect output, however good the software processing it.

**Graceful degradation** — The ability of a computer to continue operating, though at a reduced performance level, despite failures in parts of it.

**Graphics workstation** — A device which can display complex graphical images with good visual quality; includes a screen with a display that is composed of more light dots than conventional screens (known as a *high-resolution* display).

**Hacking** Gaining illegal and unwarranted access to information in computer-based systems, often through network links.

**Hard copy** See *Printout*.

**Hard disk** A rigid magnetic disk, similar to a music record, held in a sealed container and providing higher storage capacity than floppy disks.

**Hardware** The physical equipment in a computer system.

**Hardwired** Fixed electronic circuit patterns, as used for firmware (see *Microcode*).

**High-level language** A programming language designed to match the information processing needs of an application, using commands and statements that are a restricted form of the natural English-language way of expressing a requirement.

**Human-computer interaction** See *User-system interaction*.

**Human factors engineering** The study of the interaction between people and machines to improve overall operational efficiency, effectiveness, comfort and safety, particularly in working environments; can be used synonymously with ergonomics, but without the emphasis on hardware aspects often associated with that term.

**Icon** A graphic symbol on a workstation or personal computer screen which represents a particular function.

**Informal organisation** The actual procedures, groups, cliques, communications grapevines, etc, that evolve in an organisation despite the requirements of the formal organisational rules and procedures.

**Informatics** Used synonymously with information technology.

**Information centre** A unit, outside other specialist IT functions, geared to helping users solve their own computing needs and gain optimum benefit from systems they use directly, such as personal computers and 4GLs.

**Information engineering** An integrated, structured approach to the design and development of information systems, encompassing overall organisational and business environments, as well as detailed applications and technical requirements.

**Information management** The co-ordination of all information services in an organisation based on a set of policies and techniques covering information collection, organisation, analysis, processing and communication.

**Information manager** — The senior executive responsible for information management activities.

**Information retrieval** — The use of a computer-based system to search and extract information from a database or file management system.

**Information system** — The techniques and tools, often computer-based, which implement information management policies.

**Information Technology (IT)** — A variety of techniques and devices used to store, process, manage, transmit and communicate information, which can be integrated in unified computing and telecommunications information systems.

**Input** — Information translated into digital code for processing and storage by computers; as a verb, it means the act of entering data into a computer system.

**Integrated circuit** — A circuit composed of many transistors which have been reduced in size and placed together on a single physical element, typically a silicon chip.

**Integrated Project Support Environment (IPSE)** — A variety of tools and techniques unified within a common framework and user interface to cover the information system development life cycle.

**Integrated Services Digital Network (ISDN)** — A set of standards for a global telecommunications network integrating voice, data, image and text in digitised form.

**Intelligent device** A workstation or other device which incorporates its own computer processor, memory and software.

**Interactive** An application where the user is involved in a continuous dialogue with the system.

**Interface** The junction between two devices, software modules or other elements of a system.

**Interpreter** A program that translates a high-level interactive language, like BASIC, into machine code, statement by statement.

**Interrupt** When a processor's control unit switches from one mode to another, say from performing calculations to handling input and output tasks.

**Job control language** The language used to tell the operating system how to schedule and organise the processing of a computer's workload.

**Key** One or more characters that identify a data item or structure, such as a key field in a record or a key word used for information retrieval applications.

**Lap-top computer** A compact, portable personal computer about the size of a briefcase.

**Laser printer** A high-speed noiseless method of producing good quality printed output from a computer using a laser beam to form images on light-sensitive material.

**Letter-quality printing** — Printers that produce output of a high enough quality to be used for producing important business letters.

**Line printer** — A high speed, but often relatively low-quality, device that prints a complete line at a time.

**Linear programming** — An operations research technique which calculates the optimum solution to a problem where the relationship between variables can be represented as a straight line and the result relates to a single factor, such as maximising profits or minimising costs.

**Local** — Computing capability close to the actual user (see *Remote*).

**Local area network** — A means of interlinking computers, workstations, storage and other devices within a relatively small area, such as an office or building.

**Logging on/off** — The procedures needed to initiate and terminate an on-line session at a workstation or terminal.

**Low-level language** — A programming language, such as an assembler, that resembles the format of a computer's machine code, but is easier to use because it is not restricted to the use of only numerals.

**Machine code** — The numeric instructions understood by a computer processor.

**Magnetic storage media** — Devices, like disks and tapes, which store information as bits according to the magnetisation of tiny elements in the surface of the medium.

**Mainframe** The traditional large-scale computers used for corporate data processing; now generally regarded as a system whose power and capability is greater than a minicomputer, but less than a supercomputer, and which is provided with comprehensive support and software from the supplier.

**Main memory** High-speed storage which holds the programs and data needed for immediate processing; linked directly to the processor and sometimes regarded as part of the central processing unit.

**Management information service/system** 1. IT applications, like decision support systems, which assist management and staff to carry out their work.

2. The unit responsible for information systems or information management is sometimes called management information services.

**Man-machine interaction/interface** See *User-system interaction.*

**Manufacturing Automation Protocol (MAP)** An application of the OSI standard for manufacturing production activities.

**Memory** Synonymous with computer storage, usually used in relation to main memory.

**Menu** A form of user dialogue where the system's next action is determined by the user's choice of an item on a menu of options.

**Microcode** Code used in the *microprogram* that translates machine code instructions into appropriate hardware signals; a microcoded instruction set can be altered relatively easily, whereas a hardwired implementation is fixed.

**Microcomputer** The smallest and cheapest complete computers; often synonymous with personal computer.

**Microfiche** Microfilm in the form of a rectangular piece of film, like a card, which can be produced as direct output from a computer.

**Microfilm** Film that contains reduced images of a document or other information; needs special readers to be seen (see *Microfiche*).

**Microprocessor** A processor on a chip.

**Microprogram** See *Microcode*.

**Mini** Abbreviation for minicomputer.

**Minicomputer** A computer of a size and capability roughly between a personal computer and mainframe, sometimes packaged as part of a complete system, like a small business system or word processor; originally more robust and provided with less support than mainframes, but now usually similar to mainframes in many respects (see *Superminis*).

**Modelling** — The representation of a system's structure and behaviour using mathematical equations, design diagrams and software; can be used to predict likely outcome of various courses of action.

**Modems** — Devices that translate between the digital code of computers and analogue transmission lines, with one needed at each end of the line; abbreviation for MOdulator-DEModulator.

**Module** — A self-contained hardware or software unit which interfaces with other modules to form a complete system.

**Mouse** — A device which moves the cursor on a screen in the same direction as the device is moved.

**Multiprogramming** — The ability of a computer system to run more than one program at a time.

**Multitasking** — The ability of an operating system to handle more than one user task at a time.

**Multiuser system** — A computer that allows many on-line users to share the system's resources and data.

**Narrowband** — Telecommunications bandwidth that permits a limited volume of information to flow through it, less than a wideband link.

**Network** 1. The interlinking of many computers, workstations, storage devices, printers and other systems via telecommunications links, according to a structured architecture and defined protocols (see *local* and *wide area networks*).

2. A form of diagram structure used, for example, in project management and database systems.

**Node** A focal point in a network or diagram, such as a switching centre or the point on a diagram where lines meet.

**Non-procedural language** A programming language which matches the natural way of expressing applications requirements, rather than being oriented towards the algorithmic procedures of languages like BASIC, C and COBOL; fourth-generation languages, for example, are often non-procedural.

**Number cruncher** Colloquialism for an application that consists primarily of performing many complex calculations.

**Numerical control machine** A machine tool controlled by a program on a paper tape loop; computer numerical control machines are based on more sophisticated software methods.

**Object-oriented** Programming or design techniques where the basic units are objects that are meaningful to the user in terms of the application, rather than being related to detailed computer structures and requirements.

**On-line** Activity involving direct interaction with a computer over a communications link.

**Open systems** The ability to interlink computing devices and systems relatively easily and efficiently, based on the implementation of appropriate standards and system architectures; the ISO's Open Systems Interconnection is a key standard for this purpose.

**Operating system** Essential systems software which controls and co-ordinates the scheduling of work processing and use of the system's resources; the prime interface between a computer and applications software.

**Operations research** A set of techniques that model systems behaviour using applied mathematics, statistical analysis, probability theory and other disciplines often used in software applications; also known as *operational* research (see *Linear programming* and *Modelling*).

**Optical Character Recognition (OCR)** An input technique that automatically recognises printed characters, which may need to be in special typefaces.

**Optical fibre** High-speed, high-volume telecommunications medium that transmits data as pulses of light down hair-thin glass fibres.

**Organisation and methods** — The analysis and design of organisation structures and working methods for office-based activities.

**Other Equipment Manufacturer (OEM)** — A company which produces a complete system or device including important elements, such as a complete computer, made by another supplier.

**Output** — The results of computer processing translated into a form that can be understood by users, such as by being displayed on a screen or printed on paper; as a verb, it means the act of delivering results in the desired form.

**Packet switching** — A method of data transmission where information is sent in a 'packet' that includes an address at the front which is used to route the data to its destination via switching exchanges; alternative to circuit switching.

**Page printer** — Printers that produce a page at a time, usually of high quality, such as laser printers.

**Parallel processing** — A computer architecture, such as an *array processor*, which allows many processors to work on the same problem simultaneously.

**Parameter** — A variable in a program or procedure which needs to have a specific value before the program can run; parameter-driven packages provide a convenient method of tailoring software to specific user needs quickly.

**Pascal** A structured high-level language for general software developments; named after French philosopher Blaise Pascal.

**Password** A word or number, specific to an individual and/or device, provided during logging-in procedures and used by the system to check authorisation levels when attempts are made to access data.

**Payback period** The length of time it will take for the benefits of a system to pay for the investment in it (see *Discounted cash flow*).

**Peripherals** Input, output and storage devices in a computer system.

**Personal computer** A complete computer that can be used from an ordinary office desk (see also *Lap-top* and *Portable computers*).

**PERT** A technique used for managing projects involving the co-ordination of many activities and tasks (see *Critical path analysis, Gantt charts*).

**Pilot project** An application used to try out a new system and to learn lessons that make the main live application more successful.

**Plotter** Device used for producing graphs and similar drawn output.

**Plug-compatible manufacturer** A supplier that makes processors, peripherals, workstations and other

| | |
|---|---|
| | equipment which behave in the same way as similar equipment from another manufacturer when connected through a predefined interface. |
| **Point-of-sale** | The place where payment is made for goods in a retail store (see *Electronic point-of-sale*). |
| **Port** | Connection points between the internal architecture of a computer and external devices and communications links. |
| **Portability (software)** | The ability to move programs between hardware systems with minimal, if any, code changes. |
| **Portable computer** | A personal computer compact and light enough to be moved relatively easily; heavier portables are known as *luggables* (see *Lap-top computer*). |
| **Printed circuit board** | see *Board*. |
| **Printer** | Device which produces output on paper; *impact* printers create images by the physical contact of printheads on paper (see *Daisywheel* and *Dot matrix*) and *non-impact* devices without such physical contact (see *Laser printer*). |
| **Printout** | Output from a printer. |
| **Private (automatic) branch exchange** | The switching exchange used within an organisation to link its internal communications system with an external telecommunications carrier; |

manual systems are non-automatic, but PBX is sometimes also taken to refer to computer-based exchanges.

**Procedure** Part of a program that performs a specific task or calculation; an algorithm or *subroutine*.

**Process control** Application of a computer to monitor and automatically control, in real time, a continuous production process, such as in the chemical industry.

**Processor** The computer hardware unit that performs arithmetic and logic operations, controls the sequence of a system's actions and co-ordinates input, output and storage activities (see *Central Processing Unit and Parallel processing*).

**Program** A sequence of detailed instructions stored in main memory which automatically controls a computer's actions.

**Programming language** A vocabulary and set of rules used to write program code (see *High-level* and *Low-level languages*).

**Protocols** A defined set of rules, conventions and other standards that are needed to enable networked information systems to operate effectively.

**Punched card/tape** The earliest forms of input, output and storage media, which represent data according to the position of holes punched in a card or paper tape.

| | |
|---|---|
| **Quality management** | A set of management techniques and disciplines designed to give assurance that the overall organisational and working environment will produce products and services of optimum quality. |
| **Query-by-example/forms** | A means of retrieving information by specifying the items being searched for in the appropriate position of a standard format displayed on a work-station screen. |
| **Query language** | An easy-to-learn language used to prepare programs that retrieve information from a database, such as SQL. |
| **Random Access Memory (RAM)** | Main memory on a chip which allows users to read from and write to it; read/write memory is a more apt description. |
| **Read Only Memory (ROM)** | Main memory on a chip which users can only read from, say because it has a hardwired program. |
| **Real time** | The current moment; application where the computer must be able to analyse and respond to inputs instantaneously, as in military defence systems or process control tasks. |
| **Record** | A data structure which forms part of a file; usually composed of a number of fields. |
| **Reduced Instruction Set Computer (RISC)** | A computer architecture with relatively few basic instructions, which |

can provide better performance than systems with a larger instruction set.

**Relational database** A database management technique that allows great flexibility in establishing relationships between data items, which are stored in two-dimensional tables.

**Remote** Computing capability at a distance from the main computing centre or a particular user (see *Local*).

**Report generator** Software that allows users to create and change output formats easily, say for display on a screen or a printed report.

**Response time** The time taken for the computer to respond to a user input.

**Reverse engineering (re-engineering)** The development of well structured and documented software on the basis of existing unstructured and poorly documented code.

**Robot** A computer-controlled machine which carries out some, generally limited, human-like movements; typically used on a production line to perform repetitive actions involving restricted 'arm' and 'hand' manipulations.

**Scientific management** A management approach which seeks to improve the performance of the organisation as a whole, and each employee within it, by the systematic analysis and planning of working environments to optimise efficiency, based primarily on quantified scientific methods, measurements and control (see *Taylorism, Work study*).

**Semiconductor** A substance, such as silicon, that allows the flow of an electronic current to be finely controlled, which makes it suited to the construction of transistors.

**Silicon** A semiconductor material, derived from sand, which is the most commonly used substance for making computer chips.

**Simulation** The representation of the behaviour of one system by another, often using mathematical and software modelling techniques; *emulation* is a form of simulation that makes one system actually behave like another, rather than using theoretical simulation techniques to show how it is likely to behave.

**Sizing** Precise estimation of the processing power, storage capacity and other computing capabilities needed to carry out a predicted application workload to acceptable performance levels (see *Capacity management*).

**Sociotechnical management** A management approach that aims to optimise overall effectiveness by giving explicit priority to organisational, social and psychological factors, as well as the technological and economic ones emphasised by scientific management techniques.

**Software** Generic term for computer programs which control the operation of hardware.

**Software engineering** Methodologies, techniques and tools which aim to make software development a more structured, systematic, reliable and predictable process; many computer-aided software engineering (CASE) tools are available to assist with various development activities.

**Source code** Software in the language written by the user, before it has been translated into the *object* code, based on machine instructions, needed for computer processing.

**Store and forward** An electronic mail capability which stores received information until the recipient requests to see it; sometimes known as an *electronic mailbox*.

**Structured Query Language** A widely used query language for relational database management systems.

**Structured techniques** Systematic approaches to systems analysis, design and programming which emphasise the importance of building structures from discrete modules in a disciplined framework, with full documentation; uses structured graphical design diagrams to describe requirements.

**Supercomputer** Systems with the most powerful processors, used primarily for scientifically-oriented applications involving many complex calculations.

**Supermini** Systems at the more powerful end of some minicomputer ranges, overlapping with mainframe capabilities.

**Systems analyst** An IT job function responsible for analysing information management requirements and preparing detailed specifications used for selecting and developing appropriate solutions.

**Systems engineering** A structured and disciplined approach to the development of a complete hardware and software system, using similar approaches to software engineering.

**Systems house** IT services company which sells total hardware and software packages, usually incorporating elements from other suppliers.

**Systems integrator** IT services company which takes prime contractual responsibility for supplying a complete information system, made up from products and services from a number of suppliers.

**Systems software** Software, such as an operating system, concerned primarily with controlling and co-ordinating computing resources (see *Applications software*).

**Taylorism** A common way of referring to scientific management, which was pioneered by F W Taylor.

**Technical and Office Protocol** An application of the OSI standard to office activities.

**Technology agreement** A negotiated agreement between

trade unions and management specifying the conditions under which new computer-based information systems will be introduced, eg including special one-off payments, redundancy arrangements, rest periods for some kinds of stressful work, ergonomic workstation designs to promote operational health and safety, etc.

**Teletex** An international standard for electronic mail services which can link to traditional telex networks.

**Teletext** A form of videotex which disseminates information by broadcast transmission, say from a television company to TV sets with appropriate built-in teletext converters.

**Terminal** A device used for input, output and communications with a computer over a telecommunications link; can be synonymous with *workstation*, but generally of more limited and specialised capabilities than workstations.

**Time-sharing** A system which handles many on-line terminals simultaneously.

**Top-down design** A structured design approach that starts with the highest level of general concepts or objectives and subdivides them systematically into greater levels of detail.

**Transaction processing** Processing discrete user transactions made via on-line systems, for example making seat reservations.

**Transistor** Small electronic device which acts as a switch or amplifier and can be built into integrated circuits for use as computer processors and memory.

**Tuple** A record in a relational database.

**Turnkey system** A complete computer-based system delivered in a full, finalised form, ready for live operation as soon as it is switched on.

**User-system interaction** The aspects of *Human factors engineering* and *Ergonomics* concerned with the techniques of communication between the user and a computer-based information system; synonymous with Human-computer interaction and Man-machine interaction/interfaces.

**Utilities** Systems software that performs general 'housekeeping' tasks, like optimising the use of storage space.

**Value-added network** A networked service which provides IT applications, like electronic mail, in addition to basic telecommunications transmission and switching capabilities.

**Value-added reseller** A company which adds facilities and services to a system obtained directly from a supplier before reselling it to users.

**Value chain** A method of analysing activities within an organisation to show how value is added at different stages, and in different activities and functions.

**Very large scale integration** A measure of the density of integrated circuits on a chip; much greater than *small, medium* or *large scale integration,* which are chips with the relative degree of integration density described.

**Videotex** Computer-based transmission and presentation of information which includes graphics and text, such as viewdata and teletext.

**Viewdata** A form of videotex which allows users to interact with databases to retrieve information or carry out transactions.

**Visual display terminal** Same as a visual display unit.

**Visual display unit** A device with a display screen and associated keyboard.

**Voice recognition** Input technique that interprets human speech directly.

**Von Neumann architecture** An architecture built around the concept of a sequential central processing unit; named after computing pioneer John von Neumann.

**Wide area network** A network covering a wide geographical area.

**Wideband** A telecommunications channel with a high bandwidth that allows larger flows of information, organised in more channels, than narrowband links; also known as *broadband*.

**Window** A frame inside an overall workstation

screen display within which user tasks can be carried out or information displayed; multi-window systems allow many activities to take place using one screen.

**Word processing** Application of computing to the typing process, allowing for greater flexibility in editing text.

**Work study** The analysis and design of organisation structures and working methods in manufacturing operations; an evolution of Taylorism that strongly influenced O&M.

**Workstation** A computer system or device that helps people to carry out their jobs; usually has its own intelligence so it can operate on its own or linked into networks with other systems; its capabilities overlap with personal computers, intelligent terminals and VDUs.

**X.** A series of communications protocols agreed by the international CCITT telecommunications body and often incorporated into OSI standards, such as X.21 for circuit switching, X.25 for packet switching and X.400 for electronic mail.

# Bibliography

Alter S L, *Decision Support Systems: Current Practice and Continuing Challenges*, Addison-Wesley, 1980

Anthony R N, *Planning and Control Systems: A Framework for Analysis*, Harvard University, 1965

Barden R A, *How to Start in Office Automation*, NCC Publications, 1988

Barden R A, *Personal Computers for the Business*, NCC Publications, 1988

Bell R, *Management of Systems Development*, Hutchinson, 1987

Benerjee U K, Sachdeva R K, *Management Information Systems: A Framework*, Vikas Publishing, 1988

Brandon R H, *Data Processing Organisation and Manpower Planning*, Petrocelli, 1974

Brodie A, *Computer Buyer's Handbook*, NCC Publications, 1988

*Business Systems Planning: Information Systems Planning Guide*, IBM, GE20–0527–4, July 1984

Cash J L, *Corporate Information Systems Management: The Issues Facing Senior Executives*, Irwin, 1988

Chomsky N, *Problems of Knowledge and Freedom*, Pantheon, 1971

Couger J D, Zawacki R A, *Motivating and Managing Computer Personnel*, John Wiley, 1980

Davis G B, Olsen M H, *Management Information Systems: Conceptual Foundations, Structure and Development*, McGraw-Hill, 1985

Devargas M, *Introducing the Information Centre*, NCC Blackwell, 1989

Doswell D, Simons G L, *Fraud and Abuse of IT Systems*, NCC Publications, 1986

Douglas I J, Olson P J, *Audit and Control of Computer Networks*, NCC Publications, 1986

Elbra R A, *Security Review Manual*, NCC Publications, 1986

Ellison J R, Pritchard J A T, *Security in Office Systems*, NCC Publications, 1987

Enzer S, How to think strategically, *New Management*, vol 2, no 1, 1984

Finlay P, *Introducing Decision Support Systems*, NCC Blackwell, 1989

Ford N J, *Local Area Micronetworks and their Management*, NCC Publications, 1989

Gallagher J P, *Knowledge Systems for Business*, Prentice-Hall, 1988

Gandy M, *Choosing a Local Area Network*, NCC Publications, 1987

Garcia R R, *Human Factors in Systems Development*, NCC Publications, 1988

Gaydasch A, *Principles of EDP Management*, Reston Publishing, 1982

Gorry G A, Scott Morton M S, A framework for management information systems, *Sloan Management Review*, Fall 1971, vol 13, no 1, pp 55–70

Gray J, *Business Organisation*, NCC Publications, 1987

Harris S, *People and Communication*, NCC Publications, 1987

Higgins J C, *Computer-based Planning Systems*, Edward Arnold, 1985

Hook C, *Data Protection Implications for Systems Design*, NCC Publications, 1989

Hu S D, *Expert Systems for Software Engineers and Managers*, Chapman and Hall, 1987

James B, *The Systems Analysis Interview – A Guide to Interviewing in Organisations*, NCC Blackwell, 1989

Keen P G W, Scott Morton M S, *Decision Support Systems: An Organisational Perspective*, Addison-Wesley, 1978

Koontz H, O'Donnell C, Wehnrich H, *Essentials of Management*, McGraw-Hill, 1982

Marlow A J, *Computerising Your Accounts*, NCC Blackwell, 1989

Martin C J, *Computers and Senior Managers*, NCC Publications, 1988

Mason R D, Burton Swanson E, *Measurement for Management Decision*, Addison-Wesley, 1981

McFarlan F W, McKenney K L, *Corporate Information Systems Management*, Richard D Irwin, 1983

Naylor T H, ed, *Simulation Models in Corporate Planning*, Praeger Publishers, 1979

Naylor T H, Balintfy J L, Burdick D S, Chris K, *Computer Simulation Techniques*, John Wiley, 1966

Naylor T H, Thomas C, eds, *Optimisation Models for Strategic Planning*, North Holland, 1984

Nolan R L, Managing the crisis in data processing, *Harvard Business Review*, March/April 1979

Nolan R L, Gibson C F, Managing the four stages of EDP growth, *Harvard Business Review*, January/February 1974

Peltu M, *Introducing Information Systems Management*, NCC Blackwell, 1989

Peltu M, *Using Computers – A Manager's Guide*, NCC Publications, 1981

Pritchard J A T, *Electronic Filing and Retrieval: Developments in Full Text Retrieval*, NCC Publications, 1989

Pritchard J A T, *Integrated Office Systems*, NCC Publications, 1988

Pye C, *What is OSI?*, NCC Publications, 1988

Remenyi D S J, *Increase Profits with Strategic Information Systems*, NCC Publications, 1988

Robb A F, *Management Guide to Choosing and Implementing Computer Systems*, NCC Publications, 1988

Rockart J, Chief executives define their own data needs, *Harvard Business Review*, March/April 1979

Rockart J F, Crescenzi A D, A process for the rapid development of systems in support of managerial decision making, *Sloan Report WP 47–83*, Sloan School of Management, Massachusetts, June 1983

Ross S C, Penlesky R J, Doney L D, *Developing and Using Decision Support Applications*, West Publishing Company, 1988

Rowntree G, *Fundamentals of Computing*, NCC Publications, 1987

Sanders D H, *Computers Today*, McGraw-Hill, 1988

Simon H A, *Reason in Human Affairs*, Basil Blackwell, 1983

Simon H A, *The New Science of Management Decision*, Prentice-Hall, 1977

Simons G L, *Management Guide to Office Automation*, NCC Publications, 1986

Simons G L, *Viruses, Bugs and Star Wars – The Hazards of Unsafe Computing*, NCC Blackwell, 1989

Skidmore S, Wroe B, *Introducing Systems Analysis*, NCC Publications, 1988

Skidmore S, Wroe B, *Introducing Systems Design*, NCC Blackwell, 1989

Spencer J, *Computing Standards: A Practical Guide for Data Processing Management*, Blackwell Scientific Publications, 1987

Spiegler I, MIS and DBMS: where does one end and the other start, *Journal of Systems Management*, June 1983

Sprague R A, McNurlin B C, eds, *Information Systems Management in Practice*, Prentice-Hall, 1986

Sprague R H Jnr, Carlson E D, *Building Effective Decision Support Systems*, Prentice-Hall, 1982

*Stage by Stage*, vol 4, no 4, Nortan and Company, Winter 1985

Strassman P A, *Information Payoff: The Transformation of Work in the Electronic Age*, McMillan/Free Press, 1985

Szweda R A, *Information Processing Management*, D van Nostrand, 1978

Thierauf R J, Klekamp R C, *Decision Making Through Operations Research*, John Wiley, 1975

Watts R, *Measuring Software Quality*, NCC Publications, 1987

Wood M B, *Fire Precautions in Computer Installations*, NCC Publications, 1986

Wood M B, *Guidelines for Physical Security*, NCC Publications, 1986

Wroe B, *Successful Computing in a Small Business*, NCC Publications, 1987

# Index